Mirror and Metaphor:
  Images and Stories of Psychological Life

Mirror and Metaphor
Images and Stories of Psychological Life

Robert D. Romanyshyn

Originally published in 1982 as
Psychological Life: From Science to Metaphor
Foreword by J. H. van den Berg

TRIVIUM PUBLICATIONS
Pittsburgh, PA

ISBN 0-9713671-0-8

0 0 1 2 3 4 5 6 7 8 9 0 0

The first edition of this book had the following dedication:

Sadly, many of those to whom the first edition was dedicated are gone now, and yet they linger, present in another way. To honor that presence, I repeat my dedication to them here. Thank you for a heritage and a destiny, for a vocation and a vision, for love and support.

For the second edition of this work, my backward glance makes me realize that I owe words of thanks to many colleagues and friends who, over the years, have supported and encouraged my work. My former colleagues and graduate students at the University of Dallas, the Fellows at The Dallas Institute of Humanities and Culture, my colleagues, friends, and students at Duquesne University, and the friends, colleagues, and students at Pacifica Graduate Institute have my gratitude. These places have been sheltering oases for creative work.

Beyond this acknowledgement, special mention is to be made of Ivan Illich who early on encouraged me in my work, and to Kathleen Raine, who continues to do so and whose presence and work are a source of constant inspiration. Along with J. H. van den Berg, these two individuals have been mentors of the best sort.

I also wish to dedicate this second edition to my four children: Jeffrey, Andrew, Sarah, and Tim. Each of you in your own way has reminded me that creative work arises from the soil of daily life and its many demands.

Finally, I want to express my deep gratitude and love to my wife Veronica. She has been lover, companion, and friend on these journeys of soul making. To find love once in a lifetime is a gift. To find it a second time is a miracle. Thank you again for this miracle.

CONTENTS

Figures

Tables

FOREWORD

This book belongs in an important lineage, a strand of thought whose radical implication has yet to be assimilated by many. This line includes works in the 1930s and 1940s by the French professor of the history of science and philosophy, Gaston Bachelard, works such as *The New Scientific Spirit* and *The Philosophy of No.* The well-known *The Structure of Scientific Revolutions*, by the American historian of science, Thomas Kuhn, contributed to the lineage in the 1960s and 1970s. And the line has been extended in this work by Robert Romanyshyn, first published in 1982 and very appropriately being reissued now at the beginning of a new millennium.

The works of these three thinkers belong to the same family because they see through science to something deeper and more fundamental. For Bachelard it was imagery, especially images as seen explicitly by poets. For Kuhn it was paradigms, whose turns signify a seismic shift in scientific and cultural meaning. In Romanyshyn's work it is metaphor that is basic, such that a cultural history of science, including particularly the science of psychology, is a history of metaphors.

The author's provocative perspective allows him to add to the work of Bachelard and Kuhn a dimension that was not blatantly explicit in their works: namely, the psychological dimension in the cultural history of the science of the last three centuries. The effect of exposing the metaphorical character of psychological life is to restore the story of the fundamental nature of imagination that has been, for many, eclipsed in our time. It reinstates the story-quality to the history of science, which, as the author notes, has had a mythical power over our lives.

If at bottom, science is based in metaphor—or image (Bachelard) or paradigm (Kuhn)—then the cultural history of science is the story of psychology. The reason for this is that writing a cultural history is reflection, and reflection, like that in and out of a mirror, does not tell what things are, but gives an image of what they are like. Reflection does not have to do with "is," as much as it does with similitude, with "as" and "like." It has to do with making metaphors. Reflection is the soul musing about matters.

This means that reflecting metaphorically upon things or matters, including psychological things and matters, is already a psychological activity, a movement of the psyche. A person reflecting cannot ever step outside the psyche that is doing the reflecting. As C. G. Jung and George Herbert Mead would aver: *I am in a perspective, rather than having the perspective in me.* We are always in some metaphor. Cultural history is a work of the imagination. This implies that the metaphorical history of psychology as a science, as this book construes it, is itself an imaginal psychology. It is a psychology of psychology. Our life is always and already psychological. And this book conveys the insight that human life is always metaphorical; this is its reality.

Romanyshyn—like Michel Foucault and Jacques Lacan, not to mention Alice when she is in Wonderland!—begins the story of a new style of psychological existence with the metaphor of the mirror. But this is immediately amplified by other metaphors: Mona Lisa's smile; Newton's rainbow; Descartes' dreams; nightmare; a bottle of wine; the Japanese tea ceremony; desire; shadows cast by objects bathed in light; a child and her mother; hell; an eavesdropping heart that is at once divided, democratic, empty, broken, and joyous; a phonograph needle; Dante's lake of ice; Hölderlin's joyously shuddering waves; Howard Nemerov's sparrow dipped in raspberry juice; Wallace Stevens' thirteen blackbirds; a lumberjack; and lucid drunkenness!

The function of reflecting by and in metaphors reveals the shadows and twilights in enlightened knowledges. It produces a humility of knowing in the face of the real obscurity of imagined clarity. Discourse, including that of the psychological and scientific, is seen not as transparent to some-thing, but as opaque: that is, as metaphoric.

This metaphoricity uncovers a radicality of the story of psychological living as told by this book's author. Such a radicality underscores a subversion of the interior and exterior binarism. Not only is it common to think that psychology is merely interior and subjective, but similarly, it is often imagined that the inside and outside of the self are in opposition or are split off from one another, so that when I am "inside" myself I am not at that moment dealing with what is "outside."

Reading this book has the effect of overturning both of these common attitudes. Psychological life has to do with things, others and outsides, as much as it does with thoughts, feelings, intuitions and sensations inside the self. Further there is no "outside" that is not always and already "inside," and vice versa. This space of simultaneity, a reciprocal arc, places the reader of *Mirror and Metaphor* in something like an Escher drawing, in which figures are going and coming at the same time—which is of course precisely the logic of psychological existence. The reader may experience the terrain of this volume as if she or he were in a story by Jorge Luis Borges or Franz Kafka.

There is a parable by Kafka, which in my judgement expresses the deeply provocative nature of Romanyshyn's work. The parable goes this way:

> Many complain that the words of the wise are always merely parable and of no use in daily life, which is the only life we have. When the sage says: "Go over," he does not mean that we should cross to some actual place, which we could do anyhow if the labor were worth it; he means some fabulous yonder, something unknown to us, something too that he cannot designate more precisely, and therefore cannot help us here in the very least. All these parables really set out to say merely that the incomprehensible is incomprehensible, and we know that already. But the cares we have to struggle with every day: that is a different matter.
>
> Concerning this a man once said: Why such reluctance? If you only followed the parables you yourselves would become parables and with that rid of all your daily cares.
>
> Another said: I bet that is also a parable.
>
> The first said: You have won.

The second said: But unfortunately only in parable.

The first said: No, in reality: in parable you have lost. [1]

But in this volume of great insight and import, Robert Romanyshyn has won . . . in metaphor . . .which is to say in psychological reality!

> David L. Miller
> Watson-Ledden Professor of Religion, Emeritus,
> Syracuse University
> Core Faculty Member, Pacifica Graduate Institute

[1]Franz Kafka, "On Parables," Parables and Paradoxes, tr. W. and E. Muir (New York: Schocken Books, 1961), p.11.

FOREWORD TO THE
ORIGINAL EDITION

When William Harvery, in 1628, published his book on the motion of the heart and blood, he made known his conviction that a sound can be heard every time the heart beats. "With each motion of the heart, when there is a delivery of a quantity of blood," Harvey wrote, "a pulse can be heard within the chest."[1]

Harvey's view met with no approval. No one in the field of medicine from the time of Hippocrates to William Harvey ever heard the heart beat, and no colleague of Harvey showed any inclination to follow him in this unexpected and strange point. Emilio Parisano, physician and anatomist in Venice, published a pamphlet against Harvey in 1635, and in that pamphlet he made the statement that "nobody in Venice ever heard the heart beat, and nobody will be able to know what Harvey means until the time comes that he is inclined, what nobody expects, to lend us his ears."[2] Remembering this bold criticism, Emile Guyénot, in his book of 1941 on the sciences in the seventeenth and eighteenth centuries, said that evidently "human stupidity knows of no bounds,"[3] and I am almost sure that most of our contemporaries, if not all, would agree with Guyénot.

Not so R. D. Romanyshyn! In this volume Romanyshyn ventures to observe that our understanding of the history of the sciences, nay of humanity, falls short if we accept only modern insights as truth and accuse people of earlier times of "stupidity"—to use Guyénot's term. Let me consider further this point which Romanyshyn defends. To that purpose I return to my example of the audible heartbeat.

There can be no doubt that not one physician before Harvey mentioned the sound of the heartbeat,[4] or that the text of his own publication almost seduced him to make such a statement.[5] And yet in religious and artistic literature before Harvey several writers freely discussed the audible heartbeat.[6] How can this puzzling fact be understood? The answer is that nobody before Harvey saw the heart *as a pump*, with the consequence that nobody, particularly no physician, was able to hear the heart *beat* as a pump. But this is exactly what William Harvey did. He saw and he heard the heart as a pump. The religious and artistic writers discussed the heart in a different, non-medical context, in a different *paradigm*, to use Thomas Kuhn's term[7], and that context allowed them to hear the heart: to hear the whispering, wailing, loving tale of that center of the human body.

In Romanyshyn's book Kuhn's *paradigm* acquires the significance of *reality*, and this makes his book of paramount importance. Our ancestors in western civilization, before Harvey, lived in a different reality; their world was different from ours, *but as real*, and we have to take their statements to be as honest, *as true*, as ours, if we wish to understand their convictions, and our own. Romanyshyn goes so far as to state—but the reader has to read his text carefully—that "there were holes in the septum of the heart before the seventeenth century," for—I continue to quote him—"the heart with holes in the septum and the heart without such holes belong to two different styles of existence, to two different psychological worlds."

In this frame of reference the door is opened to a fresh and inspiring interpretation of human history in general and the history of the sciences in particular. Every important discovery in the field of science is, first of all, the initiation into a new reality, as real as the reality as before, and as real as the reality to come. To take a well-known example, consider that when Newton in 1665 formulated the force with which all matter on earth is pulled to its center, he not only opened a new insight into the movement of physical bodies, in particular the moon and the planets, but also manifested the truth of a new reality. This new reality was so much connected with the principles of the baroque era that the formulation of his insight would have been flatly impossible before that era.[8] It is this apprehension of the course of history that brings Romanyshyn to such statements as: "Architecture is the psychological character of an age made visible." In other words, architecture, among all other features of a developing culture, demonstrates a permanent different *reality*. Of course the question of what is *reality* arises, and Romanyshyn does not fail to meet the reader's wishes. In his book he gives an elaborate answer, particularly in his final chapter.

For the history of psychology Romanyshyn's interpretation has a specific significance. Psychology as a natural science is young. But in addition, as he shows in this work, psychology as a natural science "is a specific historical appearance of psychological life, and in it psychological life appears through a physics of nature and a physiology of the body." With this statement a new understanding of the so different psychologies of past ages immediately arises. They are not philosophical speculations, but manifestations of real life in the past, to be interpreted with as much earnestness as we give to the interpretation of our contemporary psychological insight.

The fresh judgments of Romanyshyn's book are the work of a phenomenologist. My last words of this foreword should address what this means. Much has been written about the question of what is phenomenology and many of the writings are highly theoretical. Here, however, I have to be very brief, and in any case the essence of phenomenology is readily said. Phenomenology refuses to see psychological life as an *interior event*. Romanyshyn tells about a friend who died, and who left before his death "in the corner of my study" a copy of his book. The book still remains in Romanyshyn's study. He writes: "His book, is my memory." That is phenomenology! Memory, like hope, friendship, love, disappointment, etc., is not present "in" the brain. In the brain are tissues, nerve cells, and connections: the *conditions* of what memory is. Memory is around us, in our world, in that book over there. This is the *reality* of our psychological life which his work recovers. It is the reality of the modern man or woman who no longer lives in the closed temple of egocentric isolation, but in that wide field of interaction, of communication in an emerging, turbulent world.

Jan Hendrik van den Berg, M.D.
University of Leyden

PREFACE

The ending of a work returns one to the beginning, and the preface of a work is the place where the ending and the beginning meet. Indeed at the preface the work begins again. It begins of course for the reader, but it also begins again for the author. Now at the end the author is addressed. It is the work which now speaks and not the author. In the preface it is the work now finished which addresses the reader through the author.

This work concerns the *changing* character of psychological life and the *character* of that changing reality. The former concern means that people of an earlier age had a *different* psychological life. It means that styles of dress, codes of conduct, ways of building; philosophical speculations, literary productions, artistic creations; science and its visions of nature, medicine and its visions of the body are not and never are external changes grafted onto an immutable psychological nature. It means, on the contrary, that these changes themselves are a new appearance of psychological life, a mirror through which a new reflection of psychological life appears. Our psychological life today, which is recorded as the science of psychology, is such a historical appearance. It began early in the sixteenth century with the naming of psychology as a separate science and with the rise of the new sciences of nature and the body. This work tells the story of that appearance and in so doing it recovers as *historical* what we today assume to be the *natural* state of our psychological existence. In this respect this work is offered not as a history of psychology but as a *historical reflection* which does the *psychological work* of *remembering how* we have become *what* we are. It is a psychological work, not unlike the work of psycho-analysis, performed upon the cultural dream called the science of psychology.

But there is also the second concern of this work, a concern which reaches beyond remembering. The recovery of psychological life as radically historical is also the recovery of psychological life as another reality between the material fact and the mental idea. Psychological life is not a reality inside humanity divorced from the historical events and cultural conditions which surround it on the outside. It *is*, on the contrary, these events and conditions. But, on the other hand, it *is not* these events and conditions. Human psychological life is not given *in* or *as* these events and conditions; it is given *through* them as a *reflection*. They are the *mirrors* through which psychological life appears and changes, and the second concern of this book is to show how psychological life as a reflection is a reality between the material and the mental, that is, a *metaphorical* reality. In the first four chapters of this work, this metaphorical character of psychological reality is anticipated. In the final chapter it becomes the theme.

The historical reflection which characterizes this text is a psychological work of remembering, and at the end of this work it is the metaphorical character of psychological life which is remembered. The consequences of this work are not extensively treated in this text. They remain as questions and as tasks to be done. How, for example, does the metaphorical character of psychological life affect its praxis? How does it affect the speaking, the writing, and the teaching of psychological life? What is the character of psychological truth? Who or what is the psychologist in this domain of the metaphorical? These are some of the questions raised by the work, and perhaps it is its shortcoming that they are not elaborately answered. But, on the other hand, perhaps it is prudent to be patient with these questions, and to remain for a while with this awareness of psychological life as a metaphorical reality. We are and we have been used to the scientific and philosophical ways of life. The recovery of psychological life as a metaphorical reality leads us into a way of life which is unfamiliar. It leads us into a domain of living where story rather than fact or idea informs experience, and where the imaginal understanding of the human heart supersedes the empirical understanding of the observing eye, and the logical understanding of the human mind.

Now indeed the work is almost truly finished. Its beginning and its ending have been joined. There is, however, one task which remains. A word of thanksgiving still needs to be spoken:

To Joni Caldwell who patiently and with understanding typed much of the manuscript in its many versions.

To Douglas Gerwin who read the work and offered his insights and collegial conversation.

To Tom and Bette Sheridan who offered a place of quiet peace and hospitality where so much of this work was done.

To J. H. van den Berg who informed the vision of this work and whom I wish to honor always with the word *teacher*.

And to my spouse and my companion, Janet, who had perhaps the most difficult task of all. She listened with patience and encouragement to the dream which became the work.

R. D. R.

INTRODUCTION

I am sitting at my desk, attempting to write this introduction and trying to remember the example I intended to use. The example is on the *tip of my tongue*, but I am unable to recall it. Scanning the shelves of books in my office, I notice the section on psychology. There, I imagine, I will find an answer to my difficulty, for surely the science of psychology knows about remembering and its perplexities. Rising from my chair, I cross the room to the place where the books are nestled together, and searching the many titles I choose one of the classics in introductory psychology. I choose an introductory text because it betrays most clearly the way in which a discipline organizes its knowledge and hence understands itself.[1] Opening the pages I am not disappointed, for in the chapter on "Human Learning and Memory"[2] I find a discussion of the *tip-of-the-tongue* phenomenon. The discussion is brief and not very helpful, but what catches my eye is an illustration of the phenomenon which is presented in Figure I. Now I have it! Now I understand my difficulty! Looking at the illustration I realize that the example which I cannot remember lies *inside* my head, and that it resides there in a *literal* way, as the books lie on my shelf waiting to be retrieved. And indeed this is exactly what the discussion says. To study the organization of information in long-term memory, it advises us "to see what happens when we search through the library of experience to retrieve a memory."[3] It is an interesting figure of speech, and the picture illustrates the point. My head is a library, and my memories are literally inside me. Closing the book I shudder to think how many library books are so easily misfiled, lost, or stolen, and I recall, not without a touch of horror, the electronic security systems which most modern libraries have been forced to install to prevent their shelves from being emptied.

The illustration is, I admit, a preposterous one and no one really believes what the picture illustrates. And yet the point about memory and the *tip-of-the-tongue* phenomenon is illustrated and discussed in

Figure 1. The tip-of-the-tongue phenomenon. Adapted by Claire Pate from Clifford T. Morgan, Richard A. King, and Nancy M. Robinson, *Introduction to Psychology*, p. 159

this way, and in one sense we do believe it, as we believe so many other things that are untested by critical reflection. The illustration is a metaphor and the discussion is metaphorical, but it is very likely that the illustration and the discussion enter our lives mythically, that they possess the power of myth. We believe in science and we believe that the science of psychology faithfully explicates the psychological phenomena of human life.[4] To the degree that we as readers accept psychology's account of these phenomena, we are likely to go away satisfied with what we have learned, and in this exit we will have accepted—perhaps unwittingly—two things about human psychological life as it is understood in psychology. On the one hand we will have learned that human psychological life is *interiorized* inside the subject and apart from the world. On the other we will have learned that it is *literalized* in this interiorization.[5] Both of these features are questionable, though the questioning requires some searching into the origins of psychology as a science.

I am ready now to leave my desk, and I remember the example with which I wanted to begin these remarks. It is a poem by Wallace Stevens, and I chose it because it says in the beginning of the work what I hope to have said by the end of it. In alluding to the twilight and the shadow of things, their indirection and essentially revealing obscurity, their seasons of spring and fall, transitions and changes, the poem speaks about the motive for metaphor *and* about the field of human psychological life. There is at least as much to be learned from this poem as from an introductory text in psychology.

The Motive for Metaphor

You like it under the trees in autumn,
Because everything is half dead.
The wind moves like a cripple among the leaves
And repeats words without meaning.

In the same way, you were happy in spring,
With the half colors of quarter-things,
The slightly brighter sky, the melting clouds,
The single bird, the obscure moon—

The obscure moon lighting an obscure world
Of things that would never be quite expressed,
Where you yourself were never quite yourself
And did not want nor have to be,

Desiring the exhilarations of changes:
The motives for metaphor, shrinking from
The weight of primary noon,
The ABC of being,

The ruddy temper, the hammer
Of red and blue, the hard sound—
Steel against intimation—the sharp flash,
The vital, arrogant, fatal, dominant X.[6]

I

PSYCHOLOGY AND THE METAPHOR OF SCIENCE

"In the Middle of Things"

The history of psychology reminds us that "psychology has a long past, but only a short history." This discipline, we are told, "is not a new but an ancient science, perhaps the most ancient of all sciences." Indeed we are advised that "it is safe to say that psychology is as old as the inquiring, self-conscious mind of man."[1] Despite, however, this long and ancient heritage, the remarkable fact is that the term *psychology* first appeared only in modern times, only in the sixteenth century. Although its authorship is disputed, François La Pointe points out that a strong case is often made for Philipp Melanchthon [1497-1560], friend of Luther, as the first one to use the word to describe a separate field of study. But whoever the author may be, the important point is the time of psychology's appearance. Something as old as humanity is first named in modern times. This relatively recent appearance of the term is a surprising and remarkable fact, a puzzle in need of understanding.

The most common understanding of the puzzle is that the appearance of psychology in the sixteenth century concluded a long struggle which psychology waged to free itself from the clutches of philosophy. Prior to this decisive break, psychology was *confused* with other disciplines. "The studies pertaining to the soul," we are told, "were distributed among metaphysics, logic and physics,"[2] and being so distributed psychological life was multiple and dispersed. It was, so to speak, in the middle of things, and one could find it everywhere and nowhere. But with the appearance of the term *psychology* this confusion is overcome. *The multiplicity of psychological life gives way to the unity of psychology.* The studies pertaining to the soul become a *study* of mind.

In the sixteenth century the name *psychology* appears, a name which subsequently casts a negative light on the long past of confusion. The long past is a story of error and the subsequent history of psychology in modern times is a record of its correction. But confusion is not necessarily error, and this negative viewpoint on confusion need not necessarily be adopted. In fact its adoption *conceals* an essential feature of psychological life.

James Hillman reminds us of another, more positive side of confusion. In the language of alchemy, which Hillman regards as "the depth psychology of an earlier age,"[3] the same age which sees the appearance of the term psychology, psychological life is essentially a mass of confusion, a "massa confusa."[4] Through the base metals of the earth the alchemist is working with himself, and the confused mass of materials which endlessly stews over the fires of his stove reflects the psycho-pathology of his soul. This depth psychology of an earlier age keeps alive a positive and essential feature of confusion at the very same time that the fledgling science of psychology would erase it. Confusion has a place in psychological life. Psychological life is confusion.

But even within this tradition, the significance of this long past of confusion is concealed. Confusion is not an error to be corrected. But it does become a madness to be cured. It is not explained (away) in the laboratories of science, but it is treated (away?) in the clinics of medicine.[5] Narrowed down in this fashion, the legitimate sense in which madness is confusion becomes the illegitimate equation of confusion with madness, and consequently the awareness that this long past of confusion reveals *how* psychological life appears remains obscured. The insight that this long past of confusion betrays psychological life as always mixing itself with other things is concealed. The character of *indirection*, which this long past of confusion suggests about psychological life, is not understood.

In its root sense, *confusion* means "to pour together."[6] It suggests a blending or mixing of things, and at this level it carries no connotation of either error or madness. If the long past of psychology's confusion is read in this fashion, then this past tells us that psychological life always appears with and/or through something else. We begin to suspect that psychological life is always in the middle of things. We begin to suspect that the *confusion* of psychological life is its *reflection* through other things. We begin to suspect that not only is psychological life confused with metaphysics, logic and physics, but it is also reflected in the way in which an age builds its buildings, paints its paintings, and creates its works of art. Indeed we begin to suspect that the way in which an age understands the things of the world (nature) and the human body *mirrors* human psychological life, making it a reality of reflection. And through these suspicions the naming of psychology in the sixteenth century begins to take on another significance. The naming no longer signifies a radical break between modern psychological knowledge and ancient psychological ignorance. This event no longer divides the absence of psychology from its presence. On the contrary it heralds a new appearance of psychological life. The science of *psychology* becomes a historical appearance of *psychological* life, the way in which psychological life appears in modern times. Psychology becomes the modern name, and face, of human psychological life.

In his recent book, *An Intellectual History of Psychology*, Daniel Robinson presents a critical history of psychology. It is an impressive work not only because of its scholarship but also because of its approach. Robinson is critical of the popular fashion in historical studies to trace a path of continuity between earlier ages and our own. It is a valid criticism because this fashion assumes that psychology as it exists today is psychology as it should be and that the psychologies of earlier ages were at best a preparation. In addition Robinson is critical of the opposite fashion in historical studies to dismiss the past as a well of ignorance. In this view the psychologies of earlier ages are a failure and between these ages and our own there can be only a discontinuity. The fact remains however that we stand in no exclusive relation of either discontinuity or continuity with previous times, and the appearance of psychological life as psychology leaves open the issue of the relation of this psychology to that of earlier ages. Indeed, in this work I want to avoid this issue completely because my concern is not strictly speaking historical. I do not intend to offer here a *history of psychology* in the usual fashions. On the contrary, I intend to do a *psychological* reading of the historical appearance of the science of psychology. The appearance of the term *psychology* is a unique event. It dates what the Dutch psychiatrist, psychologist, and philosopher J. H. van den Berg would call a shift in man's existence.[7] In the sixteenth century a positive confusion of studies pertaining to the soul becomes a study of mind, and with this change a new dream of human existence is born. The brief history of psychology as a science is a continuation of this dream. It is a cultural dream tied up with the modern history of things and the human body. As such, moreover, the history of modern psychology is a dream with consequences. Indeed, it requires only a little imagination to recognize the Faustian character of this cultural dream. Psychological life, which in the sixteenth century bargains away its soul to become initially a science of mental life and subsequently a science of behavior, loses not only its soul but also its mind in the later skepticism of Locke and Hume, and finally even consciousness in a consulting room in Vienna in the nineteenth century. In this respect this work is an attempt to understand the dream which psychological life has had of itself as the science of psychology.

These opening remarks have introduced three issues, each of which raises a question. First, the long past of confusion is indicative of the indirect character of psychological life. It illustrates the character of psychological life as a reality of reflection. *What does it mean to understand psychological life as a reality of reflection?* Second, psychology as a science is a historical appearance of psychological life. It is the reflection of psychological life in modern times. More specifically, a new physics of nature and a new physiology of the body are the mirrors through which psychological life is reflected in modern times. *What are the specific features of psychological life in psychology?* Third, the short history of psychology tends to conceal more than reveal the long past of psychological life. *What does the discipline of psychology conceal of psychological life?* It is through these issues and questions that we approach the cultural dream called modern psychology.

Confusion, Indirection, and Psychological Life as a Reality of Reflection: A Phenomenology of the Mirror

The indirect character of psychological life suggests that psychological life is a reality of reflection. To understand this meaning of psychological life let us consider the mirror reflection. Psychological life as a reality of reflection is like a mirror reflection, and we can begin to characterize psychological life and to recover some of its features through a brief phenomenology of the mirror.

THE MIRROR REFLECTION

It is morning. The day is beginning. As on every other day which has passed, I leave my bedroom, walk across the hall, and enter the bathroom. My head is still heavy with sleep as I stand before the mirror and reach over with my left hand to switch on the light. Now I finally raise my head to look up at the mirror. The reflection stands before me as it always has before this day. But unlike every other day which has passed by, my morning now begins to change. Today I *notice the reflection.* Temporarily disrupting my usual routines, I pause for a moment to consider the following question: "*Where* is the reflection that I see?"

Such a question hardly seems worth the time which is lost in raising it because the answer seems so simple and straightforward. The reflection is *there* on the surface of the glass, and the geometry and physics of the mirror confirm this point of view. But this explanation is not quite right, because if I pay attention to my experience of noticing the reflection, then I realize that the reflection lies as far on that side of the mirror as I am on this side of it. Despite what the *explanation* affirms, therefore, the *experience* of the mirror argues for a *depth* to the reflection. The reflection is not a flat projection lying on the surface of the glass, but the experience of a distance. Indeed, if I stay with the experience a bit longer, then I notice that this distance of the reflection is like the distance between myself and another. In other words, the reflection is not *on* the glass any more than it is *in* the mirror. On the contrary, it is like a ghostly other who inhabits that place over there. It is like an apparition who haunts that landscape of objects over there in the distance. And, indeed, what confirms this experience is the fact that in seeing the reflection I never look into the mirror as much as I look *through* it, or beyond it. In fact, the mirror itself as an instrument of projection disappears to become a medium or a pivot or an axis through which the reflected and the reflection communicate.

Certainly, however, this experience cannot be correct. Or if it is correct then it applies only to very young children and/or to the insane. Reason overcomes this confusion which would find the reflection at a distance beyond the mirror, and the physical-geometrical explanation is the epitome of that reason. The reflection lies *in* the mirror *on* the surface of the glass, an immaterial and insubstantial unreality, a *virtual* image which is, in comparison with what is *real* on this side of the mirror, only an image, a flat projection which lacks the thickness of life and which does not matter. The last point bears repeating. The reflection does not *matter*: it is unimportant and *immaterial.*

The experience of the reflection, however, does not let go of us so easily, and indeed it is the reflection itself which refuses to be dismissed in this fashion. Like a ghostly other, it seems to participate as if by magic in my life on this side of the mirror, haunting the objects over there which I also know over here. Its distance from me is a *real* distance, more real in fact than the explanation which argues this distance away in order to fix the reflection on the glass, and through this distance the reflection finds a depth and a thickness which pulses with a kind of life. It is anything but a pale and bloodless surface projection. On the contrary, if it is anything, then it is most certainly an amplification of my life on this side of the mirror, a *deepening* of it. The experience of the reflection demands therefore some additional attention.

In his essay "Eye and Mind," the French phenomenological philosopher and psychologist Maurice Merleau-Ponty discusses an interesting example from Paul Schilder's *The Image and Appearance of the Human Body.* Smoking a pipe before a mirror, Schilder observes how he feels the sleek burning surface of the wood not only where his fingers are— here on this side of the mirror—but also over there, "in those ghostlike fingers, those merely visible fingers inside the mirror."[8] The reflection of the smoker *feels* something of what the actual smoker feels, and if I now *look* at the reflection through the mirror then I must acknowledge that there is also a mutuality of vision. The reflection is no more only a something which is seen than I am on this side of the mirror only the one who sees. On the contrary, the one who sees and the seen cross; they encroach upon each other in such a way that the reflection also sees, just as I experience myself being seen by it. Indeed if one stays with the experience of the reflection, then one finally recognizes that it is impossible ever to say with absolute certainty who is the "see-er" and who is the seen. And lest this observation seem too fanciful, consider the situation of *talking* with the mirror reflection. In this instance, even more than with the case of seeing or feeling, it is impossible to say who is listening and who is speaking. Am I, on this side of the mirror, speaking to the reflection which, like a ghostly other, is merely listening? Or is it that the reflection is sometimes speaking and I am listening?

The reflected and the reflection cross each other through the mirror, and there is at the heart of the experience of the mirror reflection a *confusion* which is as inescapable as it is fundamental. In his last work, *The Visible and The Invisible*, Merleau-Ponty describes this fundamental confusion between the see-er and the seen, the touching and the touched, the listener and the speaker, as a *chiasm*, and it is explicit in his work, as it is intended to be in this one, that this chiasm, this confusion, is a positive phenomenon. I see things because I am also seeable, and I am here on this side of the mirror because the reflection is also there. One can, of course, again deny this experience with the explanation, but this denial now comes at a very high price. The see-er before the mirror who would now deny his experience for the explanation would be saying in effect that he is as see-er identical with the one who is on *this* side of the mirror, a see-er therefore who is not seen, an invisible see-er. He would in other words be affirming through his denial the Cartesian fantasy of the mirror, and like the Cartesian he would believe that the reflection is after all only a dummy and has nothing to do with him. Or perhaps even more than a dummy this invisible "see-er" would be like a vampire because he too would cast no reflection.

The *experience* of the mirror reflection compels us to affirm what the *explanation* of the mirror reflection denies: the reflection does *matter*, and in two senses of the term. It is important, and it is the visible *materialization* of oneself there in the world on that side of the mirror. The reflection "makes a difference": it counts *and* it shows a way of mattering in another fashion. It shows that *the immaterial matters*. Moreover, we might also say that the mirror reflection "de-realizes" the reflected insofar as it breaks up the too easy and uncritically accepted identification of the real with material substantiality. In summary, the reflection as it is lived and experienced collapses the too arbitrary and absolute dichotomy between the real and the unreal, the collapse which is significant for the recovery of psychological life on its own terms.

But we are not yet finished with the mirror reflection, because in addition to asking *where* the reflection is, it is necessary also to ask, " *Who* is the reflection?" This second question deepens the sense in which the reflection "de-realizes" the reflected.

"Who is the reflection?" An answer to this question is again easily provided by the physical-geometrical explanation. The reflection is a representation of the one who is reflected on this side of the mirror. It is a copy of the reflected, a visual double of the empirical me standing here on this side of the mirror.

A moment's pause, however, now persuades us that this is not the case. On the contrary, when I look in the mirror I never see merely a double of myself on this side of the mirror but rather *a figure in a story*, as illustrated in Figure 2. It is a character that I see when I look "in" the mirror, a figure who may be a saint or a sinner. At times the figure may be the youth who has slipped away from my life; at times it may be the old man who too quickly approaches with the declining years. But whoever the figure may be, the reflection is never of the empirical person who stands on this side of the mirror. The lined face, sagging chest, and balding head tell a story, and in this sense the reflection gathers together these features, which would otherwise merely be statistical facts about the person reflected, and weaves around them a tale. In the wrinkled face and baggy eyes the middle-aged man may see the absence of an admiring glance, just as in the soft mouth and seductive eyes the young woman may read the furtive intentions of another's desire. *The reflection, then, is of*

Figure 2. The reflection as a figure in a tale. Adapted by Claire Pate from R. Brent Bonah and Sheila Shively, *The Language Lens,* p. 15

Figure 3. The reflection re-figures the person. Drawing by Claire Pate

a figure and not of the person, and even if one insists that the reflection is only a pale copy of the reflected that too is a way of spinning a tale. The one who sees through the reflection only a duplicate of himself on this side of the mirror is the one who tells the tale of science.

It seems obvious from these few remarks that the reflection as a figure transforms the reflected. The figure in the story is a figure for someone, and that someone is not the empirical person on this side of the mirror. On the contrary, when I see a reflection I see a figure through the eyes of a specific type of other, and it is this other and not the empirical person who sees the figure. The young woman, for example, sees an alluring reflection through the eyes of an adoring man, and it is *this adoring man and not the young woman* who temporarily stands on this side of the mirror. The reflection as a figure in a story *infects* the reflected, and the one who sees the reflection is caught up in the story. The reflection "de-realizes" the reflected as it transforms the one who is on this side of the mirror into a character in the tale. This feature of "de-realization" is illustrated in Figure 3.

The example of the mirror indicates two features about the reflection which are significant for understanding psychological life. On one hand the mirror experience illustrates that the reflection matters. The image counts. It has weight. On the other hand the example indicates that the reflection also transforms the reflected. The image de-realizes the reflected. It re-figures it. Each of these features of the reflection challenges some of the customary and natural ways of regarding reality and psychological life. In the next section I want to consider the significance of these features and these challenges. But before I do this one additional remark about the mirror reflection is to be made.

Everything which has been said about the experience of the mirror reflection is usually unnoticed or forgotten in our natural and habitual ways of thinking and in the explanations for the mirror reflection which grow out of them. To use this example, therefore, we have had to remember what we live forgetfully, an effort which further characterizes the reflection as a re-covered reality in two senses of this term. The reflection is always in need of being recovered from the forgetfulness of habit and routine, but it is also always destined to be re-covered (covered over) again. This third feature is also significant for our understanding of psychological life, and it too is to be considered in the next section.

THE MIRROR REFLECTION AND PSYCHOLOGICAL LIFE

The significance of psychological life as a reality of reflection is conveniently illustrated by the mirror reflection. This example points out three features of psychological life, each of which challenges our ordinary conceptions of what is real and what is psychological.

The Immaterial Reflection Matters

The mirror experience presents the *immaterial* reflection as a weighty *matter.* In the experience of the reflection the image, this non-material and insubstantial appearance, counts and has weight. The image is important and significant. With the mirror experience the reflection enters our life as a reality.

This feature of the reflection, however, poses a problem. From the point of view of everyday, natural, empirical reality the reflection is not real because the real is identified with the material substantiality of the reflected. The experience of the mirror reflection, therefore, challenges this natural tendency to define the reflected as the only real and consequently to dismiss the reflection as unreal. Indeed, the experience forces a reversal of this natural tendency. It invites and even demands that we move from an empirical understanding of reality which excludes the reflection to another understanding of reality which includes it.

But to include the reflections of reality in an understanding of what is real is to open the way for a psychological perspective, since psychological life makes its appearance as a reality of reflection. Indeed the whole point of the mirror example was to help us to see some of the features of psychological life as a reflection. The example, therefore, draws us toward this conclusion. As a reality of reflection, psychological life matters. It is important and it is real. To be psychological in this way is to insist that psychological life is not on the other side of reality. To be psychological in this way is to refuse the dichotomy between the empirically real and the psychologically unreal. To be psychological in this way is to remember that psychological life shows itself through the empirical world, that it is a deepening of this given world, that the given world in its substantial materiality is the material of human psychological life. Indeed, to be psychological in this way is to see the empirical attitude as a special and specific expression of psychological life. To regard the world in its material substantiality as an objective reality in itself on the other side of which there is the subjective is to adopt a specific historical appearance of psychological life. One point of this work is to unfold this story, that is the psychological story of psychology as an empirical science. At the moment its unfolding requires that we consider more fully the relation between empirical reality and psychological life. What does it mean to refuse the placement of psychological life on the other side of the empirically real and to insist that psychological life shows itself through and is a deepening and re-figuring of the empirical world? To answer this question we must return to the example and broaden it.

In the mirror example there is the person standing before the mirror, the mirror, and the reflection which is as far on that side of the mirror as the person is on this side of it. The mirror is over there, an

object or thing in the world, while the person who is over here we cus-
tomarily regard as a subject. However we may express it, the issue is the
same: there is the person and the mirror, a subject and an object, man and
world. Let us, therefore, speak of persons and things, and then let us
formulate our question in this fashion: *What is the place of the reflection in relation to persons and things?* In order to be clear, however,
about our major concern, let us remember that when we are speaking
about the reflection we are speaking about human psychological life.
Hence our question is: *What is the place of psychological life in relation
to persons and things?* Furthermore, in order to broaden our scope let
us keep in mind that in daily life the mirrors which reflect psychological
life are more often than not the things of the world and other people.
In the next two chapters these mirrorings will be made explicit. At the
moment I am interested only in acknowledging that the example we are
using is a special and specific case of a more general theme.

We recall from the example that the reflection is a deepening and re-
figuring of the reflected, and these two points already indicate the place
of the reflection with respect to persons and things. For example the
depth of the reflection emphasizes that the reflection is not the mirror
itself. The reflection is not in the mirror or on the glass. Its depth,
therefore, preserves the reflection from an identification with or reduction to the mirror. And yet, while the reflection is preserved in this
fashion, it is obviously the case that without the mirror there is no reflection. The reflection shows itself through this thing. It is through this
object that the reflection appears. With respect to psychological life,
then, we may say that while it shows itself through the given material
world, it is not reducible to or identified with the things of the world.
In other words, there is no psychological life apart from the material
world of events and things, any more than there could be a reflection
without an object or thing to bear and contain it. The given world of
material events and things is in this sense the vessel of psychological life.
But on the other hand this given world is not literally our psychological
life, any more than the thing which bears the reflection is the reflection.
Our psychological life is not *in* things, or because of them, it is given
through them.

The mirror example which is guiding our understanding of psychological life as a reality of reflection forces upon us, therefore, a paradox. Psychological life is and is not the empirical world. As troublesome as this paradox may be, however, it nevertheless has the benefit of avoiding either a reduction of the psychological realm to the empirical order or the dualism of the empirical world *and* psychological life. Indeed, in place of this dualism (or reductionism) the paradox offers a *difference*. Psychological life is different from the empirical world, even while it is through the world of empirical events and things that it appears. The paradox, therefore, allows and respects the relation which does exist between the empirical world and psychological life without losing a sense of their difference.

There is no question that this way of presenting psychological life challenges ingrained assumptions. I would point out, however, that much of what is being said here about the relation of difference between the empirical world and psychological life finds its counterpart in contemporary physics. If from the side of psychological life we are forced to admit that there is no psychological life apart from the material world of events and things, then from the side of contemporary physics we are forced to acknowledge that there is no material world of events and things apart from human psychological life. And just as this view of psychological life does not reduce the psychological order to the order of material events and things, this view of contemporary physical science does not intend to reduce the material order of the world to psychological life. On the contrary, contemporary physics is simply acknowledging the relation between the empirical world and psychological life (between the observer and the events observed) without forgetting their difference. This is the point of view which the American physicist John Wheeler seems to adopt when he speaks of the "Leibniz logic loop." "The analysis of the physical world, pursued to sufficient depth," he writes, "will lead back in some now-hidden way to man himself."[9] Contemporary physics and the view of psychological life presented here seem to agree on this point: we can neither speak about the world without speaking about ourselves, nor speak about ourselves without speaking about the world. To understand psychological life, therefore, we must learn how to read our many ways of reading the world.

If the depth of the reflection teaches us something about the relation between psychological life and things, then the reflection as a re-figuring of the reflected tells us something about the relation between psychological life and persons. The reflection is not the person but a figure in a tale, and yet the person who is re-figured in that way is the one who lives the story. Between the empirical person and the reflection as a figure, then, there is once again a relation of difference. Without the person there is obviously no figure, but the figure is just as obviously not identical with or reducible to the person. Thus, just as the depth of the reflection preserves it from identification with or reduction to the mirror-thing, the reflection as a figure is preserved from any identification with the person. With respect to psychological life this preservation means that human psychological life is not the same thing as the life of the person, even though it is always a person who bears psychological life. Since I will consider this point in more detail in the following section, I will limit my remarks here to one additional point. The recognition that human psychological life is not identical to the life of the person is in accordance with the original genius of depth psychology. The genius of Freud was to recover beyond the official life of the person (the life of the ego) the main currents of psychological life. It was the dreams and the emotions of his patients which revealed their psychological stories, and to enter these stories Freud had to develop a technique which would allow him to listen beyond the official language of the person. Even though this technique leads to the notion of an instinctual unconscious in Freud, we need not follow depth psychology along this path.[10] We can, however, take notice of how the mirror experience evokes again the initial insight of depth psychology insofar as it teaches us that psychological life as a reality of reflection is not identical to the official life of the person.

The mirror experience tells us that the reflection matters, and with respect to psychological life this first feature forces us to acknowledge that psychological life is real. This acknowledgment in turn forces us to reconsider the relation between empirical reality and psychological reality. In more specific terms this acknowledgment leads us to the question concerning the place of psychological life in relation to persons and things. I have suggested here that the relation between empirical and psychological reality is a relation of difference, that psychological life occupies a paradoxical place with respect to persons and things. Were I to summarize these remarks now, I would say that psychological life is a different reality. It is, if you wish, a third between persons and things, man and world, subject and object. Between persons and things, man and world, subject and object, a story appears, a story which is expressed in terms of a way of seeing and of speaking about the world. The story which appears is the appearance of psychological life. We will do well to remember this characterization of psychological life as a third and to recall that psychological life as a reality of reflection, as an image, is neither subjective nor objective.

The Reflection Re-figures the Person

The mirror reflection deepens the reflected, and this deepening transforms the material person before the mirror into a character in a tale. The mirror reflection is not a duplicate of the reflected person on this side of the mirror but the image of a figure in a story. In brief, the reflection *re-figures* the person.

Psychology as a science is a study of persons, and as such it concerns itself with the empirical events of an individual's biographical life. The mirror reflection indicates however that psychological life as a reflection which matters is wrapped up in figures. It is not the empirical person which *matters* for psychological life. *The figure matters.* And it is not the empirical events of one's biography which are psychological, but the way in which those events are gathered together to weave a tale. Through the things of the world, with others, and across time psychological life tells its stories, and in those stories the person who I am is *re-figured.* For example, the American anthropologist Loren Eiseley has written an autobiography entitled *All the Strange Hours,* in which we come to know this complex and sensitive man through the several different figures which make up his life. There is no one person to be found between the covers of this book, no one person whom the reader can directly see as the subject of this individual history. Rather the man one comes to glimpse as Loren Eiseley appears only indirectly through the figures of the "drifter," the "thinker," and the "doubter." Each of these figures inhabits a landscape of things and others, and collectively these figures are the person. In this regard the person I am, the ego, the self which recognizes itself as a coherent self and is so recognized by others, is not the condition of the existence and appearance of the figures but their consequence. Stated in another way, the person whom philosophy recognizes as the coherent, stable source of action and meaning is *not* a psychological reality. *Person* is a philosophical notion; *figure* is psychological.

Obviously, however, I am not suggesting here a denial of the notion of person, nor do I intend to enter into a discussion of the logical primacy of person over figure. My point is only that while person as a philosophical notion is a viable reality in the experience of one's life, it is *not* a legitimate notion for a psychological discipline. To meet psychological life on its own terms requires respect for the figures who are one's psychological life. If person has a *logical* primacy, figure has a *psychological* one.

One can appreciate this difference immediately by wondering about who writes this book. Obviously, it is a person, and yet this question is not settled with this reply. Indeed the question and answer are deepened if one also recognizes the figures who author this work. It is not necessary here to be specific about them. It is enough to say only that they lurk in the dedication, as they most often do. Indeed, when one reads a book, one should pay attention to the dedication. It provides another slant on the work.

Perhaps, however, I should provide a specific example of this difference. An illustration is apparent in Eiseley's work, specifically in the *tone* of his book. A person, Loren Eiseley, writes this work, and yet he who writes the book is in his remembering re-figured by the figures who are remembered. The reader hears the story through that figure who glances back in a particular way. It is an old man who is sensitive enough to realize it without regret. And indeed it is this way of figuring the story of a life which makes it so memorable and so moving because in some small measure we are all always figures who see with the eyes of an "old man" when we glance backward at our past. This tone is the mood of that figure, a mood which may be the tone of all autobiographical reminiscence.

Eiseley's autobiography is neither about one particular person nor authored by one particular person. Taken psychologically, the subject and author of the work are multiple and not one. But in addition to this point about person and figure, we should also note another point. As autobiography Eiseley's work is certainly not *fiction*. Fiction is neither what he writes nor what he intends. But neither is it *fact*. It is, on the contrary, an exceptional illustration of *psychological* story, and this marvelously moving little book portrays with eloquence and rare beauty that landscape which lies between fact and fiction, the domain of psychological life. It is moreover a landscape which one inhabits every day of one's life, and though we dwell there with less eloquence than Eiseley we dwell there nonetheless. The things which make up my life, for example, are *psychologically speaking* not my possessions. I do not own them. On the contrary they embody the figures of my life, those companions who have accompanied "me" along the way. To look at these things is to catch the reflections of those figures. The figures dwell there. The material things of the world are the home of one's psychological life. The world is alive psychologically.

Earlier I spoke of how the reflection matters. The sense of this phrase can now be extended. Psychological life as a reflection which matters is a deepening of the reflected, and this deepening is a re-figuring of the empirical, factual events of one's life as a story and of the person as a character in a tale. This view is obviously critical of scientific psychology's understanding of itself as a study of persons. Just as the psychological world is neither empirically real nor unreal, psychological life is not the life of persons. On the contrary, figures which are neither fictional nor factual belong to the psychological world in much the same manner as persons belong to the empirical world of facts. If psychology is to be psychological it must respect this difference. It is, however, a difference which the fantasy or dream of scientific psychology conceals.

The Reflection as a Recovered Reality

The drama which takes place before the mirror, the re-figuring of the person as a character in a tale, is naturally forgotten. In daily life the reflection is taken for granted. It is simply assumed and passed over in our daily habits and routines. One does not notice the story which is reflected. On the contrary the story is lived through. Indeed, in order to realize the significance of the reflection as a reality which matters, the attitude of everyday life must be temporarily *disrupted* and an effort at *recovery* must be made. The mirror reflection is a remembered reality. It is a recovered reality.

Psychological life, like the mirror reflection, is also covered over in our daily habits and routines. In the natural attitude[11] of daily life we live on an empirical level with things, with others, and with our own bodies, which means that we take these realities *matter of factly* as *matters of fact.* The cup is simply the cup, as my friend Thomas is simply Tom, or as my right hand is simply a hand, and it is only in the disruption of this matter-of-fact attitude, this literal cast of mind, that the cup and Thomas and my right hand reflect a tale. The *broken* cup,[12] for example, suddenly reflects those quiet moments of the evening when my wife and I sit together drinking tea. Through its shattered pieces the dreaming figure of the late evening is reflected.

Like the mirror reflection, therefore, psychological life is a recovered reality, and it is the moment of disruption which allows the recovery. An interruption of the natural course of life is the eruption of the psychological, and indeed psychological life is always something of an *opus contra naturam,*[13] a work against the natural attitude of forgetfulness so characteristic of everyday life. Re-membering, which means a gathering together again when it is written in this fashion, is an index of psychological life, and it is not surprising that modern depth psychology begins with remembering and its difficulties. Freud's psychology, which is in many respects not modern psychology at all, first remembers psychological life through the disruptions provided by symptoms and dreams.

But the reality of psychological life which must always be recovered from forgetfulness, from its hiddenness in habit and routine, is destined to be covered over again. *Recovered* means not only "found again" but also "hidden again." The mirror reflection whose significance is recovered must eventually be abandoned in order that one may pursue the tasks of the day. One cannot stay forever, or even for very long, before the mirror noticing the reflection. Indeed to do so may even be dangerous. Narcissus, after all, lingers before the mirror—forever—and we are aware of his fate. His involvement with the reflection leads to death. Does this figure present us with a warning about psychological life? Is psychological life inextricably bound up with the theme of death?[14] Be that as it may, in daily life we do not and cannot linger with the reflection. The children must be driven to school and one's business affairs must be arranged. In the course of the day one necessarily slips back into the empirical course of events and the significance of the reflection is again forgotten. Later, perhaps, the story and the figure are recovered again, through the mirror of things or others, for example. But just as surely as they are recovered they are covered over again, making psychological life rhythmic in its hiddenness and revelation, and rhythmic perhaps in its interplay between living and dying.

This second sense of recovery emphasizes the hiddenness of psychological life, which is after all only another way of speaking about the indirect character of psychological life. Insofar as psychological life shows itself through the world, it also hides itself in the world. The world, we might say, holds many secrets, and most, if not all of them, are about us. Moreover, insofar as psychological life hides itself in the world, this third and final feature of psychological life as a reality of reflection bears a consequence. It means that psychological life requires a discipline which is redone in every age. As the world changes, so does psychological life change. As the way in which we understand the things of the world and the human body changes, the way in which psychological life reveals and conceals itself changes.

SUMMARY

What does it mean to understand psychological life as a reality of reflection? This has been the question addressed in this section, and in answer to it three features of psychological life have been presented. Psychological life as a reality of reflection is a *recovery* of how the psychological dimension of human life *matters* by *re-figuring* the world of fact as story and the person as a figure in a tale.

The Moving Earth and the Human Corpse

In 1543 two events occurred which are of decisive significance for understanding the history of modern psychology as a so-called separate science, a story which Husserl has called a "history of crises."[15] On one hand Corpernicus' treatise dealing with the revolution of the earth around the sun was published.[16] On the other hand, Vesalius' book on the fabric of the human body, that work which in many respects inaugurated the modern approach to anatomy, also appeared.[17] What is the relationship between these two works, one which transformed the world of things and the other which changed the human body? And what is the significance of their relationship for the appearance of psychological life in modern psychology?

Copernicus must imaginatively stand on the sun to move the earth,[18] and the true significance of this achievement lies less in a stellar revisioning of the heavens and more in a shift in attitude, in a new way of standing which this achievement demands. Galileo recognizes this latter point very early, praising Copernicus in this fashion: "I cannot find any bounds for my admiration, how that reason was able in Aristarchus and Copernicus, to commit such a rape on their senses, as in despite thereof to make herself mistress of their credulity."[19] It is not Copernicus' new geometry of the heavens which Galileo admires, but rather reason's rape of the senses.

To move the earth Copernicus must disregard the appearance of things, and in place of the *experience* of the earth as the stable and central ground of humanity's place in the heavens he mist substitute an *idea* for it. This remarkable achievement requires a new posture in relation to which appearances are deceptive, and if Copernicus is not yet a Cartesian, practicing a methodic doubt with respect to appearances, he nevertheless takes that first step which is to reach its philosophical climax some seventy-five years later in Descartes. With Copernicus reason rapes the senses, allowing him temporarily to disregard the appearance of things and so to dispense with the living human body as ground of knowledge. On a moving earth a body which still "sees" a rising and a setting sun is an impediment to knowledge. Indeed, as van den Berg suggests, in order to do science one must abandon one's body.[20] This methodic distrust of experienced appearances is the power of modern science *and* the nourishing soil of modern psychology. This methodically practiced doubt is the condition for the success of the natural sciences *and* the reason for modern psychology's history of crises, as the rest of this book tries to show.

But what is this body which is abandoned, and where "on earth" is it to be found? It is the corpse, and it is to be found on Vesalius' dissecting table. The body which Copernicus leaves behind in order to move the earth becomes the body of modern anatomy and physiology. Copernicus' new world is complemented by Vesalius' new body. Modern physics and physiology are identical twins.

There is not, however, a causal relationship between these two events. The body which Vesalius cuts into is as much ground for Copernicus' achievement as the latter is for the former. Vesalius' work honors the anatomical corpse and not the living human body, and in this way his work allows Copernicus to take his first step of dispensing with the body. Copernicus does not refigure the geometry of the heavens without Vesalius' new vision of the body. On the other hand, however, Vesalius' new body could not appear on a stationary earth. The anatomical body can dwell only on the moving earth. It is the corpse, whose "life" is no longer understood in terms of the world but rather in terms of the mechanisms of the physiological body, which haunts the Copernican earth. It is *on* this earth which moves daily round that sun and *in* this body as a corpse that psychological life makes its appearance in modern psychology.

A moving earth and a corpse lying on a dissecting table are the two concrete events through which we can imaginatively recover the reflections of psychological life in scientific psychology. A physics of the world and a physiology of the body reflect psychological life in modern times. Lest, however, this effort seem initially unwarranted, consider how this same relation appears in the works of Galileo and Newton, and most explicitly perhaps in those of Descartes. It appears, for example, in Galileo's doctrine of primary and secondary qualities as described by Edwin Burtt,[21] and Norwood Hanson[22] notes how Newton's *Opticks*, which presents a physics of light, presupposes a physiological eye which in turn explains the psychology of seeing. For Descartes we need only look through the pages of *The Dioptrics* to see how his psychology of seeing presumes these same terms. Speaking of his theory of vision, which is his psychology of seeing, Descartes advises us that we can be more certain of its facts if we demonstrate them by taking "the eye of a newly dead man."[23] Descartes could not be more explicit. It is the eye of the corpse through which we are to see the life of vision.

Perhaps, however, there is an even better place to spy the moving earth and the human corpse in the imaginal background of modern psychology: Descartes' posthumously published *Treatise of Man*. The explicit intention of this work is to bring together in one system physics, physiology, and psychology, and in this work psychology cannot be understood apart from the new cosmology (Copernican), physics (Galilean), and physiology (Vesalian-Harveian) of the sixteenth and seventeenth centuries. Originally intended as the second part of a three-part work entitled *The World*, the *Treatise of Man* clearly demonstrates that while its intention "was the interpretation of physiological function in terms of matter in motion,"[24] a physics applied to physiology, its consequence is a psychology suited to people who have lost their place in the world and whose psychological life, therefore, is no longer lived through their relation to the world but rather *in* the body. In discussions of pain, touch, taste, smell, hearing, breathing, seeing, and other dimensions of human life, one finds the same movements toward the *inside* of the body and away from the world as it is lived and experienced painfully, touchingly, tastefully, and so on. Writing to Father Mersenne of this intended work in 1629, Descartes clarifies the direction taken by this psychology which appears on the grounds of a Copernican earth and in the shadows of a human corpse. "In my *World*," he writes, "I shall speak somewhat more of man than I had thought to before," and then announcing what he plans to do beyond what he has already written, he adds, "Now I am dissecting the heads of different animals in order to explain what imagination, memory, etc. consist of."[25] The point is clear. The ground of modern psychology is a lifeless world and a dissected corpse. Imagination, memory, etc., reside *inside* the heads of animals and of humans. Experience is *inside* the body.

What happened in the sixteenth century continues today, but in a way which is more hidden because it is more easily assumed. What was a project for Descartes has become a commonplace for us, and one still finds these same kinds of events in the imaginal background of psychology. For example, in an article written by B. F. Skinner, entitled "The Machine That Is Man,"[26] the corpse still haunts modern psychology. It is of course an animated corpse, because there beats within it the heart as a pump first described by William Harvey in 1628. But it is nevertheless a corpse. And with respect to the Copernican earth as indicative of the world of modern psychology, it is easy enough to show that it is this earth which whirls under psychology's feet, accounting in part perhaps for why much of modern psychology is a dizzying array of multitudinous facts and theories. In an introductory textbook where the meaning of psychology as a science is being discussed we find this passage: "It was once common sense that the sun, rising always in the east and setting in the west, must daily pass around the earth. It was common sense that the earth, stretching out apparently endlessly in all directions, must therefore be flat. The youngest schoolboy," the author continues, "nowadays knows better."[27] Perhaps, however, the most convincing example appears in an article entitled "Subjective Contours" which appeared in *Scientific American*.[28] The title of the article betrays the author's point. An incomplete figure like the Ponzo illusion (Figure 4) can give rise to a visually experienced figure, a triangle, which is, however, only *subjective*. That is, geometrical figures which are left unfinished and are arranged in a certain way can give the appearance of another experienced figure, the contours of which have no *physical* basis in reality. We "see," therefore, something

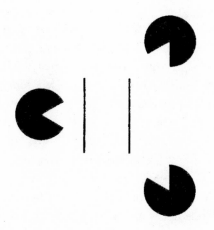

Figure 4. The Ponzo illusion. From "Subjective Contours," by Gaetano Kanizsa. Copyright © 1976 by Scientific American, Inc. All rights reserved.

which is not there to be seen. The point, however, is that these experienced figures are *not* there to be seen from the perspective of the incomplete figures as defined in physical-geometrical terms, *and* from the perspective of the eye defined by physiology. The triangle which is not physically present but which we nevertheless "see" in the Ponzo illusion does not register on the retina, and it is from the point of view of this eye that what we "see" is defined as subjective, and even at places in the article as an illusion. One's experience of seeing becomes a subjective reality, that is, a reality with no basis in physical reality, in a psychology done within the context of physics and physiology.

These three brief examples all illustrate the same point. In modern psychology psychological life appears in a world defined by physics and within a body defined by physiology. This particular reflection of psychological life was true at the beginning of modern psychology in the sixteenth century and remains true today. And the consequence of this reflection is that psychological life appears as an *interior event.* The interiorization and the literalization of psychological life as an event are two features to be explored.

INTERIORIZATION: MONA LISA'S SMILE

In psychology as a science, psychological life is reflected through the physical world and the physiological body, and through these mirrors psychological life is *interiorized*. This interiorization is one feature of psychological life in modern times, and Mona Lisa's smile offers some visible evidence of it. The painting was executed in 1503, well within the same period when the term *psychology* appeared, and it reflects this relation between a science of nature, including the human body, and modern psychology. Mona Lisa's smile and the landscape behind her merit our concern.

Van den Berg writes that the landscape behind the smiling woman "is the first landscape painted as a landscape," that is, "an exterior nature closed within itself and self-sufficient, an exterior from which the human element has, in principle, been removed entirely." It presents, he says, "things-in-their-farewell,"[29] by which he means things which no longer provide a place for humans to dwell. These are strange things, things newly imagined, nature as it has never been seen before. It is a landscape "almost hostile in its sublime indifference," which, as the poet Rilke says, foreshadows the Galilean world,[30] a *neutral* landscape which will better reflect the space of scientific objects which fall equally fast than it will the experiences of human life. And in the midst of this landscape looms the figure of Mona Lisa. She dominates the landscape even while she turns her back on it and faces us with her smile.

How is one to understand this smile? Enigmatic, it haunted da Vinci's contemporaries even as it continues to intrigue us today. Who can look at this painting and not be captivated by that smile? Who can look at it and not wonder what it reveals and hides? And yet we are at a loss even to begin to answer such questions. Indeed, we do not even know where to look for a clue within the confines of the painting. The smile of Mona Lisa is and remains a secret smile, and nothing around her, nothing in the landscape, reflects its meaning. "Her smile seals an inner self," van den Berg writes; "she is the first," he continues, "who is estranged from the landscape."[31]

Estranged from the landscape? Here is a clue.[32] Mona Lisa faces us with a smile which dominates the painting, and the force of the painting turns us as viewers toward that smile *and* away from the landscape, even as Mona Lisa herself has turned her back on the world. It is the smile and only the smile we are meant to see. We are not invited nor are we meant to see through it a world which is its reflection. On the contrary, as Walter Pater remarks, we are meant to see only the smile and behind it, in a world beyond time, "a *beauty wrought out from within* upon the flesh, the deposit, little cell by cell, of strange thoughts and fantastic reveries and exquisite passions." Her smile is a dream from within. And even if we do manage to see the landscape, then all that we see is a neutral, sublime indifference. Mona Lisa's smile does not fit the landscape. "She is older than the rocks among which she sits," Pater says, and "like the vampire, she has been dead many times, and learned the secrets of the grave."[33] Her smile is of another time and another place. It has no place in the world.

The smile and the estrangement belong together as one theme, as a theme of separation between man and world. Mona Lisa's smile is perhaps the first face which simultaneously invites us to look away from the world and to gaze inside. It is perhaps the first modern face which invites a new way of seeing, a way of seeing which says in effect that if we are to understand the smile we must retreat inside. It is a way of seeing which invites a blindness for the world. Indeed, Mona Lisa may be, as Pater says, "the symbol of the modern idea,"[34] the symbol of a life of Cartesian thought and of Freudian dreams divorced from the world. Modern psychology is the practiced discipline of this strange way of looking, and the painting portrays the emergence of modern psychology as a separate and independent discipline on *this side of the world*. The world as landscape is now something to look at, something to inspect, and in the face of this world one now sees only one's exclusion, an exclusion which invites one to gaze inside. There is nowhere else to turn but inside. Mona Lisa turns in this way and so does Descartes, who in 1619 crosses a threshold into a small stove-heated room in Germany to dream alone his new dream of reason. Like Descartes' *cogito* Mona Lisa's smile betrays a communion with herself and with herself alone. Modern psychology is the discipline created by this exclusion, a science of the inner self which appears in the midst of an alien world. And even when in more recent times psychology proclaims itself the science of *exterior* behavior, it remains haunted by the smile of Mona Lisa, since the rejection of this inner domain *in fact* is still the acceptance of it *in principle*. The world as defined by physics and the body as defined by physiology establish psychological life as an interior domain, and the denial of the interiority of psychological life without re-visioning body and world leaves untouched the science of psychology as a science of the homeless and the dispossessed. Mona Lisa's portrait is the visible expression of this dispossession. Her smile is the face of modern psychology.

Newton's Rainbow

The smiling of Mona Lisa cannot be divorced from the turning of her back on the world. Turning away from the world, she turns inside, and one is not able to find the meaning of her smile through the landscape in which she dwells. While "her" back is turned (which is also our back) the world is changed, and in such a way that the meaning of her smile can no longer be supported by the world. An event which occurred in 1666 illustrates this world which appears behind "her" back and the relation of this foreign landscape to a smile which belongs only on this side of the world.

In 1666 Isaac Newton goes into a darkened room and through a small hole which he makes in his window shade a ray of the daylight sun streams through. Placing a prism between the shade and the opposite wall in his room, Newton sees the spectrum. White light, the light of the sun, is really the composite colors of the spectrum. Going into the dark and turning his back on the light outside his room, Newton sees what others outside his room in the world do not see. He sees the sunlight as composed of "Difform Rays, some of which are more refrangible than others."[35] A remarkable achievement, Newton's scientific explanation of color is a clear example of the power and precision of early modern science. But that *achievement* is not my concern. On the contrary, I am concerned with the manner in which this achievement is understood, and with the implications of this understanding. Newton does not stay in his darkened room where the spectrum appears. He goes outside again and sees the spectrum in the rainbow.

In describing this experiment, Newton announces that it makes evident "why the colours of the rainbow appear in falling drops of rain."[36] This is an astonishing claim. In one sentence tucked innocently enough within the body of this article Newton claims to have unweaved the rainbow in a darkened room. The issue is not whether the claim is correct or incorrect. Indeed the claim is both right and wrong. Rather the issue is how the claim *forgets* a *difference*.

> Nature and Nature's law lay hid in night.
> God said, "Let Newton be!" And all was Light.[37]

These are the words of homage which the eighteenth-century poet Alexander Pope wrote in praise of Newton and his new science. They are well deserved even if a little extravagant. Newton has not been universally praised, however, and we hear in a later poet's voice a different claim. John Keats says it this way:

> Do not all charms fly
> At the mere touch of cold philosophy?
> There was an awful rainbow once in heaven:
> We know her woof, her texture; she is given
> In the dull catalogue of common things.
> Philosophy will clip an Angel's wings,
> Conquer all mysteries by rule and line,
> Empty the haunted air, and gnomed mine-
> Unweave a rainbow.[38]

Pope and Keats look differently upon the same achievement. Like Newton, Pope does not see a difference between the rainbow and the spectrum, or if he does it is a difference which does not matter. Keats, on the other hand, does see a difference. How, we must ask, can the difference be denied? And what is the difference which Keats sees?

For Newton the spectrum in his darkened room is a matter for the eyes alone. Indeed it is a matter for a very special eye, the prismatic eye, the eye of anatomy and physiology. To "see" the spectrum one must look with this special eye, and seen with this eye, the spectrum is *only* a visual spectacle. The colors of the spectrum, for example, provide no warmth. Pope sees the rainbow in this same way. Like Newton, he "sees" the rainbow only with his eyes. The difference between the rainbow and the spectrum can be denied, therefore, if one pretends that seeing is a matter only of what meets the eye, and if one treats this seeing eye only as an organ of vision.

There is, however, another point in the denial of this difference. Newton intends to look only with his eyes and to treat his eyes in this special way. The arrangements which he makes and the procedures and instruments—like the prism—which he uses are evidence of this intention. His intention is concrete and explicit. Pope, however, *misses* the intentional character of this vision. He brings no prism to the rainbow. The consequences are first that a particular way of seeing or *how* one sees is forgotten, and second that in this forgetfulness *what* is seen defines the way things really are in themselves. *What* one sees is taken literally. In fact this forgetfulness is true even of Newton. While his intention to see in a particular way is explicit and concrete in the conditions of his experiment, he discounts these conditions. He denies that there is a relation between *how* he sees and *what* is seen. Wanting to avoid the charge that the prism *creates* the spectrum he uses two prisms for what he calls an "*Experimentum Crucis*,"[39] and on the basis of the results of this experiment he concludes that the conditions—specifically the prism—do not count in the vision of light as a spectrum. And yet while this experiment proves his point—the spectrum is *not created* by the prism—his specific conclusion does not follow. The demonstration that the prism does not produce the spectrum does not mean that the spectrum exists in itself apart from those conditions. In other words, the "*Experimentum Crucis*" does not warrant a neglect or forgetfulness of these conditions. It is, however, precisely these conditions which are forgotten by Newton and by Pope. Each forgets that *what* he sees—the rainbow as a spectrum— is in relation to *how* he sees. Thus to deny the difference between the rainbow and the spectrum, not only must one look solely with one's eyes and treat one's eyes in a special way as organs of vision, but also one must forget how one is seeing. One must forget this because to remember how one is seeing the rainbow would mean that the rainbow is as much *unlike* the spectrum as it is *like* it, that it is as *different* from it as it is the *same*.

But how else does one see if not with the eyes? Here we must go to Keats, who looks at the rainbow in another way. Keats sees a difference, and to see the difference between the rainbow and the spectrum we must see how Keats looks.

The rainbow arches across the sky, and to see it is also to see the change in the brilliance of the light and to *smell* the freshness of the summer day. With the rainbow *seen* in the sky there is also a *touch* of the air on one's skin, and one cannot help but notice a change in the rhythm and *sounds* of the day. Looking at the rainbow slows down the tempo of the day, and indeed a rainbow which does not temporarily suspend the pace of the day is unthinkable. A rainbow is a temporary respite from the concerns of the day, the world's promise of a richer horizon.

Keats, and anyone who has ever seen a rainbow, looks in this way. It is all of these experiences, of sight and sound, of touch and smell, and of mood, and all of these experiences belong together. One *sees* the rainbow as much with the skin as one does with the eyes, and as much with the nose and the ears as well. Indeed this is why a blind person can see the rainbow even without eyes, because seeing is not simply an event of the empirical, anatomical body. On the contrary, seeing is an embodied vision. One sees with the eyes, but it is with the embodied eye that one sees. Indeed one is *unable* to see in this latter way *only* if one pretends that one's eye is a prism, *only* if one first allows the eye to become the eye of anatomy and physiology. Newton's vision, and Pope's too, is, therefore, a very special vision, and their eyes are paradoxically penetrating and strangely blind. Keats' eye, on the other hand, is the living eye, the eye which if it sees as a prism sees itself seeing in this way. It is an eye which practices a double vision, and it is this embodied eye which sees the difference between the rainbow and the spectrum.

The difference or lack of it between the rainbow and the spectrum depends upon how one looks. How one looks, however, has consequences, especially for psychology. If one forgets how the rainbow becomes primarily a visual spectacle, one's experience of all the other dimensions which comprise seeing a rainbow—its touch, smell, sound, mood, etc.— is *not supported* by the world. Newton's rainbow supports only the empirical eye, and hence like Mona Lisa's smile all these other experiences retreat *inside*. They become conditions or properties of the subject, destined to lead only a *mental* existence. These experiences become *only* experiences, and in the history of modern psychology *experience* comes to mean subjective, not real, simply what one feels, and at times even an illusion. We should not be surprised to learn, therefore, that the term *hallucinate* makes its first appearance in the English language in 1604,[40] right between Mona Lisa's smile and the appearance of Newton's rainbow. It appears in Robert Cawdrey's *A table alphabeticall of English wordes*, and some forty years later in 1646, only twenty years before Newton's rainbow, *hallucination* makes its first appearance in the specific context of psychopathology.[41] The term appears because man's existence has radically changed. The human body has become a system of organs with specific and limited functions, the subject has withdrawn from the body, and the world of nature has been transformed from a subject of belief to an object of reason. In the same period of which we are speaking, Pierre Bayle banishes any miraculous interpretation of heavenly events.[42] Comets do not portend any unnatural reality. The phenomenon of hallucination appears, therefore, precisely when man's relation to nature becomes essentially a matter of judgment. Its appearance coincides with the beginning disappearance of the miracle, that is with the world which solicits our belief.[43]

Newton turns his back on the world in which we, including him, live, and while our backs are turned the experienced world becomes the world defined by science. There is no indictment against science in phrasing things this way. On the contrary, I am only stating the anthropological conditions necessary to do science. To do science one must turn one's back upon the world in which one lives. And yet what Newton does while his back is turned on the world he does in time; and at another time, a later time, he must turn around again and return to the world, even if it is only to take a walk in the waning hours of the day. But the return is now complicated because the rainbow which appears in the sky is not the rainbow which Newton has unweaved in the darkness of his room. The latter is a refraction of light, and it is this rainbow which is *real*. The former as a way of being in touch with the world, as an experience of the world as a richer horizon, is by implication *unreal*. These experiences, like the smile of Mona Lisa, have no place in the world. These experiences have no place in a rainbow which is a spectrum. They are only experiences which belong to the subject. They exist inside the subject. They are immaterial. They do not matter.

After a soft rain, on a clear summer day, in the late afternoon I see another rainbow in the sky. I see the rainbow and I think about Newton in his darkened room over three hundred years ago. I know what Newton achieved. I know this rainbow is a spectrum. I know all this and the consequences which it has for the rainbow I am seeing. And yet I still see the rainbow. I cannot help but see it. I look at it, the day slows its pace, the light changes color and grows subtly softer, and I am at peace. In the light of Newton's spectrum this nonreality refuses to disappear. Even after Newton the difference between this rainbow and the spectral rainbow remains.

In 1503 an artist paints a smiling woman who has turned her back upon the world. In 1619 a philosopher crosses the threshold of a room and closes his door upon the world. In 1666 a scientist turns away from the light in order to study it. They all embody a new psychological life. During this time a shift in psychological existence occurs. That shift and that new style of psychological life are recorded as the science of psychology. In such a world, in which rainbows nevertheless continue to matter, a new science is needed to explain why what we experience is not real and what is real is not what we experience. Modern psychology is that science. It originates in order to save the hypothesis of the scientific world.[44] And it saves that hypothesis by making the experience of the world an event inside the subject. As such, moreover, it even effects a return to the world. It teaches us how to return to the world as defined by science by living inside and away from the world. It even charts the interiorized landscapes of human life which begin to appear in the face of this world as defined by science, and with Freud gives those landscapes a depth and a history. Psychological life, as it appears in modern psychology, psychological life as it is reflected through a physics of nature and a physiology of the body, modern psychological life becomes an illusion or a dream.

On the inside psychological life is made up of the immateriality of dreams or illusions. To count as a science this reality must matter in the sense that it must be empirically real. Put it another way, the dream must be interpreted and the illusion must be explained. The second feature of psychological life as it appears through the science of psychology achieves this transformation.[45]

LITERALIZATION: DESCARTES' DREAMS
AND THE PSYCHOLOGY OF NIGHTMARE

On November 10, 1619, René Descartes, twenty-three years old at the time, crosses a threshold to enter a small, stove-heated room near Ulm, Germany. He has just attended the coronation of the Emperor Ferdinand at Frankfurt, and he has spent the previous twenty months under the tutelage of his friend, Isaac Beeckman, whom he credits with having awakened him from a deep sleep of ignorance. According to his own account of this day, he is filled with enthusiasm, and on that night there is revealed to him in a series of dreams the foundations of a new science and his vocation. His dreams are worthy of our attention. In order more fully to appreciate the impact of the dreams I present them as if Descartes himself were narrating them to us now.[46]

I am walking through some streets. Phantoms appear before me. I am terrified. My right side feels weak. I cannot lean on it, and in order to continue walking I must lean toward the left side. I try to straighten up but then a tempestuous wind whirls about me and spins me around on my left foot. I try to drag myself forward but feel that I am going to fall at every step. On the path before me there is a college with an open gate. I enter it and try to reach the church of the college in order to pray. I pass a man whom I know but I fail to

greet him. I try to return to acknowledge him but the wind vio
lently flings me against the church. Someone in the middle of the
college court now calls my name. He says that another acquaintance,
Monsieur N., has something to give me. I imagine that it is a melon
and that it has been brought from some foreign country. Other
people are now gathered around me for conversation. They stand
straight and are steady on their feet. But I am still bowed and stag
gering. As the wind becomes less strong I wake up. I am in pain and
I fear that this dream has been the work of some evil genius.

Upon awakening Descartes prays for two hours for protection and
preservation. When he falls asleep again he has a second dream which
again fills him with terror. A sharp and piercing noise which he takes for
a clap of thunder awakens him and he sees sparks of fire scattered throughout his room. Then a third dream follows in which he sees on his table a
dictionary and a work entitled *Corpus poetarum.* The latter is open at a
passage which reads: *quod vitae sectabor iter?* (What path shall I follow
in life?). An unknown man appears and hands him some verse. The words
Est et Non catch his eye.

Jacques Maritain offers an interesting interpretation of these dreams
in the context of Descartes' new conception of reason, and in passing he
cites the brief remarks which Freud made about them.[47] A more detailed
interpretation, along phenomenological lines, is offered by Bernd Jager.[48]
The interpretations, interesting as they are, are not however the concern
of these remarks. On the contrary, I begin with these dreams, which
actually are nightmares, in order to illustrate how the nightmare *appears*
in human experience before it appears in psychology.

The Cartesian figure of these nightmares exists in a situation with
other figures. The figure inhabits a world. It is a panicky world, and the
figure is caught up in a terrifying story. He is in danger and he feels
helpless. There are unknown and impersonal forces which push and pull
at him, which whirl him around, and he cannot move. If he tries to
advance or flee it is only with great effort and only very slowly that he
gets anywhere. More often than not he is rooted to one spot. The
dream figure in the nightmare is passive and frozen. This figure is unable

to act. He is, on the contrary, acted upon. He is confronted with phantoms, addressed by others, spun around and thrown about. He dwells in
a world in which he is unable to stand or to find his way.

In these respects Descartes' nightmares are typical of the experience
of nightmare which any of us may have. A nightmare is essentially *a
terrifying story lived in a panicky world.* Descartes, however, adds an
ironic note to this discussion because of the claim which he makes for
these dreams, and because of the place he occupies in the history of
thought, including the rise of modern psychology. They were "the
most important thing in his life,"[49] and according to Maritain the meditations which followed the dream are the core of Descartes' philosophy.
This philosopher whose *Treatise of Man* involves a psychology based on
a mechanistic physiology begins his thought with a dream. Given what
the dream will become when it is viewed within a Cartesian framework,
Descartes could not have made a more incongruous beginning. The oneiric
disturbances which inaugurate Cartesian philosophy are unrecognizably
transformed in the psychology of dreaming which emerges from it. To
appreciate this change, and the second significant feature of modern psychology, let us ask what a science of psychology today makes of the
dream.

In a published textbook entitled *Fundamentals of Psychology,* the
authors discuss the psychology of nightmare. The discussion appears in a
chapter entitled "Physiological Foundations of Behavior," and within
the context of some remarks made on the four stages of sleep. Defined
as a disturbance of sleep in an individual who is partly awake, the authors
add that a nightmare is an increase in heart, eye, and brain function.
Moreover, all of these physiological responses last less than one minute.
Finally the authors state that "the most terrifying nightmares seem to
occur as the individual is coming out of deep sleep into the lighter stages
of sleep."[50]

It is obvious from this account that there is an essential difference
between the way in which nightmare appears in one's *psychological* life
and the way in which it appears in *psychology.* In the account given of
Descartes' dream, the dreaming figure embodies a world. In the account
given by the science of psychology the dreaming figure is the body of

physiology. What is an experience of a world becomes in psychology a bodily event inside the dreamer. The embodied figures who populate the nightmarish world become the physiological body of the dreamer. The story of a world and the figures who embody the story are stuffed inside the brain, and the pumping heart, of the dreamer. And placed on the inside in this fashion, the experience of nightmare is made concrete, literal, and real in the workings of physiology. *In* physiology the interiorization of psychological life becomes *real*. In physiology it is *concrete*. In physiology this interiorizing of experience is taken *literally*. Psychological experience *really* does occur as these concrete, empirical, factual, physiological events. Psychological experience is these events. The *interiorization* of psychological life finds its literal expression in physiology. The interiorizing of psychological life finds its necessary complement in this *literalizing* of it. Psychological experience as it appears in psychology is not only interiorized away from the world, it is also literalized inside the physiological body. The consequence of this feature of literalization needs to be discussed.

The embodied figure in a nightmarish world lives in panic. Terrified, beset by dangers, the dreaming figure is hyper-alert, ever watchful and in flight. The physiology of nightmare more or less reflects this world. There is, for example, an increase in brain and eye activity and the heart beats faster as well. These organs of the body mirror the dreaming figure's world. They are the way in which the body lives this world. *But these events inside the body are not the experience of the nightmarish world.* The physiology of nightmare does not equal the experience of it. It is not the brain which is hyper-alert, any more than it is the eye with its rapid movements which is vigilant and watchful. The *embodied figure* is alert and circumspect. The increased heart rate is not the dreaming figure's panic. This figure is not in terror because his or her heart beats faster. On the contrary, it is when the figure is fearful, when the dreamer is in a fearful world, that the heart rate increases. In short, it is the experience of nightmare as an embodied world which makes sense of the physiological events inside the body and not these events which make sense of the experience. *In themselves* the events are meaningless and neutral.

Psychology, however, focuses on the events and (in)tends to see the experience *in* them. For psychology these events are the facts of the experience. They are the literal transcription of the experience.[51] They are the data of psychology. They are psychology's facts. When one recognizes, however, that *it is not the experience which is seen in the events* but *the events which are seen through the experience*, then the character of psychology and its data are revealed. Its intended focus is a pretense and its belief in the facts of the experience is a way of making-believe. In other words, its focus is an intention to pretend that two different senses are one.[52] Its focus is a way of making-believe(able) that the experience is (like) these events.

A metaphor is a piece of make-believe which makes reality believ-able. A metaphor is a way of seeing something through something else. A metaphor is an intentional pretense in the original sense of that latter word as a profession of the way in which things appear. A metaphor is a way of likening one reality to another. In all these respects, therefore, psychology's focus on nightmare is *originally metaphorical*, and its data are not facts but metaphors.[53] Psychology, however, forgets this vision. Focusing on the events of physiology as the facts of psychology, it for-gets that these events are primarily ways of seeing psychological life. Focusing on *what* it sees, it forgets *how* it sees. And in this forgetfulness what originally matters metaphorically is taken literally.

An explicit illustration of this theme is provided by the authors whose discussion of nightmare initiated these remarks. Commenting on what the science of psychology knows of nightmare, they state that the most *terrifying* nightmares occur in the lighter stages of sleep. Terror, how-ever, is not a matter of stages of sleep as measured by brain activity. Terror does not belong to the functioning of physiological events. On the contrary it belongs to the experience of nightmare, to the appear-ance of nightmare as a world. To establish this "fact," therefore, it is necessary to see it through the experience, and to see it through the experience is originally to see the physiology of nightmare metaphori-cally. Psychological life originally appears metaphorically, even if the science of psychology forgetfully envisions it literally.

The difference between a metaphorical and a literal understanding of the body for a psychological discipline matters.[55] What is undoubtedly productive as a metaphor can be misleading when taken literally. To conclude these remarks I offer a final example of how the literalization of psychological life can be misleading.

The psychology of nightmare indicates that the time of a nightmare is usually less than one minute. For anyone who has ever had a nightmare this suggestion comes as surprising news, because certainly this time does not apply to the experience of nightmare. It is on the contrary the time which belongs to the measured physiological events. To claim, therefore, that it is the duration of nightmare as it appears in human life is to engage in that forgetfulness which takes the relation between the embodied world of nightmare and these physiological events literally. And in this instance, literalization leads to a false understanding of the endless eternity of nightmare's terrifying world.

Literalization is the second feature of psychological life as it appears in the science of psychology, and it is the counterpart of the first feature of interiorization. In both features a concealment of psychological life is revealed. A question emerges, therefore—the third and final one of this chapter. If psychological life is revealed in psychology as an interior, literal fact, then what is concealed in this revelation? To put the question in another way: what does the discipline of psychology conceal of psychological life?

Psychology's Concealment of Psychological Life

Interiorization and literalization are two features which characterize the appearance of psychological life in modern psychology. Each of these features, however, conceals psychological life more than it reveals it. On one hand the feature of interiorization conceals the appearance of psychological life as a reflection through the world, and as such it conceals how psychological life is a deepening and figuring of the material world which allows this world to matter in another way, as a story of human life. On the other hand the feature of literalization conceals the original metaphorical character of human psychological life. To illustrate this theme of concealment, and to demonstrate the specific concealments of psychological life in psychology, I offer an example.

Last year I unexpectedly lost a friend through death. He was a young man, and we had been friends for a long time. Before he died, he had given to me a copy of a book which he had recently finished, and he had written within it an inscription of our friendship. Today that book is the only piece of material remembrance I have of him, and I have placed it in a corner of my study. It rests solitary and alone on a table. Nothing else surrounds it. It is a simple memorial to a friend.

There have been times in the course of these days since he died when I have recalled my friend. Sadly, however, these moments have become rarer and are always brief. But on occasion when I enter my study I am called by that book which rests upon the table, and in those moments I remember him deeply and vividly. In those moments he is there in the room with me. His book is my memory. That book is my departed friend. Through the book my remembrance of him is a world. Through the book my memory of him has a place. That book is the reflection of my experiences of memory and of sadness. That book mirrors the story of our life.

Surely, however, one wants to object that this description pertains to my feelings, and that these feelings are private and belong to me. And surely one wants to add to this objection that the book is after all only a book, only an empirical material reality, which remains unchanged in spite of the addition of my feelings to it. Psychology certainly would agree with these objections. Psychology knows about feelings and their projection.

But I cannot take these objections seriously, any more than anyone can who preserves memories through the things of the world. The book *matters*, and the loss of it would matter now almost as much as the original loss of my friend. I do not deny that my feelings are revealed in this account, and that my feelings as feelings are private and belong to me. But I do insist that these feelings are not the experience. I do insist that *the feeling of an experience* is not the same thing, either logically or phenomenologically, as the *experience of a feeling*. And so insisting I would add that while my feelings are private and invisible, my experience is public and visible for others to see. Through that book which sits on that table, others are able to experience something of the sadness of a departed friend. Through that book others can and do participate in this psychological story of friendship and early death, even if not in detail or with the same depth. This psychological experience is, therefore, visible as a world, and the world through which it appears, this material book, does matter in another way. It is not exclusively an empirical object which receives my projections. It is on the contrary another kind of object, a psychological object, which reflects an experience of my life. That book, I said, *is* my departed friend. I am speaking psychologically. It is a metaphor. That book appears psychologically as a metaphorical reality.

Review and Preview

The world which mirrors psychological life is textured metaphorically. Psychological life as a reality of reflection is psychological life as a metaphorical reality. The long past of confusion of psychological life with other matters bears witness to this reflection. The short history of psychology as a science conceals it. In order to present a psychology which is faithful to how psychological life appears (a psychological psychology), it seems necessary to recover how material things, others, and the human body are realities of reflection. It seems necessary to *recover* material things, others, and the human body in their metaphorical character, that is, as psychological realities. The chapters which follow address these themes.

II

REFLECTIONS OF THE PSYCHOLOGICAL WORLD: THINGS

Introduction

The recovery of psychological experience on its own terms, as a metaphorical texture rather than a scientific fact, begins with a remembering of what the science of psychology forgets. It begins by remembering that things, others, and the human body are realities of reflection which matter. In this chapter I am concerned with the recovery of the psychological world of things. Things reflect our psychological experiences. Psychological experience is a world. The converse, however, is also true. If *psychological experience is a world*, then it is because *the world is also psychological.* Psychological life as a reality of reflection means that matter matters in another way. Hence this chapter involves two related issues. On one hand it illustrates how psychological experience is a world. On the other hand it illustrates how the world is psychological.

Psychological Experience Is a World: The Visibility of Experience

WHAT IS A THING?

It is in the neighborhood of things that I begin a recovery of psychological experience as a world. Such a beginning requires, however, some justification because the question which locates us in this neighborhood of things seems so easily answered. Anyone, it seems, knows what things are. Things are trees, cars, desks, pencils, coffee cups, houses, furniture, and whatever, but not dogs, cats, mice, other people, pigeons, geese, or flies. The matter, however, is not so simple, for what do we do with a statement like, "I have some-*thing* to discuss with you." Are words things? Are the issues which we discuss things? Is a book a thing, and if so how is it a thing? And what about a poem? Martin Heidegger wrote an entire book with this question of *What Is a Thing?* as its title because, he says, we have forgotten what things are—if we ever really knew—and as a consequence we do not know what poems are either. And in an essay from another work, entitled "The Thing,"[1] Heidegger tried to remind us of what is forgotten. *Thing*, in its original experience and languaging, means a *gathering, the assembling of a world*, and it has been through another kind of languaging that thing has come to mean a question of discourse between people (*res publica*) and/or any entity whatsoever (*ens*). Although I do not adopt here the specific sense in which Heidegger means thing as the gathering of a world—it is the gathering of the fourfold of gods and mortals, earth and sky—I do adopt this notion of the thing as the assembling of a world in order to recover a sense of how psychological experience is a world mirrored through things. Things do gather a world, and through things the world of experience which is gathered is reflected. "Man cannot plan the world without designing himself," the architect Rudolf Schwarz says,[2] and Merleau-Ponty notes that "It is through my relation to 'things' that I know myself . . ."[3] The question of things involves, therefore, not only what poems are but also what we are. Things are everywhere, we are surrounded by things, and how we understand things reflects how we understand ourselves. The world holds many secrets, and most, if not all of them, are about us.

A BOTTLE OF WINE

The scene is a winter evening with the snow gently falling outside. In the street beyond his window a man hears the soft crunch of boots on the snow-covered pavements, and from this distance the warmth of his room has an inviting appeal. The room seems even more inviting in anticipation of an expected visit by an old friend. A fire burns brightly in the fireplace and beside it at a proper distance there stands a bottle of good wine recently purchased for the occasion. Awaiting his friend's arrival, the man sits down to write some letters. The phone rings. It is his friend telling him that the weather will prevent his visit. Chatting for a moment, they arrange for another day before saying good-bye. Crossing to the window, the man pulls the curtain aside and looks out on the cold, damp snow which only shortly before reflected the warmth of a prom- ised evening. But now the evening that was planned and expected has changed, and along with it so has the room. The evening now seems longer and emptier, and the room somewhat more quiet and less com- fortable than before. Throwing some logs on the fire to recover some of the warmth of the evening, the man picks up a book and begins to read. The evening passes slowly. Later, when he raises his head to think about a passage in the book which remains unclear, his eyes catch sight of the bottle of wine near the fire. At that moment he realizes once again that his friend will not come, and he returns to his reading.

This is an extraordinarily simple episode taken from everyday life, an incident which is described by J. H. van den Berg in his book *The Phe- nomenological Approach to Psychiatry.*[4] Considering this incident, van den Berg asks what happens at that moment when the man looks at the bottle of wine and realizes that his friend will not come. Putting our- selves in the place of that man, let us take up this incident as a question for psychology to understand.

Certainly, van den Berg says, at that moment I see a green bottle with a white label upon which is printed the name Médoc. In addition I even see that the bottle is corked and that a lead capsule encloses its opening, and in principle this kind of description is almost endless, as one could add many other details of the bottle. But, as van den Berg writes, it "becomes rapidly clear . . . that in this way I shall certainly not come nearer to what happened when looking up I saw the bottle standing there." The nearness which this enumeration of the physical details of the bottle brings is at the same time a distance from the experience of the bottle which I see. What one sees at this moment is "very definitely not green glass, white label, lead capsule, etc." On the contrary what one sees is "a disappointment that my friend had not come, the loneliness of my evening."[5] *Through* that bottle of wine I see the world of conversation and warm friendship which has now become a world of disappointment and loneliness.

Van den Berg is right, however, in recognizing that a psychology based in the attitude of science would find this description "too poetical an explanation,"[6] and indeed it is true that at that moment one does see a green bottle with a white label. But in agreement with van den Berg one must also recognize that this objection presumes a special kind of vision which emphasizes the neutrality of seeing. It is a vision which treats seeing as an event *in* the physiological eye focused on a physical world—the world of green bottles and white labels. It is a vision which treats the seeing of one's loneliness through the bottle of wine as an *immaterial* feeling projected onto a neutral, material world. It is a vision which treats this other way of seeing as a consequence of the subject's vivid imagination. And in light of this special vision, poetry is the only name which seems to apply.

But in addition one must also recognize that if the charge of poetry applies to the account of loneliness, it applies to the account of science as well. That style of vision which sees a green bottle with a white label is also an experience, and as such it is also a matter of reflection. Its account is not simply an explanation of the event of seeing. It is also a story about seeing as an event. It is a way of experiencing which is also reflected in how the bottle is seen.

The difference between the two accounts is not, therefore, a difference between poetry and science. Van den Berg's account, regardless of the objection which he knows will be made, is no more a piece of poetry than the account of science. On the contrary *both* accounts are *psychological.* The bottle of wine reflects the world of science as much as it reflects the world of loneliness, and hence the difference between the two accounts lies elsewhere. It lies in the recognition of the psychological as a reflection. Van den Berg's account explicitly acknowledges that psychological experience is a world. Psychology's account hides it. Van den Berg's account reveals psychological life as a reality of reflection. Psychology's account conceals it. Van den Berg's account recovers psy-

chological life. Psychology's account forgets it. Psychology locates the
psychological *in* the events of seeing and forgets that it is its vision of
seeing as an event which is psychological, a vision which again is reflected
through the world.

This difference, however, is not the only one to be noted, for even if
the account offered by psychology is *recovered* psychologically, another
difference remains. The psychological story which the science of psychology tells is more general and more neutral. It is a psychological
account for everyone and therefore for no-one. Few, I imagine, are *moved*
by it, or are able to see themselves through it. It is *formally* psychological, but it lacks the *moving* quality of that other tale and the way in
which that other account *figures* the experience. A stranger, for example, lost in the snow and knocking on the door would experience
something of the drama of loneliness. Spying the bottle of wine resting
on a table near a dimming fire, he might wonder to himself, even if he
would not speak it, "I see you were expecting company." He would see
through that bottle of wine the outlines, if not the details, of the world
of my evening, just as he would glimpse something of the lonely figure
who inhabits the scene. Certainly he would see this as surely as he would
see a brief refuge from the coldness of the night. And were I to venture
at that moment the opinion that what he sees is a green bottle with a
white label so many measurable feet from the heat of a fire, he would
not be so cold as not to see in this account a cool distance and alienation.

There is a difference therefore between the two accounts in how we
are affected. If the account offered by modern psychology is useful,
pragmatic, and even a source of power within a scheme of scientific knowledge, it lacks that disruptive quality which reminds us of one of the
many dramas of human life. Recovered psychologically, it nevertheless
fails to affect us precisely because it lacks that disruption which awakens
us from the sleepiness of our routines, from the numbing inertia of our
habits, in order to mirror for us the stories and figures whom we live and
who we are. And in this respect is there not always something positively
disruptive in the appearance of psychological life, and is it not always
through those moments which touch us deeply, which move us with
emotion, which *re-figure* our experiences that psychological life does

appear? Is it not in our dreams and in our wishes, in our failures and in our mistakes, in our passions and in our disappointments that our psychological lives hidden in the world become reflected through it? Is not psychological existence always on the other side of the ordinary, the expected, the taken-for-granted, and the routine? Is not psychological life, as a reality of reflection which matters, always the break-up or breakdown of the material world which allows it to matter in another way, psychologically?

An unopened bottle of wine sitting near a dying fire with a snow heavily falling outside begins to recover for us how psychological experience is reflected through the things of the world. Woven through the fabric of the world, our psychological experiences are deepened and figured through those things which surround us and constitute our existence. The material realities of everyday life are the material of psychological experience. But the things of the world deepen and figure not only individual experiences, but also the *typical* experiences of human life. Buildings are mirrors of psychological experiences carved in stone, and through them a city, a culture, and an age reflect their own typical psychological styles. To illustrate this theme I move from a bottle of wine to a cup of tea.

A CUP OF TEA

In a simple and moving little book entitled *The Book of Tea* Kakuzo Okakura describes the ancient tea ceremony of the Japanese. Recalling that the original characters used to name the tea room mean the "Abode of Fancy," Okakura explains how this name is reflected in the construction of the tea room itself. It is, he writes, "an Abode of Fancy inasmuch as it is an *ephemeral* structure built to house a poetic impulse." Later symbols, he continues, refer to it as the "Abode of Vacancy" and the "Abode of the Unsymmetrical," and in each naming there is a *materialization* of the meaning and experience intended by the name. The name Abode of Vacancy is visible through the absence of ornamentation, while the name Abode of the Unsymmetrical is made visible through the presence of some things purposely left unfinished "for the play of the imagination to complete."[7] But perhaps more than any other feature of the tea room, it is the doorway or the threshold which demonstrates how this structure reflects a typical experience. Describing the movement along the path which connects the tea room itself with the place of waiting, Okakura tells us how the guest will "silently approach the sanctuary, and, if a samurai, will leave his sword on the rack beneath the eaves, the tea-room being preeminently the house of peace." Then, he continues, "he will bend low and creep into the room through the small door not more than three feet in height," a proceeding which "was incumbent on all guests—high and low alike,—and was intended to inculcate humility."[8] Can the figuring and reflection of experience be more visibly demonstrated? The threshold of the tea room demands a particular posture, and through the doorway and the posture the experience of humility is made visible and is embodied.

Matter mirrors man, and there is as much psychology reflected through a building as there is "in" a brain. Architecture is the psychological character of an age made visible, and the tea room offers a concrete example of a cultural psychological experience made visible. But what is true of this example is also true for us today in our own culture. Universities house our typical experience of higher education, just as hospitals reflect the way in which we understand the experience of illness and its relation to health. In a similar manner our experience of the sacred and its relation to the profane is visible through church architecture. The changing styles of church architecture are for van den Berg an accurate reflection of human experiences of spirituality.[9] Churches, schools, office buildings, zoos—a city's psychological life is present through its buildings and its streets, and anyone who would know the character of a city—and its people—must learn to read its architecture. New York City is not Los Angeles. The difference is made visible through the architecture which is the city, and the difference which is made visible is a difference in psychological life. Architecture as the reflection of typical psychological experiences is the concern of an authentic environmental psychology, that is, an environmental psychology which understands that we are shaped by the environment *only because* in designing it we have committed ourselves and those who follow to an expression of who we are. Building and environments do not primarily condition behavior. On the contrary, as stages of action they invite, solicit, and even allow this or that kind of human reply. They reflect a story in which we are asked to play a part, a story whose lines and characters however have been written by others who have come before us. In building the world we betray ourselves. Architecture is the embodiment of *typical* psychological experiences cut in stone.

But these few remarks on architecture as the mirror of typical psychological experiences risk becoming too abstract. Let me conclude these remarks, therefore, by moving from the Japanese tea room to the rooms of a contemporary American house. Here too we find the reflection of typical experiences, albeit in a less dramatic way. Within a typical house, each room gathers its space together in a characteristic fashion; and within that space even the time of the room flows differently. The dimensions of the rooms of one's house are never given solely by the ruler, and the clocks which tick in different rooms are not the measure of time as it is lived. Time, in fact, flows differently in each room of the house. The time of the den is not the time of the dining room, and the time of the latter is itself different in the evening from what it is in the morning. Moreover, we live these different spaces and times without having first to know them. Indeed it is not necessary to know these differences as one knows a mathematical formula, because within each room these different experiences are materialized through the particular things which are placed in that room. The dining room, for example, which gathers its space and time primarily around the place of the table, mirrors a different experience than the bedroom, which gathers its space and time primarily around the place of the bed. To appreciate the difference it is sufficient to imagine your next family dinner in the bedroom. It fails not merely for practical but also and more importantly for psychological reasons. The bed mirrors an experience which is not conducive to such a family gathering. It reflects the experiences of intimacy and dreaming, while the dining room table gathers together the experiences of community and conversation. Each room through the things which compose it demands a certain re-figuring of experience, and only the most insensitive bore would be able to sleep and to dream at the dining room table. On the

other hand we need only recall the figure of Louis XIV, whose palace at
Versailles, that magnificent expression of seventeenth-century life and
culture, was centered about his bed.[10] What better way to reflect the
fantastic spirit of this *grand siècle* than to place its heart on this center
of dreaming? Despite his many shortcomings in the political arena, Louis
XIV was a sensitive environmental psychologist.

NEWTON'S SPECTRUM

Two examples have illustrated how the things of the world reflect
human psychological life, and each of them has demonstrated that human psychological experience is visible as a world. This *visibility of
experience* is not, however, a content to be seen. Psychological experience is not a thing, and one's loneliness, for example, is no more *in* the
bottle of wine than what is in the bottle of wine can erase one's loneliness. The reflections of experience are not *in* the things of the world, in
the way that my notes are in the drawers of my desk. The visibility of
psychological experience is not an empirical spatial reality, any more than
the mirror reflection is an empirical spatial reality. Psychological experience is not something to see any more than the mirror reflection is
something to see. It is a way of seeing, a seeing-through, as one sees
through the mirror reflection a figure in a story. To speak of reflections,
to speak of the visibility of experience, is to speak about the deepening
and figuring of experience *through* the things of the world. I continue
this theme now with another example which illustrates how even the
objects of science reflect, deepen, and figure human psychological life.

Recall that in the year 1666 Isaac Newton enters into a darkened
room and that through a small hole which he cuts in his window shade a
ray of the daylight sun streams through. Turning his back on the light
outside his room, Newton places a small triangular glass prism between
the shade and the far wall in his room, and there on that opposite wall he
sees the spectrum. Going into the dark he "discovers" the light. The
spectrum, however, is not something merely waiting to be discovered. It
is not simply lying there in the sunlight waiting to be seen. Starting with
the achievement, *and never contesting its validity as an empirical fact*, I

want to emphasize that the spectrum is not only or even primarily an observed fact. *On the contrary it is also and primarily a way of seeing.* It is not simply an event. There is a story told through the event. As such, the spectrum reflects an experience of seeing which allows us to ask: "What is the experience of seeing which is reflected through the spectrum?"

The answer to this question is found in the details of the experiment. It is found in the arrangements which must be made and in the procedures and instruments which must be used in order to make the spectrum appear. In turning one's back on the light, in making the room dark, in cutting a small hole in a window shade, and in using a prism, sunlight as a spectrum appears *and* is revealed as a way of seeing. The experience of seeing is told through these procedures. *The story of this experience is embodied in these actions.* If one looks by turning one's back on what one wants to see, if one looks by reducing the seen (darkening one's room to study light), by narrowing one's vision (cutting the hole), and by seeing only with the eye (the prism), then one's experience of seeing is marked by a particular *style.* That style is *Newtonian.* And notice that in this account we have passed from the empirical *person* of Newton who does the *experiment* to a *figure* who has an *experience.* The spectrum reflects a figuring of experience, and anyone who sees in this way has already taken up this style of embodiment, this psychological attitude or style toward this world of light called a spectrum. To see the spectrum in the rainbow is to look with a Newtonian eye, and it is that kind of figure who inhabits that kind of world.

Beginning with the spectrum as a way of seeing, we recover its psychological character. Beginning with the spectrum as a reflection of an experienced world, we recover the figure who inhabits that world. It is not the person of Newton who sees the spectrum. It is *a Newtonian figure* who sees it. *The recovery of psychological experience as a world is a re-figuring of the person psychologically. It is a figure and not the empirical person who inhabits the psychological world.* The figure is the counterpart of a psychological world, just as the person is the counterpart of an empirical, scientific world. The recovery of psychological experience through the things of the world means not only that the world *matters* in another way, but also that the person *matters* in another way. The person matters as a figure in a story. The psychological world is simultaneously the *de-realization* of the material world—its deepening and reflection—and the *re-figuring* of the person.

EXPERIENCE TAKES PLACE AND MAKES SENSE: A BRIEF CONSIDERATION OF DESIRE

The three examples which have been presented intend to demonstrate how psychological experience is visible as a world. All these examples illustrate that experience is not a content either in the world or in the subject but a way of making content. Human experience, in other words, is a sense of the world, a way of making sense, the way in which the world is sensible, and psychologically this way of making sense specifically means a deepening and figuring of the world.

In this work our task is to reanimate those embodied sense-giving acts which originally do figure the world in a psychological way. But, as we have seen, this task is complicated by the rise of the modern sciences of nature and the body and by the appearance of modern psychology within this context. The modern sciences radically transform the ways in which experience makes sense and takes place, and modern psychology is the arena where these transformations and their consequences become the theme. On one hand, the appearance of modern psychology is brought about by the dilemma associated with these transformations. Its emergence is nothing less than a historical acknowledgment that human embodied experience no longer takes place through the world nor makes sense of it. On the other hand, modern psychology emerges as the proposed solution to this dilemma. If experience no longer takes place through the world nor makes sense of it, then sense can be made of experience in a retreat from the world. In other words, experience can be made sensible again if its is placed inside the subject on this side of the world.

It is important here to recognize the shift which occurs with these transformations of the sense and place of experience. When our experience no longer makes sense (of the world), the making sense of experience now becomes our place. This shift involves not only a retreat from the world to the subject as the place of experience, but also and perhaps more importantly a new sense of the person as subject, a sense in which each of us becomes the author of experience, the one who now gives sense to the world and makes it sensible. To appreciate this point one needs only to recall here the previous remarks on Newton's spectrum. The spectrum is the world of light *made sensible* by Newton. One can *"see"* this world of light *if* one becomes a Newtonian figure, and *when* one does become a Newtonian figure this world of light *makes sense*. It is easy to understand, therefore, that with the interiorization of experience we not only lose our place in the world but also must begin to create our own place. We may well wonder here about the dangers inherent in this position, but such a concern would take us beyond the limits of this work. Let it suffice to say that this new position has been a mixed blessing. We cannot deny the fruits of modern science and technology which inaugurate (or are the offspring of) this new attitude toward experience and the world. But we also cannot ignore the consequences of losing one's place in the world. In Chapter 4 I will consider how this loss of place has radically altered the human heart. Here I want to offer a specific illustration of how experience does make sense of and does take place through the world.[11] My example is the experience of desire.

The centrality of desire in modern psychology seems evident. On one hand it appears in the psychology of motivation under the guise of needs, and on the other hand it appears in Freudian depth psychology under the rubric of instincts. But wherever and however it appears, desire enters modern psychology as a condition of the body or as a subjective feeling. In either case, therefore, desire is tucked away inside the subject on this side of the world.[12] Indeed, the experience of desire is so divorced from the world that in Freud's psychology desire appears in opposition to the world. Desire is the enemy of culture, and hence "as a man of desires I go forth in disguise."[13] In modern psychology, then, desire places humanity on this side of the world and perhaps even in opposition to it. This proclivity has its roots in the very origins of modern psychology. John Locke echoes this psychology of desire when he writes that the "uneasiness a man finds in himself . . . is what we call

desire . . . [and] the chief, if not the only spur to human industry and
action is uneasiness."[14] Locke wrote these words in 1690, at a time when
the new sciences of nature and the body were on the rise. Do they echo
the voice of a new psychology in which desire has become an interior
restlessness because we have lost our way in the world, our sense of things?
An affirmative answer seems difficult to give because desire seems so readily
to concern the interior uneasiness of the human heart. Modern psychology seems so right in its focus. John Locke's words seem beyond re-
proach. But I will suggest that what seems so natural to us is in fact a
historical shift in the sense of desire, and that this shift is forgetful of
how desire radically concerns our place in the world.

To recover this original sense of desire we must return to etymology
because etymology is not only the history of a word but also, and perhaps more importantly, the story of that word as a way of experiencing
the world. The science of philology presumes this experience of language, a psychological speaking, and hence etymology can be a way of
recovering psychological life.

In its origins *desire* springs from the Indo-European root *sweid,* which
means "to shine," and it is related to the latin word *sidus* which means
"star or constellation of stars."[15] More specifically, *desire* is formed on
analogy with the appearance of *sidus* in the term *con-siderare* which
means a careful observation of the stars. Observing the stars, we lift our
gaze toward the heavens, suggesting that the appearance of the phenomenon of desire in human life is coincidental with raising oneself up from
the earth in order to dwell upon it in another way. In the upward gaze
the earth becomes a place for us to dwell. Through the heavens the
earth becomes a human place. Desire situates us upon the earth. Humans, and not the animals of the earth, *con-sider* the heavens. Desire is a
phenomenon of *human* life. It is the dawn of *human* consciousness.

There is, moreover, an even more specific sense of this upward gaze
because this careful consideration of the heavens originally described the
priestly function of the Roman augur. In his careful consideration of
the heavens his task was to foretell the future. The movements of the
stars and the wanderings of the birds spoke of human destiny. His upward gaze intended, therefore, a way of speaking, a pre-dicting, a saying

of what is to come. In his look he read a fate; he saw a future. The careful consideration of the heavens establishes the earth not only as a human place, but also as a place in time, as a temporal (and temporary) place. Time is born out of desire, and an original way of being on the earth, which this story of desire tells, is originally our way of being in time. The psychological story of desire is originally a tale about time. Desire may even be the first name of time, its original psychological name. To be on the earth in a human way is to be in time. Without desire there is no time. The fantasy of eternity, of eternal life, is the extinction of desire. We dwell upon the earth in a human way as beings of desire, and as human beings of desire we go forth in time. This understanding of the upward gaze, this vision of the heavens as transforming the earth into a temporal place upon which human beings can dwell, is already found in Plato's *Timaeus*. Here is what he says: "The sight in my option is the source of the greatest benefit to us, for had we never seen the stars and the sun and the heaven, none of the words which we have spoken about the universe would ever have been uttered. But now the sight of day and night, and the months and the revolutions of the years have created number and have given us a conception of time, and the power of inquiring about the nature of the universe."[16]

Language, number, time, and the power of human rational thought spring forth in this upward movement from the earth toward the stars.

Desire, however, is formed on *analogy* with consideration, and hence if there is a moment of likeness between them there is also a moment of difference. *Con*-sideration is a way of being *with* the stars, and through its likeness with this term desire transforms the earth into a *human place*. *De*-sire, on the other hand, means *away from* the stars, and thus in this difference between desire and consideration we begin to hear the suggestion of a journey. In considering the heavens I stand up upon the earth, and in this standing it grounds me and gives me support. Considering the heavens, the earth gives me a place. But what supports me and grounds me in this moment of consideration cannot be the focus of my concern. To look upward toward the heavens in this moment of consideration I must assume this ground. I must presume it and take it for granted. To consider the heavens I must (temporarily) *forget* the earth as a human

place. In this moment of consideration I must live this earth in a forgetful way. Considering the heavens I trust the earth which *stands under*
me. In this moment of consideration I might say that the earth *understands* me.

The moment of desire however remembers what is originally forgotten. *De*-sire is a movement *away from* the stars and back to the earth.
It is the moment of a return, of a turning back toward that earth from
which I have considered the heavens, and in this moment of return I
come to understand what originally understands (stands-under) me. A
heritage which gives me a place becomes a destiny and with desire I am
placed back upon the earth in a different and in a more profound way.
This moment of desire, this moment of return, *deepens* the earth as a
human place. It deepens it because in this return I now take up the earth
through that initial consideration of the heavens. In the return I now
see the earth *through* the heavens. In this return the earth is taken up as
a *reflection* through the heavens. It is deepened as a reflection, and in
this deepening as a reflection the earth is transformed from a *human
place* into a *psychological home.* In the moment of desire, in this moment of difference between con-sideration and de-sire, I take up my
place upon the earth in a *humanly psychological* way. The *analogous*
relation between desire and consideration seems essential, therefore, because the two moments of likeness *and* difference reveal how the very
dawn of human consciousness is *psychological.* The analogous relation
reveals how human inhabitation of the earth is originally and essentially
psychological. It reveals that we are not human *and* psychological, but
human precisely because we are psychological.

The *two* moments of likeness and difference are essential to an analogy, and to forget either one of them is to misunderstand the phenomenon to which the analogy alludes. In the specific case of desire a forgetfulness of the difference would enforce an angelic view of human
psychological life. Desire, then, would place us as wanderers amongst the
stars, as visionary dreamers drifting through the heavens. On the other
hand a forgetfulness of the likeness would enforce a beastly view of human psychological life. Desire, then, would find us mired within this
thickness of nature, as rapacious plunderers of the earth. Remembering

both moments, however, allows us to see that human psychological life is neither of the angel nor of the beast. Remembering in this way allows us to see that as psychological beings we belong neither to the heavens nor the earth. Or, perhaps better said, this remembrance allows us to see how psychological life places us *between* the heavens and the earth. Recovering the story of desire as a world, we discover that we are travelers on a journey toward home, and that paradoxically this journey and this home consist in a remembrance of what is forgotten.

The phenomenon of desire, when it is recovered psychologically as a world, tells the story of a *homecoming*, and the experience of time which is born out of desire is primarily tied to a sense of coming-home. Through desire, which originally speaks about our place in the world, we return or are returned to the earth to prepare it as a human habitation. Through desire we *cultivate* the earth as home. Cultivation belongs to the story of desire. Like the farmer who plows the land in order to make the earth ready to receive the sky, we who desire till the soil of our lives, and in these acts of cultivation we prepare a place for that which calls us forth. Cultivation means "to move around, to sojourn, to dwell," and in its extended root form, *kwelos*, it is related to *telos* and means the "completion of a cycle."[17] We who desire move over the earth, inhabit it, build upon it, and through these acts of culture and cultivation we complete that cycle between "being with" and "being away from" the stars. Cultivation is the axis around which consideration and desire pivot. Cultivation is the manner in which we who desire are between the heavens and the earth. Culture is not the opposite of desire.[18] On the contrary, the cultivation of desire is the emergence of culture, of our way of recovering the earth as our home.

But the home which we build for ourselves out of desire, the place which the man and woman of desire cultivate in order to receive what shines forth, remains forever incomplete. The farmer prepares the soil every season, and the journey toward home which the story of desire tells is never finished. Our psychological home is always *between* the heavens and the earth. It exists in that cyclic journey between departure and return. It exists in that separation and distance between earth and sky, a distance however which is never a matter of mere miles but is always

a matter of the radical difference between them. If desire is the story of
a homecoming, then it is the story of a home which is present *before*
one's *consideration* of the heavens but paradoxically also absent until
after this *consideration*. It is a home which does not exist but paradoxically always is, a home which is not a fact but more like a promise. It is
a nostalgic home, this home of desire.[19] It is the home out of which
dreams of paradise and tales of the gardens of Eden are born. It is the
home we have never had but have always lived.

How can a home which never was always be? How can desire continuously call us to a place which always and never is? How can desire be
a story of homecoming when that home does and does not exist? Here
again the etymology of the word helps us because, as the story of a
journey between the heavens and the earth, this story of desire necessarily links earth and sky. Desire is the joining of earth and sky, but this
joining always occurs over there on the horizon. It is on the horizon
where the earth and sky do meet, and it is as a horizon that our psychological home appears. The horizon is not empirically real. But neither is
it a dream or an illusion. On the contrary it matters in another way and
it exists always as a promise. It is everywhere on earth and nowhere. The
home of which desire speaks is, therefore, always a promised place, but it
is a promise which is always visible on the horizon. Situated between
earth and sky, we who desire nevertheless are given a visible expression of
their union. The horizon is like a covenant, and there on the horizon lies
a visible hope that there is a sense in this journey toward home. Desire
places us within a world of hope. Without desire there would be no
hope. And yet without this hope there would be no desire. Could the
farmer, for example, continually prepare the soil in a landscape where
earth and sky did not meet? Could desire, as a story about our place in
the world, appear in the absence of a horizon?

I do not mean to suggest with these remarks that I have given an
exhaustive psychological account of the experience of desire. My intention has been only to illustrate that experience does make sense of and
does take place through the world. Regardless of our modern tendency,
therefore, to place desire as an interior uneasiness, the original sense of
this experience narrates how we are placed upon the earth. The word

recovered as a world helps us to remember our original way of being in time and making place. But these places which we make for ourselves in time and out of desire always remain below what shines out above us, and like the horizon where earth meets sky everywhere and nowhere, the places of one's desires always exist between promise and fulfillment. The world of desire is between dream and reality, and through the cultivation of our desires we reveal our ways of recovering the earth as home. In the uplifted gaze of our consideration the earth becomes a human place, and in the moment of desire that place is inevitably and forever transformed into a psychological home. From that moment the world is always more than a fact *and* more than a dream, and we who desire are from that moment neither realists nor dreamers. The story of desire as a world reveals a heritage which is a human destiny: the recovery of the earth and our place upon it as a *psychological* home. It is a home which, like the horizon, is neither a fact nor a dream.

CONCLUSION

Matter mirrors man. Psychological experience is visible as a world. The things of the world, from wine bottles, through the architecture of Japanese tea rooms, to scientific objects like Newton's spectrum, reflect experience, and through those reflections our experiences are deepened and figured in a psychological way. "The world is our home, our habitat, the materialization of our subjectivity,"[20] van den Berg writes, and "it is through my relation to 'things' that I know myself" according to Merleau-Ponty.[21] But if we wish to avoid misunderstanding this psychological way of experiencing the world as a *projection* of an idea or a feeling upon a neutral, material, empirical reality, then we must show that *psychological experience is a world* because *the world is psychological.* The recovery of psychological experience as a reflection of the world means that matter matters in another way. The mirror reflection, which was used in the previous chapter to illustrate psychological life as a reality of reflection, *de-realizes* the reflected. If matter mirrors man, then it is because matter does matter in another way. The recovery of psychological experience as a world is complemented, therefore, by a recovery of the world as psychological.[22]

The World as Psychological: Shadows and Reflections

THE SHADOW "OF" THINGS

It is late afternoon and I am standing at the window of my office looking out over the landscape which spreads itself below me. A solitary tree dots a spacious field of yellowish-brown grass which here and there retains a tuft of green. I look, and as I continue to look I begin to see the shadow of the tree which stretches on that field. Before I had not really noticed this shadow, but now it has captured my gaze. The shadow shimmers slightly, and as I continue to look I see it lengthen, spreading itself just a little bit further through the grassy field. How long can I look? It does not matter because I have already seen something of the tree which I had never seen before. I have seen it breathing; I have seen its pulsing life. Next morning, when I return to my window, what I first saw yesterday is confirmed. The shadow of the tree is somewhat smaller, slightly lighter, and visits the other side of the lawn. During the course of the day the shadow has expanded and contracted, and it has changed place. During the day the tree has changed.[23]

The shadow lengthens; the tree is changing. To say one is to say the other. Through the shadow I see the changing tree. But more than this should be said because the shadow is not merely the shadow *of* the tree, *its* appendage as it were, but the tree as it *lives* through the grass. The shadow *visits* the other side of the lawn, and in this visitation we have a visible suggestion of the communion of grass and tree. What appears in terms of how it appears must be taken seriously, and thus if we go back to the window in my office, then what we see *through the shadow* is a *con-fusion* of the grass and the tree, the *reflection* of one through the other. The shadow is the *figure* of the tree through the grass. It is the way the grass *figures* the tree.

I *know*, of course, that the shadow belongs to the tree, and with this knowledge I am tempted too easily to say that the tree projects its shadow on the grass. But it is not a question of what we know here, but of how we see. The language of the psychological eye is different from the language of the philosophical mind, and the former demands that we say that the shadow is the visible evidence of how the grass reflects the tree and of how the tree deepens itself through the grass. Indeed the shadow is evidence that things imagine each other and that imagining is not just an activity or capacity of the subject. Through the shadow of the grass is the image of the tree, just as the tree is the image of the grass. Things do with each other what they do with us, and what we do with ourselves when we look through a mirror. The image is a deepening and figuring of one thing through another.

The shadow however is only the *effect* of the light, and at high noon and in the dark it *disappears*. These seem serious objections, serious enough in fact to make one wonder if the description claims too much for the shadow. Each of them, therefore, deserves some attention.

Certainly at high noon and in the night the shadow disappears, and with this fact everyone will agree. This fact however does not invalidate the meaning of the shadow. On the contrary it actually indicates the temporality of the psychological world. At noon and at night shadows disappear. At these times the world is *different*. Shadows belong to the morning and to the evening, to dawn and to twilight, and at these times we can see the world imagining itself. In the beginning and at the end of things, things reflect each other, while at high noon and at night they do not. There are times, therefore, when the world is openly psychological, and there are times when the psychological character of the world is hidden.[24] The appearance and disappearance of the shadow only confirms, therefore, how the psychological is a *recovered* reality. There are times when the world as psychological is revealed and times when it is concealed. At high noon the light of the sun is *above* the world and at night it dips *below* it. At such times the world is psychological in a hidden way. It is, we might say, psychological in a Cartesian and/or Freudian way. It is psychological as an idea or a fact. At dawn and in twilight, however, the world is psychological in a metaphorical way, as the Stevens poem quoted earlier suggests. These psychologies differ. They differ as much as these worlds do. At dawn and in twilight for example one speaks differently than one does at high noon or in the darkness of the night, a difference which is as noticeable as that between metaphorical speech, factual speech, and logical speech.

The other objection is that the shadow is only the *effect* of the light, and here two points are to be made. First, as an explanation of the phenomenon it is of course correct, but the explanation ignores the phenomenon as it appears. It discounts its significance. In this explanation it is only the thing itself which counts and the shadow does not matter. But the thing counts in itself and the shadow does not matter only at certain times of the world. The explanation ignores the shadow as it appears therefore because it looks at it only in one moment. It takes this one moment of the world's way of being psychological and fixes that one meaning.

The second point to be made to this objection is that it assumes a dichotomy between things and the light. There is the light and there are things which are lighted. This dichotomy is however a special vision. It is a "Newtonian" vision which makes light a separate thing and concludes with respect to the colors of things that an object "may be made to appear any colour"[25] since color belongs not to things but to the light. But there is no more a real dualism between things and the light than there is a dualism between the reflection and the reflected. On the contrary there is a relation of deepening so that each is what it is through the other. Just as the reflection deepens and re-figures the reflected and thereby allows the reflected to matter in another way, light is the depth of things and things are the way in which light matters. This is what Merleau-Ponty means in speaking of "lighting-things lighted" as a "structure."[26] Things and the light belong together and to change one is to change the other. At night when the light changes, so do things. Things and the light are not two items in a relation. They are a relation. I see one through the other. On a brilliant sunny day, for example, I do not look at the sun, but I see it through the grass and the trees where it plays, and if I do look at the sun itself then it is for a special reason for which I adopt a special moment of vision. The shadow, therefore, is not so much the effect of the light as it is an acknowledgment that a thing is what it is through the light. It is an acknowledgment that light matters by shadowing things, just as things are deepened and re-figured through shadows.

Shadows are the *depth* of things. This depth, however, is not hidden inside the thing. On the contrary it is a depth of radiation, a transgression of the thing beyond itself and beyond its own form and boundaries. Merleau-Ponty speaks of "a radiation of the visible" and he says that "All flesh, *and even that of the world,* radiates beyond itself." There is a dehiscence of the visible, a "system of exchanges," a "reflexivity of the sensible."[27] The depth of a thing is its *shadowy* life through other things, its *re-figuring* through other things. The shadow is not a projection of the tree *on* the grass but a reflection of the tree *through* the grass. It is the visible expression of the tree through the grass, the coherent *de-formation* of the tree through the grass, its re-figuring. The shadow is the *de-realization* of the visible, the thing's way of saying that *it is* and *is not* what it is.

The painter Paul Cézanne always wanted to paint one moment of the world's being. The failure to do so is the success of his paintings. In an essay entitled "The Elusive Goal," the art critic Liliane Brion-Guerry tells us that the greatest obstacle in Cézanne's struggle to paint the harmony among things was the rigidity of the form of things, their fixed spatio-temporal dimensions. But in his last oil paintings, and particularly in his watercolors, Cézanne realized something of this elusive goal. Through the play of light he freed things from their encasement within their borders, and through light and shadow he began to see the contraction and expansion of things. He began to see how "all matter is penetrated by air and vibrations of light,"[28] and in this vision of things he neared his elusive goal. He painted a moment of the world's being, a moment however which refused to be still. He painted that moment when things are born and die through each other, that moment which reveals the psychological world as a reality of reflections.

THE REFLECTION "OF" THINGS

In his essay "Eye and Mind," Merleau-Ponty contrasts the vision of science, psychology as a science, and painting, which he says "gives visible experience to what profane vision believes to be invisible." By profane vision he means a way of seeing—everyday perception and the science of perception in psychology—which "forgets its premises," a way of seeing which forgets that the see-er is caught up in the seen and that the seen reflects the see-er. The visible existence which painting celebrates means therefore nothing less than that circuit of reflection between vision and the visible which also exists among things. Indeed, Merleau-Ponty says that the painter can paint how he is caught up in the fabric of the visible because "there is a reflexivity of the sensible." Just as some of Matisse's drawings, for example, depict the painter in the act of painting, betraying not only what the painter sees of things but also what the things "see" of the painter, the frequent use of mirrors in Dutch painting reveals "within things the labor of vision," the way things reflect each other. Quoting Bergson, Merleau-Ponty notes that in "painting themselves we could seek a figured philosophy."[29] The canvas of the painter shows what profane vision forgets: how things *re-figure* each other through their mutual reflections.

It is clear through his examples that Merleau-Ponty is speaking of a style of painting rather than of painting in general or even of a period of painting. That style, however, is significant for the issues considered here because it portrays the way in which the world is psychological. Describing a pool of water on a sunny day and a row of trees which stand above the pool, Merleau-Ponty broadens this theme of the psychological character of the world.

Looking at the water, he says, "I cannot say that the water itself—the aqueous power, the sirupy and shimmering element—is in space; all this is not somewhere else either, but it is not in the pool. It inhabits it, it materializes itself there, yet it is not contained there; and if I raise my eyes toward the screen of cypresses where the web of reflections is playing, I cannot gainsay the fact that the water visits it, too, or at least sends into it, upon it, its active and living essence."[30]

Just as the shadow betrays *the tree through the grass*, the reflection "of"[31] the water through the trees suggests that the water is more than a body of liquid over there in some definable empirical place. The reflection reveals how the water is a thing precisely because it is a reflection. The water reflected through the trees is as much the water as the liquid in the pool, and without this reflection it would not be a thing. This *reflection* makes the water *real* in the sense that through it the water is a thing of this world, a thing of the human world. A thing without reflections would be like a person looking in a mirror and seeing no reflection. Neither would belong to the human world. The reflection therefore counts as much as the reflected in saying how *things* are. The water "in" the trees *matters* as much as the water "in" the pool. Indeed, the water is "in" the pool because it is reflected through the trees. The reflection is the way in which water *matters*.

"How unimportant a thing would be," the Spanish philosopher Jose Ortega y Gasset says, "if it were only what it is in isolation." Contrary to this isolation, however, Ortega claims that "there is in each thing, a certain latent potentiality to be many other things, which is set free and expands when other things come into contact with it." Through each other things are what they are, and "one might say that each thing is fertilized by the others; that they desire each other as male and female; that they love each other and aspire to unite, to collect in communities, . . . in worlds." "When we open our eyes," he continues, it seems as though things "expand, stretch, and break up like a gaseous mass torn by a gust of wind." Gradually, however, things stabilize, and there is a "settling down and focusing of the outlines [which] results from our attention." Our vision puts things in order and spreads "a net of relationships between them." Our looking directly *at* things de-animates them; our eyes become closed. But with patience and with a less focused kind of looking a thing will gradually become "more clearly perceived because we shall keep finding in it more reflections of and connections with the surrounding things." And when we see in this way, when we catch the reflections of one thing through many other things, it is the *depth* of the thing that we see. The depth of a thing is "what there is in it of reflection of other things, allusion to other things." This depth is the most profound meaning of a thing. A thing matters in "its co-existence with other things." Hence it is never sufficient "to have the material body of a thing." Besides this empirical materiality "I need, besides, to know its 'meaning,' that is to say, the mystic shadow which the rest of the universe casts on it."[32] I need to know its existence through other things. To see the thing I have to see it through its reflection.

Ortega's words, like Cézanne's paintings, indicate that things through shadows and reflections *mirror* each other as they mirror us. Things reflect our experience and they reflect each other. To say one is to say the other. Stated in another way, a re-visioning of psychological experience as a world inevitably means a recovering of the world as psychological. To recover experience psychologically is to see how the world does *matter* in another way.

Johannes Kepler, Tycho Brahe, and Sigmund Freud

It is the last moment of the night, the moment before the dawn, and on the hillside stand two men. One of them is Johannes Kepler, astrologer and astronomer in the Copernican tradition. The other is Tycho Brahe, also a watcher of the stars and other heavenly bodies but a watcher in the Ptolemaic and Aristotelian tradition. Both men are waiting for the "same" event, this coming of the dawn, and yet each will see in this same event a "different" world. For when the night ends and the day begins, Kepler will see on the eastern horizon the earth turning away from its fixed local star, the sun. Brahe, on the other hand, will see on that same horizon the rising of the sun.[33]

This example borrowed from Norwood Hanson recapitulates the concerns of this chapter. The disagreement between Kepler and Brahe about what they see has had fateful consequences for the meaning of psychological life in a world of nature defined by science.

Kepler, who "stands"[34] on a moving earth sees the dropping of the eastern horizon. Brahe, who stands on a stationary earth, sees a moving sun. This difference illustrates the history of modern science, and today we are the descendants of the early morning disagreement on that hillside. Kepler "won" that argument and Brahe "lost" it in the sense that the difference between them became a difference between what is real and what is experienced. Despite, therefore, the sunrises and sunsets we do see, and despite the poetic visions which such sunrises and sunsets inspire, we know that the sun does not rise or set at all. We know that the earth moves. We *know* this even if we do not *see* it. We know it even if our experience is of another sort.

But of what sort is Brahe's experience, and our own? Stated in another way, how did Kepler "win" the argument? Or how is Brahe wrong?

The difference between these two figures obviously presumes some basis of agreement between them. Both men must witness the *same* event for otherwise there would be no *difference*. The difference between them betrays an event which is the same for both men, even while the same event is a difference. Kepler and Brahe are looking in the same direction. Their postures betray a common focus on what is happening over there in the world. They see the *same* thing but they see *it differently*. The questions raised above hinge on this *it* which they see. How is the event which they see and over which they disagree the same?

The sun emits photons which cross space, enter earth's atmosphere and finally impinge upon the retinas of Kepler and Brahe. Standing on the hillside, Kepler and Brahe "see" photons on their retinas. The event is the *same*, therefore, if two pairs of eyeballs stand on that hill, if seeing is only a matter of what meets the eyeball. Trust your eyes, Kepler may say to Brahe, echoing the earlier words of Copernicus, who appealed to his readers to look at the matter of the moving earth with both eyes. And yet this advice is precisely what Brahe would give to Kepler. The eye has changed between Kepler and Brahe. It is a different eye about which each one speaks. Brahe and Kepler not only stand on a different earth, therefore, but they also inhabit a different body. Return to that morning hillside, and you will see the figure of Brahe in conversation with the eyeballs of Kepler. Then you will know why they disagree and ultimately why Brahe is wrong. Brahe *sees through* rather than *with* the eye, to borrow a distinction made by the poet William Blake,[35] and it is only if Brahe looks in Kepler's fashion, only if he looks *with* the eye, that he will see what Kepler sees.

Brahe and Kepler can see the same event if Brahe adopts Kepler's style of vision. The difference is erased *if* the figure of Brahe becomes a Keplerian figure. Historically we know that Brahe did not adopt Kepler's vision, and psychologically we know that our vision of that morning event on the eastern horizon is *always* experienced by a Brahe type figure, even if we can scientifically know that event in Keplerian fashion. It has not been possible therefore to erase the difference. On the contrary, it has been necessary to move it *inside*. Beginning with the event as it is defined by physics, beginning with photons of light traversing space and impinging on the retina, beginning with a physics of nature and a physiology of the body, the difference which originally is seen there in the world becomes a difference which belongs to the subjects of Kepler and Brahe. If the events of the human body are of the sort defined by physiology, then any differences in the experience of these events must belong inside the subject. Brahe lost the argument because his experience of that event on the eastern horizon has no place in the world as defined by physics. And with the argument he also lost how psychological experience is a world, and how the world is psychological.

What Brahe lost however can be recovered, because Brahe's experience of that event is no more inside him as a private, subjective reality than Kepler's vision is of the objective world as it really is in itself. On the contrary both accounts reveal not only *what may be seen*, but also *a way of seeing*. Kepler's vision is no less *a way of experiencing the event* than Brahe's, and in each instance what is seen over there on the eastern horizon *reflects* the see-er. Despite science's claim that it deals with a reality as it is in itself apart from its relation to humanity, despite its claim that it deals with a world which casts no reflections, Kepler's vision is no less psychological than Brahe's, and Brahe's vision matters as much as Kepler's, even though they matter for different reasons. Philip Frank, the philosopher of science, has said of this event that "sense observation shows only that in the morning the distance between horizon and sun is increasing, but it does not tell us whether the sun is ascending or the horizon is descending."[36] This increasing distance is the *same* event which Brahe and Kepler see. And yet neither one of them sees only this bare fact. On the contrary, through that increasing distance each one sees a different world. With that bare fact each one spins a different tale about a different world. Kepler's tale is the story of the world of science. Brahe's take is the story of the world as it is lived. Each story includes a vision of human psychological life. In Kepler's account psychological life is interiorized on this side of the world inside the anatomical body.

In Brahe's account psychological life is reflected through the world.

To recover the world of science as a psychological story about the world is neither to dismiss the achievements of science nor to challenge their empirical validity. On the contrary, it is only to remind us about how psychological life appears in this story. It is undertaken in order to remember what the story of science forgets about psychological life. The power of modern science lies partly in its ability to forget differences in order to envision a neutral world without reflections, one which is the same for everyone. It succeeds because it can establish a democracy among things. It succeeds because it can shift the differences among human experience of the world away from the world inside the subject. It succeeds because finally it can pretend that such differences do not matter. The science of psychology shares this democratic vision, and it even furthers it by explaining those differences inside the subject as events which occur in the homogenous body of anatomy and physiology. The Keplerian eye which sees a moving earth in the increasing distance on the eastern horizon is the democratic eye of anatomy and physiology. It is the anonymous eye which is the same for all, the eye which is defined exclusively by its function. Seeing with this eye the science of psychology "gazes"[37] upon a neutral world, and what is reflected from this world is our sameness and equality. But uncritically accepting the world as defined by science, modern psychology forgets that there is a reflection here, and hence it assumes that our differences are not given through the world and that they really are a matter of the inside. In its forgetfulness of the world, including the world of science, as a reality of reflection, and in its democratic vision, the science of modern psychology systematically displaces our differences. Our differences retreat inside. Freud's psychoanalysis is the science of these interior differences, and in this respect we may say that depth psychology was already born in that conversation between the figures of Johannes Kepler and Tycho Brahe. Our differences which no longer have a place in the world have become our symptoms, and indeed it often seems that now it is only our symptoms which make us different. Depth psychology is the inevitable consequence of the science of psychology.[38] It is a witness of the disappearance of psychological life as a world and of the world as psychological. And it is a witness of how the science of psychology forgets that human psychological life "makes a world of differences." Human psychological life matters, and it matters as a landscape of differences.

Conclusion

Psychological life is a reality of reflection. Through the things of the world psychological experience is visible. The recovery of psychological life in this way is, however, also the recovery of the world as psychological. If matter mirrors man, then it is also true that matter matters in another way. *Psychological life matters and matter matters psychologically.* Shadows and reflections are evidence of the latter point. They are evidence of the psychological reality of the world. They are moments in which the psychological character of the world is revealed. One would miss the point of the chapter, however, if one were to think of shadows and reflections as things to see. They are not things to see but ways of seeing, and in this same vein the psychological world which has been recovered in this chapter is not another world alongside of or in addition to the empirical, material world. The psychological world is no more another substantial reality than it is an insubstantial reality. It is, on the contrary, the reflection of the material world. It is the way in which the empirical, material world is deepened and re-figured psychologically.

III

REFLECTIONS OF THE
PSYCHOLOGICAL WORLD: OTHERS

Introduction

Experience, psychologically understood, is not only experience *of* things but also experience *through* things. Matter mirrors man, and the way in which we understand the things of the world reflects the way in which we understand ourselves. What is true of us and things in this way is, however, also true of the relationships among us. "I borrow myself from others," Merleau-Ponty writes; "man is [a] mirror for man."[1] I see myself through others *and* I understand the other through myself. Moreover, I am a self because I am simultaneously also an other, just as the other is simultaneously a self. Self and other are mutually reflexive terms. They are realities of reflection.

The American philosopher and social psychologist George Herbert Mead has written extensively on the co-presence of self and other. He states, for example, that the "others and the self arise in the social act together." In addition he has emphasized the reflexive character of these terms. Thus he notes that human intelligence "arises in those early stages of communication in which the organism *arouses in itself* the attitude of the other and so *addresses itself* and thus becomes an object to itself."[2] Mead's approach, however, strongly implies that this reflexivity is an *act* of reflection, an attitude which the organism reflectively adopts, an act of cognition. He emphasizes only one moment of reflection, that moment when the organism bends back upon itself and takes up the attitude of the other. Reflection, however, has two moments, and in addition to this moment of "bending back upon" there is that moment of "being given back by" the mmirror of others and the world. In this moment the organism does not arouse within itself the attitude of the other. On the contrary in this moment the organism is impregnated with the other. It is not a moment of reflective cognition as much as it is a moment of embodied perceptual life. Before I know the other and take up her attitude toward me, my body knows the other and weaves her styles and gestures into the fabric of my own behaving.[3] The smile on the other's face quickens my stride toward her before I reflectively take up her attitude toward me. My legs and the general inclination of my body know the other before I do, and my style of walking betrays how I *already* know myself through the other before I know that I know it.

Self and other as realities of reflection are lived before they are known. The transgression of boundaries between me and you, this mutual impregnation of styles of conduct, this relation of mirroring, is an essential and primary reality of human life. It originates well before the end of the first year of life and its presence is not eradicated by the appearance of rational adult conscious life. In this chapter I want to illustrate the appearance of this self-other relation of mirroring in the periods of infancy, childhood, and adulthood. Then I want to consider three implications of this recovery of self and other as realities of reflection. First, this recovery forces us to reconsider the notions of behavior and experience. Second, it suggests that the mode of psychological understanding is imaginal rather than empirical or rational and that the form of this understanding is the story rather than the scientific fact or the philosophical idea. Third, this recovery allows us to reconsider the meaning of unconsciousness and its place in human psychological life.

Self and Other: Realities of Reflection

THE INFANT BEFORE THE MIRROR

In an essay entitled "The Child's Relations with Others," Merleau-Ponty considers the appearance and development of the "specular image," the image "in" the mirror, and at the outset he emphasizes that this specular image originally appears as a kind of "quasi-reality."[4] It originates with an affective vitality. It *matters*. In addition Merleau-Ponty also emphasizes that the appearance of the specular image is co-incidental with a developing consciousness of the other. The two incidents are related to each other. They appear together. The reflection of oneself through the specular image and the recognition of otherness go hand in hand. Because one's self "casts"[5] a reflection, we might say, there is the appearance of the other. With the specular image an initial sense of otherness is born. The other as other appears at approximately the same time that the child notices the specular image, *and* this image is originally noticed not as a duplicate of one's self but as an other. This reflection is a *deepening* and *re-figuring* of oneself which allows one to *matter* in *an-other* way.[6]

Before the age of three months the infant shows no clear reaction to the specular image and at approximately five months the initial reaction is one of simple fixation. After approximately six months, however, a definite conduct begins to appear and at eight months the infant clearly shows a reaction of surprise to the image. "At thirty-five weeks the child still extends his hand toward his image in the mirror and appears surprised when his hand encounters the surface of the glass."[7] The gesture indicates the expectation of an encounter. The reflection is not yet unreal. On the contrary, the image is impregnated with a life and vitality of its own. Moreover, Merleau-Ponty notes that infants treat the image of another person in much the same manner as they treat their own. At six months an infant reaches out to touch the image of his father in the mirror, and he is surprised when his father speaks to him and the voice comes from behind. In both instances the specular image is anything but "an appearance that counts for nothing against the unique space of real things."[8]

For the science of developmental psychology these conducts, all of which occur before the first year, describe a lack or insufficiency on the part of the infant, and this lack defines the goal of development to be a reduction of the image to a simple appearance. At approximately one year this goal is apparently reached. A child of one year, for example, "steps before a mirror with a straw hat which she has been wearing since the morning." According to the observation which Merleau-Ponty reports, the child then "puts her hand not to the image of the hat in the mirror but to the hat on her head." The behavior indicates that the child has learned the difference between the reflection and the reflected. The latter is real and the former no longer *matters*. The child has now become a little adult. *Now* "the mirror image is no longer anything but a symbol."[9]

But this reductive analysis of the mirror image, an analysis which presumes a view of things as physical objects in neutral space, is not even true of the adult. This learned difference does not dissolve the original vitality of the image. It does not replace what was an error with the truth, and even an adult, Merleau-Ponty notes, "will hesitate to step on an image or photograph." Indeed, "if he does, it will be with aggressive intent,"[10] indicating thereby that the reflection does matter. A difference between the reflection and the reflected is learned, therefore, and one truly does exist, but there are two ways of regarding this difference. On the one hand we can take it as an indication of the difference between *what is real* and *what is fictional*, that is, unreal, and eventually we can consign to the latter all experiences which are not real in a strictly empirical sense, including myths, stories, dreams, and metaphors. Or we can take this difference between the reflection and the reflected as an indication of the difference between *what is real* and *what is psychological*, and eventually we can develop out of this difference a sense of how the psychological as a reflection is a deepening of the real. Merleau-Ponty's essay is compatible with the latter direction. In immediate life the image, he says, is always something which "*solicits* our belief."[11] The image, the reflection (psychological life as a reality of reflection) is a matter of belief, and belief matters.[12]

In spite of what is learned, the specular image retains the power of a "quasi-presence" even beyond the first year and in this context Merleau-Ponty considers the following events. At twelve to fifteen months, for example, the child is seen rehearsing movements in front of the mirror, and at around the same time a child sitting in front of a mirror with his mother and asked to point to her will, while laughing, point to her in the mirror and then turn to look at her. "The specular image has become the subject of a game,"[13] Merleau-Ponty writes, and as late as thirty-one months children are observed *playing* with the mirror image. These observations of play are central in understanding the significance of the specular image. The child's playful conducts indicate that there is a vitality to the image even after the first year *and* that the image is more than a double of oneself. Playing with the image the child is playing with an other and not with himself. The specular image figures as a character in a tale. The surprise with which the image is first encountered is retained although transformed as play.[14] The quasi-reality of the image is made psychologically real in the game.

These playful conducts with the specular image strongly suggest that the reflection is a deepening of oneself through an other. The specular image is never totally reduced to an encounter with one's own self. In fact its significance in the *life* of the infant is appreciated only to the extent that it is understood as an encounter with an other. Hence this is why Merleau-Ponty emphasizes the "de-realizing function"[15] of the specular image. Undoubtedly through the image a new knowledge of oneself appears, a self-knowledge. But this self-knowledge is given through the viewpoint which an-other has on one, a viewpoint which is visibly present as the specular image. Through the specular image one first glimpses the way one is seen by others. One first glimpses the viewpoints of the other, which means, however, that the specular image momentarily transforms one into the other who views one in this way. The reflection de-realizes the reflected, and between them there is a crossing or a confusion of self and other. The self who I am is no longer safely encased on this side of the mirror. It is, on the contrary, already "infected" with the viewpoint of that other who views the reflection. In like manner the reflection is not simply a duplicate of oneself. It is an ideal self, an imaginary self, *an other self,* a self who is already possessed by others. The specular image makes the self who I am and who looks at the reflection an other, even as the specular image presents my-self to me as an other. "At the same time that the image of oneself makes possible the knowledge of oneself, it makes possible a sort of alienation."[16] The specular image with which the infant plays *is* and *is not* the infant. Between the infant and the reflection there is a relation of identity and difference. The specular image bears the countenance of a *familiar-stranger.*

AN ILLUSTRATION FROM CHILDHOOD

The specular image reveals that the reflection matters psychologically in its otherness. It is the difference which matters psychologically. The reflection is an other and the other reflects the self who I am. In brief, the self is a phenomenon of indirection and this is the essential point which the specular image demonstrates. This indirection, this reflection of self through other continues beyond these encounters with the mirror. It is found also in the child's relations with others. Merleau-Ponty calls this phenomenon "syncretic sociability,"[17] and he illustrates it in the following fashion.

A little girl is seated beside her mother and another child. She is visibly uneasy in this situation. Quite unexpectedly this little girl slaps her companion. When she is asked why, she answers that her companion hit her. Is she lying? The sincerity of her reply to the initial question is sufficient to rule out that it is a lie or a deliberate trick. And certainly we do not advance far toward understanding this child's behavior if we merely say that she is bad or naughty. But then how are we to understand this piece of aggressive behavior? For his answer Merleau-Ponty returns to the observation of the little girl's uneasiness. She is visibly anxious and it is her anxiety which "impregnates her view of the little girl sitting beside her." "The child," he continues, "[is] living her anxiety, and the gestures appropriate to lessening it, *not as interior events but as qualities of things in the world and of others.*"[18] Her anxiety is experienced as a world. It is reflected through it, through the physiognomy of that world and those who share it. Her aggressive behavior bears witness to the style of her world. In particular it bears witness to her experience of the other whom she slaps, another who reflects her anxiety.

This example is admittedly quite simple, and yet it is illustrative of a common enough theme in daily life. I choose this example, moreover, because on the basis of the little information provided it seems obvious that the little girl is *mistaken* in her experience of the one whom she slaps. She lives her anxiety through the other, but it seems that the companion does little to deserve this experience. The little girl is in error, but her error is informative about the phenomenon of syncretic sociability.

Because the little girl is mistaken we may be tempted to say that her behavior is the consequence of a *projection*. But syncretic sociability in general, and in this particular case, is not explained by projection because projection always presupposes what it needs to explain. The little girl must already experience her anxiety through the other if she is to project her experience onto her. Apart from the fact that the theory of projection never tells us how what is inside a person can leave her and become attached to another, the theory also ignores those very features of the world which make an explanation by projection initially plausible. The theory begs the question of its own possibility, because *before* there can be any projection the world and others must appear in such a way as to present a landscape in which one can behave in this or that particular fashion. Projection, therefore, is no *explanation* at all for the phenomenon of syncretic sociability. In fact, it presupposes it. At best, therefore, the term has a *descriptive* meaning. It is not a mechanism inside the person which explains the behavior, but a style of conducting oneself with others in the world. It describes a way of being with others which is not sustained over time. The anxious little girl slaps her companion and she is rebuked. Her slap, which testifies to her experience of the other, is not affirmed by her mother. The error of her behavior does not refer, therefore, to a feeling which hides within her, but to a way of seeing herself with and through others which is not borne in time. Projection describes a kind of syncretic sociability in which one's way of being with others is closed off to the horizon of time. It is not a spatial phenomenon. It is a temporal one.

The failure of the theory of projection to explain syncretic sociability, even in its errors, points back to this phenomenon as an originary aspect of human life. The little girl's erroneous behavior is the disruption of a norm which is highlighted by this very disruption. Her confusion in the negative sense points to a confusion in the positive sense which exists between us in the heart of every situation. "To the very extent that it is convincing and genuine, the experience of the other," Merleau-Ponty notes, "creates . . . a *mixture* of myself and the other."[19] We exist within a circuit of reflections. One is infected by the other, so to speak, and there is no absolute inoculation against this contagion by the other.

But surely this phenomenon is destined to be overcome in adult life. Surely this confusion (mixture) is destined to be corrected by adult experience. If syncretic sociability is not essentially an erroneous phenomenon, then certainly it must be only a childish one. Here again, however, we are mistaken if we regard it in this fashion. "Syncretic sociability is perhaps not liquidated," Merleau-Ponty writes, and indeed "this mutual impingement of the other and myself at the heart of a situation in which we are confused . . . [is] met with again in adult life."[20] The phenomenon is of course transformed between childhood and adulthood insofar as experience places more distance between us in place of that earlier "dizzying proximity to others."[21] But the phenomenon nevertheless remains. Having illustrated this relation of reflection between self and other in the periods of infancy and childhood, it remains to demonstrate its appearance in the world of adults. We may anticipate this appearance however by recalling here a remark of Goethe: "For each of us our circle of friends is what we ourselves are."[22]

A VISION OF HELL

At the end of his play *No Exit*, Jean-Paul Sartre has Garcin, one of three characters in the play, say the following:

> This bronze. [Strokes it thoughtfully.] Yes, now's the moment; I'm looking at this thing on the mantelpiece, and I understand that I'm in hell. I tell you, everything's been thought out beforehand. They knew I'd stand at the fireplace stroking this thing of bronze, with all those eyes intent on me. Devouring me. [He swings round abruptly.] What? Only two of you? I thought there were more; many more. [Laughs.] So this is hell. I'd never have believed it. You remember all we were told about the torture-chambers, the fire and brimstone, the "burning marl." Old wives' tales! There's no need for red-hot pokers. Hell is—other people![23]

I begin with this dramatic example because Sartre's play vividly demonstrates this relation of reflection between self and others in an adult world. It matters little here that this world is hell, and one does not have to accept Sartre's conclusions that this reflection is hellish in order to see the point. Garcin sees who he is through the eyes of others, Estelle and Inez, just as they see through each other and Garcin who they are.

The action of the drama takes place in a comfortable sitting-room. Garcin, a coward who proclaims himself a pacifist and who deserted his friends at the outbreak of the war, enters first and is shortly followed by Inez, a cynical lesbian murdered by her lover. Estelle, the third character in the drama, enters last. She is an elegantly dressed vain woman, a woman of supposedly high taste who has murdered her baby.

In the beginning of the drama each of the characters reacts differently to the situation. Inez is initially indifferent and seems callously resigned. Estelle, on the other hand, pretends confusion and is sure that a mistake has been made in her case. Garcin struggles to make the best possible arrangement of this situation, and he wavers in his behavior between a pretense of self-control and a nervous preoccupation. In moments of silent brooding, for example, his mouth twitches, and Inez brutally reproaches him for this expression of fear.

As the drama progresses the dialogue among the characters gradually corrodes their initial postures. Inez's indifference gives way to a sadistic honesty in which Garcin's and Estelle's illusions are destroyed. All of them are criminals and murderers, she shouts, and to Estelle she says that no mistakes are ever made and that each of them is damned for something. Moreover when Garcin pleadingly searches Estelle's eyes for confirmation of his manhood, Inez mockingly reminds him that Estelle will say whatever he wants to hear because of her own desperate need to be regarded by any man, however cowardly and miserable he may be. Garcin's pretended heroism slowly dissolves therefore in these bitter reflections of Inez. Unable to convince *himself* that he is not a coward, he is also unable to find this confirmation through Estelle because of Inez. Indeed the moment before he realizes that hell is other people, he desperately asks if night will ever come to this room. Inez gives him the answer, and at that moment Garcin is faced with the realization that she will always see him and therefore that he will always see himself as a coward through her. Estelle, finally, becomes increasingly desperate as her confusion and pretended innocence are stripped away by Inez and Garcin. The

murderer of her child, her only care is that she not be left without something or someone to reflect her beauty. Without a mirror she cannot
exist, she says, and when she discovers that none are to be had in this
room she cries out that she cannot do without one for all eternity.

But Estelle does not need an actual mirror to see herself any more
than Inez or Garcin can escape their reflections in this mirror-less room,
because each is a mirror for the others. Inez in fact explicitly offers to be
a mirror for Estelle and invites her to see herself through her eyes. Estelle,
however, cannot look. Her fascination with Inez is also a fear because she
cannot tame, as she says, the reflection of herself in Inez's eyes. Through
Inez she fears what she may see of herself, and hence she turns away from
her toward Garcin. With Garcin she knows who she is, a woman whose
beauty can be reflected in a look of desire, and it is only through a man's
desire that she can see herself. Inez, however, cannot allow Estelle to be
with Garcin, since she needs Estelle for herself. Her desires, however, find
only fear, rejection, and hate in the eyes of Estelle. Inez, therefore, must
continually unmask Garcin's feeble efforts to love Estelle as so many desperate attempts on his part to find through her a conviction of his he-
roic life. Garcin himself then has nowhere else to turn but to Inez, and
with her he must spend an eternity seeking to change the reflection of
himself as a coward. Thus when the door unexpectedly opens near the
end of the play, Garcin is unable either to leave or to help Estelle push
Inez outside the room. He needs Inez as much as Inez needs Estelle and as
much as Estelle needs Garcin. They are mirrors of each other, three
circuits of reflection:

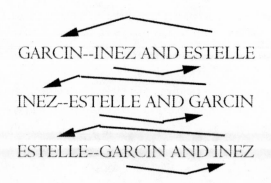

GARCIN--INEZ AND ESTELLE

INEZ--ESTELLE AND GARCIN

ESTELLE--GARCIN AND INEZ

Sartre's play is a dramatic example of the relation of reflection between self and others even if it is one-sided in its interpretation of this reflection. If hell is other people, if the presence of reflection is hell, then heaven must be the absence of reflection. But this absence is not heaven as much as it is the condition for the appearance of unconsciousness in human life. This theme will be considered later in the chapter. For the moment I point out a more immediate theme. Insofar as the relation of reflection between self and other in the adult world is illustrated by a drama, it turns our attention toward the themes of behavior and experience. A drama presents human actions, and Sartre's play is performed less in terms of self and other and more in terms of concrete behaviors and experiences. Through the example, therefore, we can move from self and other as realities of reflection toward an understanding of behavior and experience in this way. The example leads us to this first implication of the recovery of self and other as realities of reflection.

Some Reflections on Behavior and Experience as Realities of Reflection

Psychology defines itself as the science of behavior, and as such it purports to be a rigorous study of an observable, empirical event. Behavior is a thing to be studied, and like other things in the physical world it occurs in a locatable, real space. Over there is the behavior to be observed while here is the observer, and between them there exists a relation only of spatial proximity. Nothing seems more certain than this fact of science which is also a fact of daily life: I see what you do, just as you see what I do.

The matter, however, is not so simple because the *doings* which one sees are unspecified in their meaning. Indeed in the definition of psychology as a science of behavior, the term *behavior* is an empty category. It is empty because no one ever really sees *behavior*. On the contrary one sees "John *kissing* Mary," or "Frank *pushing* Ralph," or "James *collapsing* in a chair," which is not unlike what the psychologist sees as John's compulsive eroticism, or Frank's counter-phobic aggression, or James' chronic depression. What you and I see and what the psychologist sees are not unalike because in each case no one is observing behavior. Rather in each case one is interpreting through one's experience of the behavior the meaning of the action. Kissing, pushing, slumping are interpretations. They are not neutral observations. Behavior is not an event which is observed but an action which is interpreted. And in fact there is no such thing as a neutral observation. Observation is always and already an interpretation. "Seeing is an experience," the philosopher of science Norwood Hanson says, and "People, not their eyes, see. Cameras, and eye-balls, are blind," he adds, and "there is more to seeing than meets the eyeball."[24]

The science of psychology would have little difficulty accepting this position. Neutral observation, the neutral observer, is neither a popular nor a defensible position today. But there is more at stake here than this issue of a neutral observer. In fact the issue is not unlike physics suddenly throwing into question the sense in which it understands the terms *matter* or *energy*, because what is at stake is the sense in which one of psychology's fundamental terms, *behavior*, is understood. If one allows that observed behavior is always behavior interpreted through the observer's experience, then one can no longer hold to the definition of psychology as simply the study of behavior. Rather one must say that psychology is the study of *experienced behavior*, a definition which means that psychology is as much an expression of the observer's experience as it is a study of the behavior observed. Stated in another way, this change in definition amounts to the recognition that *behavior reflects experience. One's experience is visible through the other's behavior*, and this includes your experience and my experience of Mary's behavior *and* the psychologist's experience of that behavior as well. Consequently the psychologist's theory, which is after all a methodical experience of the other's behavior, is as much a part of the definition of psychology as a science as are the facts of that science. The behavior observed reflects the theory of the observer. It reflects the observer's vision, the observer's way of seeing. A *dichotomy* of fact and theory is untenable. It is as untenable as a dichotomy between behavior and experience. Every observed fact reflects a theory just as every behavior reflects an experience of that behavior. An example will illustrate my point.

HARVEY LOOKS AT THE HUMAN HEART

William Harvey was an English physician who in 1628 published his epoch-making text entitled *An Anatomical Disquisition on the Motion of the Heart and Blood in Animals.*[25] In that text Harvey laid the foundations for modern medicine by describing the human heart as a pump. The achievement is undoubtedly important. But it is also interesting as a piece of scientific behavior, a case study in the behavior of science. Let us look at Harvey's behavior, and let us begin by imagining the scene when Harvey first saw the pumping heart. Our imagining here is guided by a description of his discovery which Harvey himself provides in the preface of his work.

Although the text was not published until 1628, Harvey tells us that for more than nine years he had known the heart to be a pump. In fact the first public utterance of this bold thesis occurred on April 17, 1616, in a class which he gave in his official capacity as Lumleian lecturer attached to the Royal College of Physicians of London. Twelve years, therefore, actually separated his vision of the heart and the publication of this vision, and it is easy to imagine that this first pronouncement was preceded by many years of diligent labor. Thus sometime before 1616 Harvey first saw the heart as a pump, and it is this moment I wish imaginatively to describe.

The year is not yet 1616 and William Harvey, not yet thirty-eight years of age, is a young physician trained at Padua and practicing in London. In the evenings after seeing his patients and dining with his wife he retires to a small laboratory located in his home where he is busily engaged investigating the motions of the animal heart. He has stooped over countless animals and dissected them, and his room bears witness to this labor. Cold-blooded toads, frogs, small fish, eels, crabs, shrimps, and snails lie about the dissecting table, along with the hearts of their warm-blooded mammalian cousins: dogs, cats, and hogs. But Harvey is not able easily to catch the rhythm of this movement, which comes and goes, as he says, in the twinkling of an eye and like a flash of lightning. He continues to work, however, and on this night sometime before 1616 he looks down upon one more animal and he sees with his eyes and feels with his hands the rhythmic movement of a moribund heart.   It is a moment of *scientific* truth and of personal triumph and we can understand without too much difficulty the look on Harvey's face as he raises his head away from the open chest of that dying animal.   He knows now that the blood flows throughout the body, that it courses in a circle, and that the heart is a pump.   He knows it, he sees it, and sometime later he will speak it in that public lecture.   And yet twelve years will intervene between that day in April 1616 and the publication of his views in 1628.   In these twelve years he will converse with the king and become his friend, and he will walk the evening streets of London between his patients' houses and his home, knowing what he has seen and marshalling more evidence on behalf of his daring vision.   But in this same period of time he will not raise his voice above a cautious whisper to proclaim his views.   Only a select circle of colleagues will hear of his discovery.   For twelve years he will remain tentative and perhaps even diffident in the elaboration of his conviction.

How can one understand this piece of behavior?   How can one understand Harvey's reluctance to publicize his views?   The way in which I have imaginatively described this historical occasion already implies a certain understanding.   Harvey's reluctant behavior, his caution, is an exemplary illustration of the workings of modern science.   His behavior embodies the posture of the true scientist, careful, diligent, and dispassionate in the long search for truth.   Harvey is the figure of that scientist, and his behavior is understandable in those terms.   But other understandings are possible and perhaps even demanded.   His behavior can be observed in other ways.   Let us introduce three witnesses to this scene, a modern-day behavioral psychologist, a psychoanalyst, and a physiological psychologist.   Then let us listen to Harvey's understanding of his own behavior.

For the behavioral psychologist an understanding of Harvey's reluctant behavior is framed in terms of the social conditions which shape and determine behavior.   Insofar as behavior is a function of its consequences, we may presume that Harvey has had some singularly unpleasant experiences in initially professing his views.   His diffidence is a consequence of his previous encounters with others.   His reluctance is a piece

of learned behavior, a consequence of his conditioning. No credit therefore can be given to a man of science whose caution is the ennobling
feature of a patient seeker of truth. And even if one were to claim that
his caution is an expression of the best trait of the scientific posture, then
the behavioral psychologist would answer that this scientific training is
and has been the conditioning factor. For the behavioral psychologist,
Harvey's reluctant behavior shows a previous history of reinforcement.

The psychoanalytic psychologist, however, will see a much different
behavior and quite probably will not be impressed with the explanation
offered by the behaviorist. Harvey's behavior is much richer than this
previous account allows, and if it is to be understood then it must be seen
in terms of its *symbolic* structure. Harvey has looked upon the dead and
dying bodies of animals, and in his practice he has certainly gazed upon
the dying struggles of his fellow men. As a physician he knows death, and
he has come to know life through his studies of the corpse. But the heart
is somehow different, and the human heart holds a special significance in
the life of men. Harvey himself recognizes and acknowledges this special
place of the heart in the larger anatomy of things when in the dedication of the work to King Charles I of England he calls the heart the
foundation of life, the sovereign of everything which is living. It is this
heart, however, which he sees as a pump, and *as such* the human heart is
like any other heart. It is like the hearts of the animals which he has so
laboriously studied and dissected. Its special place, therefore, is something of an illusion, for how can what is so common be also so special?
King Charles I, to which this work is recommended and dedicated, will
be beheaded in 1649 by the non-kingly forces of Oliver Cromwell, and
by that time Harvey will have given up his earlier view of the heart's
central place. Could it be, the psychoanalytic psychologist might ask,
that Harvey has already seen in this earlier work something of what he
should not see? Could his reluctance be explained by a knowledge which
he knows in some way is already forbidden? He is friend to a king whose
kingdom will soon be divided, and in this work he sees, among other
aspects of the pumping heart, the tough, fibrous wall which *divides* the
heart. Does this vision of a divided heart anticipate the division of a
kingdom? Is his reluctance the consequence of an ambivalent vision?

Certainly this explanation is more dramatic than the behavioral account, but just as certainly it would be dismissed by our third witness. The physiological psychologist would be less inclined toward such fanciful explanations and would prefer to find a reason, a cause for Harvey's reluctant behavior, in the workings of the body. Harvey's reluctance is a kind of fear, and fear is an emotion whose sources are traceable to the sympathetic nervous system. His fear then is ultimately understandable in physiological terms, just as his *vision* of the pumping heart can be explained in terms of the anatomy of the human eye. Ironically, moreover, this last witness could call Harvey's work in defense of this account, because it is this work which in many ways prepares for this kind of explanation. It is the physiological body which Harvey opens up, and it is this same body toward which the physiological psychologist turns in observing Harvey's behavior.

But if *Harvey's work* can be called to the physiological psychologist's defense, Harvey himself cannot be. It is true that fear has played a large role in the story of this twelve-year delay, and Harvey himself explicitly says as much in his preface. But fear for Harvey is not yet the physiological workings of the body. It is rather an expression of his sense of isolation, just as his eventual triumph over the fear is an expression of the growing support he finds among his fellow physicians. In Harvey's eyes fear is a social phenomenon which colors his relation with his colleagues and with the medical tradition of which he is a part. His fear is not a consequence of these social conditions—his present relations and the traditions of the past—but a way of envisioning them.

I admit, of course, that I take some license in the presentation of this example, and I recognize that one may claim that I have oversimplified the position of the witnesses. But the positions per se are not the issue here, for I wish to illustrate only that each of these positions including my own and Harvey's is a way of experiencing Harvey's behavior, *and* that the behavior of reluctance reflects each of these experiences. All the explanations are ways of experiencing this behavior, and in each case one is not simply observing facts which are already there waiting to be seen. On the contrary, in each instance one observes the behavior through an experience. The dedicated scientist, the conditioned man, the guilty visionary, the physiological mechanism, and the man who is simply afraid—all of these observations say as much about the observer's experience as they do about the behavior observed. In each case the behavior is observed because the experience of the observer makes it visible in a particular fashion. And conversely the experiences which make the behavior visible in these five ways are themselves visible through the observed behavior.

But surely this account of behavior and experience cannot be accepted, because on one hand it leads to chaos and on the other hand it confuses *public* knowledge and *private* opinions. With regard to the first objection the argument is that one cannot have five different interpretations of the same behavior in a valid science of behavior. The criteria of validity in science intend to insure that what an observer sees is what is really there to be seen. With five visions, and even more with other witnesses, these criteria evaporate. This argument necessarily presumes however that behavior is a neutral fact whose meaning lies in or with the behavior ready to be discovered. It presumes that validation can occur *outside* the way in which the behavior has been observed. Now I am not dismissing here the notion of validation, but I am questioning the way in which it is understood as well as the presumption of behavior as a neutral, empirical fact which occurs in the physical world. The fact is that behavior is not a fact in the sense of an identity closed within itself and immune to the ways in which it is seen. The fact is that behavior is a reality of reflection and as such it is characterized simultaneously and paradoxically by identity and difference. The example certainly illustrates this point. What is needed then is a way of conceptualizing this reality and a rethinking of the notion of validation in accordance with what the reality of behavior demands.[26] A psychological science of behavior has to accept behavior on its own terms, that is, in terms of how it appears. It will not do to decide in advance what kind of reality behavior should be in order to cast it into some pre-established mold.

Concerning the second objection, the argument is that the observations of the three witnesses are public knowledge, while Harvey's observation and my own qualify as subjective opinions. But what makes those three observations any more public than the other two? The science of psychology must be mute on this point, because in principle each of the observations is identical in form. In each instance behavior is observed through an experience. In each instance it is not only something to see but also a way of seeing. Thus we cannot dismiss in principle any of these five observations without dismissing all of them. But we can dismiss one or another of them on the grounds of preference or intention.[27] One's preference however does not make one's observation public knowledge and the others' private opinions. All the observations are public knowledge provided that one can indicate to others how to stand in order to see what one sees.

The two objections do not invalidate what the example clearly demonstrates: behavior is made observable through an experience, and that experience of the behavior is visible *as* that behavior. But now we appear to have opened up a third dilemma, because if the experience of a behavior is visible *as* that behavior, then this phrasing seems to imply an identification between one's experience and the other's behavior. It seems to suggest that my experience *is* your behavior, and/or that my behavior *is* your experience. No such identification however is intended. The relation of reflection between behavior and experience emphasizes in fact a *de-realization* of the reflected through the reflection. If your behavior reflects my experience, then it does so by re-figuring it in a deeper way. To put it briefly, your behavior *makes a difference* to my experience, a matter with which we are all readily familiar in daily life. A second example will illustrate this point.

A STUDY IN HUMAN EMOTIONS

In 1962 Schachter and Singer conducted a study entitled "Cognitive, Social, and Physiological Determinants of Emotional State," designed to dispute the classic James-Lange theory of emotions. The authors wanted to demonstrate that an emotion is "a joint function of a state of physiological arousal and of the appropriateness of a cognition."[28] More specifically the authors made three hypotheses. First, they hypothesized that given a state of physiological arousal for which subjects have no immediate explanation, the subjects will describe their emotions in terms of the cognitions available to them. Second, they assumed that given a state of physiological arousal for which a completely appropriate explanation exists, the subjects are unlikely to label their emotions in terms of alternative cognitions which may be available. Third, they suspected that given the same cognitive circumstances, subjects will react emotionally only to the extent that they feel a state of physiological arousal.

The test of these three hypotheses required the manipulation of the physiological state of the experimental subjects, the control over the information which the subjects received as explanations for their bodily states, and the creation of experimental situations from which alternative explanatory cognitions could be derived. Informing the subjects that the experiment was designed to test the effects of a vitamin supplement on vision, a physician injected each of the subjects with either epinephrine (adrenalin) or a placebo. The second requirement was met by having the experimenter provide various explanations of the expected effects of the injection. Epinephrine is a sympathomimetic drug whose effects include a marked increase in systolic blood pressure, heart and respiration rate, and such bodily feelings as palpitations, tremors, and occasionally accelerated breathing. One group, hereafter called epinephrine informed (Epi Inf), was given this information by the experimenter and the physician. A second group, epinephrine ignorant (Epi Ign), was told that there would be no side effects. The third group, epinephrine misinformed (Epi Mis), was given incorrect information by the physician and the experimenter. This group was told to expect numbness of the feet, itching, and a slight headache. Finally a fourth group which received the placebo injections was told, like the Epi-Ign group, to expect no side effects. In other words this group received no physiological stimulant and was told not to expect any reactions. For the third requirement the investigators used experimental cohorts who were introduced to the subjects as co-subjects in the experiment. After each subject received the injection and instructions, the experimenter returned with the cohort and indicated that there would be a twenty-minute delay in order to wait for the vitamin supplement to enter the bloodstream. The cohort, who did not know which injection or what information the subject had

Table 1. Design of the Schachter-Singer Experiment

Hypotheses	*Group*
1. Physiological arousal but no immediate explanation: Subject is expected to describe emotions in terms of the available cognitions (euphoria or anger).	Epi Ign & Epi Mis
2. Physiological arousal with a completely appropriate explanation: Subject is expected to be immune to the experimentally created situation.	Epi Inf
3. No physiological arousal and no immediate explanation: Subject not expected to react emotionally.	Placebo

Table 2. Expected and Obtained Results for Condition of Euphoria

Expected Results

Epi Mis $\geq$ Epi   Ign $>$ Epi Inf $=$ Placebo

Obtained Results

Epi Mis $\geq$ Epi Ign $\geq$ Placebo $>$ Epi Inf

Table 3. Expected and Obtained Results for Condition of Anger

Expected Results

Epi Ign $>$ Epi Inf $=$ Placebo

Obtained Results

Epi Ign $>$ Placebo $>$ Epi Inf

received, was instructed to behave either euphorically or angrily during this waiting period. In the situation of euphoria, cohorts would, for example, doodle on some scratch paper and then crumple that paper to engage actively in a "basketball game." In addition they might make and fly a paper airplane, use a rubber band and wads of paper for a slingshot, or twirl a hula hoop. During all of this activity the cohort would engage the subject in conversation and periodically invite the subject to join the games. For the situation of anger the cohorts were instructed to respond with increasing irritability to items on a questionnaire which they and the subjects were told to answer during the delay. At the end of this sequence the cohort would tear up the questionnaire and storm out of the room. Table 1 summarizes the design of the experiment matching each of the hypotheses with its respective group or groups.

The results of the experiment are summarized in Tables 2 and 3. Table 2 gives the expected and obtained degrees of emotionality for the situation of euphoria. Table 3 gives the expected and obtained degrees of emotionality for the situation of anger.[29]

The tables indicate that the authors expected more demonstrated emotionality for the misinformed and ignorant groups than for the group that was informed about the effects of the injection. They expected in other words that the misinformed and ignorant groups would be more affected by the cohorts' behaviors than the informed group. The obtained results confirmed this expectation. Moreover, Table 2 indicates that the authors assumed that the misinformed group would be more susceptible to the cohorts' behavior than the ignorant group. They were *misinformed* by two authority figures rather than *uninformed*, and the investigators assumed that this wrong information would make it more difficult for these subjects to fall back on the injection to account for their experiences. To do so they would have had to dismiss the "information" which they did receive. They would have had to discount the "information" of the experimenter and the physician. Schachter and Singer assumed this would be a difficult task, and hence they further assumed it would be easier and more likely for these subjects to account for their experiences in terms of the cohorts' behavior. This misinformed group in other words was more likely to be susceptible to this influence than the uninformed or ignorant group. This latter group, without information, could more easily use the injection to interpret their experiences, and hence they were less likely to be susceptible to the cohorts' behavior. Again the results which were obtained confirmed those which were expected. Finally, the tables suggest that the authors expected that there would be no difference in either situation between the informed and the placebo groups. In each case they expected that there would be little, if any, demonstrated emotionality. The informed group and the placebo group were expected to remain immune to the cohorts' behavior. The authors reasoned this way because the informed group was given an adequate explanation for their bodily feelings by the physician and the experimenter. They counted on the influence of this information. For the placebo group the authors tentatively assumed that no physiological arousal was involved. In this case, however, the obtained results did not sustain this expectation, and in the instances of euphoria and anger the placebo groups were consistently more affected by the cohorts' behavior than the informed groups. In summary, the first two hypotheses were sustained. The third one, however, was not supported by the results of the experiment.

On the basis of these results Schachter and Singer drew two tentative and general conclusions. First, they concluded that their experiment did demonstrate the influence of the experimentally created situations on the subjects' experiences of their emotions. In the absence of a completely adequate cognitive explanation, the two groups, Epi Mis and Epi Ign, did interpret their feelings in terms of the cohorts' behaviors of euphoria or anger. As the authors themselves state: ". . . given precisely the same state of epinephrine-induced sympathetic activation, we have, by means of cognitive manipulations, been able to produce in our subjects the very disparate states of euphoria and anger."[30] Regardless, therefore, of the common physiological state, one set of Epi Mis and Epi Ign subjects interpreted their experiences as euphoria while the other set interpreted their experiences as anger. Clearly, then, the effect of the created experimental situation, the effect of the cohorts' behaviors on the subjects' experiences was demonstrated. Second, Schachter and Singer concluded that the greater degree of emotionality in the placebo group compared with the Epi Inf group made it "impossible to evaluate un-equivocally the effects of the state of physiological arousal . . ."[31] The placebo group was apparently influenced by the experimentally created situations, by the cohorts' behaviors, much as the Epi Mis and Epi Ign groups were, *even in the apparent absence of a physiologically induced state.* In fact while this placebo group consistently manifested a lower emotional level than either the Epi Mis or Epi Ign groups, this differ-ence was *statistically significant* according to the authors only in the anger situation. This result brings into question the precise role of physi-ological arousal in the genesis of emotions.

For the purposes of the present discussion it is the first conclusion which is important. The second conclusion, however, is not completely separable from the first one, and hence some remarks need to be ad-dressed to it.

Considering this unexpected second conclusion, the authors acknowl-edge that the placebo injection does not guarantee a neutral physiologi-cal state. They say, for example, that while "there is no question that epinephrine effectively produces a state of arousal, there is also no ques-tion that a placebo does not prevent physiological arousal."[32] Acknowl-edging this fact, Schachter and Singer then report that indeed *some* of their placebo subjects did manifest a state of physiological arousal, ap-parently created by the very situation of the experiment. A needle injec-tion is arousing enough, and when that is added to the behavior of the cohorts we can easily imagine the subjects' situation. Moreover, it was precisely those placebo subjects who did manifest a physiologically aroused state, as measured for example by pulse rate, who reported more emotion than the Epi Inf subjects. Those placebo subjects who showed no sign of a physiologically aroused condition reported no greater emotion than the Epi Inf subjects. The authors state that "the emotional levels of subjects showing no signs of sympathetic activity are quite comparable to the emotional level of subjects in the parallel Epi Inf conditions." There seems no doubt then of the body's necessary role in the genesis and experience of emotions. Physiological arousal and situation are both "essential to an emotional state."[33] Nevertheless, there is also no doubt that the body which is involved in emotions, the emotional body, is not

the unambiguous body of physiology. The *same* physiological condition of epinephrine-induced sympathetic activation is manifested in the
different psychological experiences of euphoria and anger. The *same*
physiological body lends itself in *different* ways to various situations.
Acknowledging as much, Schachter and Singer explicitly state that while
their study "does *not* rule out the possibility of physiological differences among the emotional states,"[34] it most certainly speaks very strongly
against it. They reject therefore any *specific* correspondence between
experience and physiology, even while they leave open the possibility of
a *general* correspondence between them. But the precise nature of this
relation is not the subject of their conclusion. Nor is it our concern in
this chapter. To conclude this part of the discussion, therefore, I will say
only that this classic study of emotions strongly suggests a need to recover the body in a psychological way. This need is the theme of the
next chapter.

With respect to the first conclusion which Schachter and Singer
draw from their study, it seems clear that their results confirm that one's
experience is visible through the other's behavior *and* that this reflection
of experience through behavior is not an identification of experience
with behavior. There is no hint that the subjects *mimicked* or *copied* the
cohorts' behavior. On the contrary there is only the indication that the
Epi Mis and Epi Ign subjects *made sense* of their feelings *through* the
behavior of the others, the experimenters' cohorts. These subjects either
were told to expect no bodily feelings or were misinformed about what
they would feel, and the first hypothesis suggested that in the absence of
any immediate or appropriate explanation for their bodily feelings the
subjects would understand them in terms of the cognitions available to
them through the cohorts' behaviors. The confirmation of this hypothesis strongly suggests, therefore, that the behavior of the cohorts provided a mirror through which these subjects' experiences could be reflected. Indeed we might say that for each of these subjects a bodily
feeling of an experience became *the experience of a feeling* through the
behavior of the other. Moreover, we may also say that this relation of
reflection applies as well to the Epi Inf group. In their case, however, it
was not the behaviors of the cohorts which reflected their experience

but the *authoritative* behavior of the physician and the experimenter. Their immunity from the cohorts' behaviors does not disprove the relation of reflection. It shows only that the mirrors lie elsewhere. While Schachter and Singer provide no direct data on this point, there are some indirect data which support it. The greater degree of emotionality of the misinformed group as compared with the ignorant group leads one to suspect that the "information" provided by the experimenter and physician did figure in the subjects' interpretation of their experiences. Moreover, as I previously indicated, the investigators themselves assumed this possibility. It was built into the very design of their experiment, specifically with respect to the first two hypotheses.

Schachter's and Singer's subjects were influenced by the behavior of the cohorts. Their experiences were affected by the euphoric and angry behavior displayed before them. This influence takes the form of a *contagion*, and in fact at the very end of their study Schachter and Singer use this metaphor to further discuss their results. It is a suitable metaphor. A relation of reflection between me and you means that we infect each other with meaning, and it may very well be that the biological theory of contagion draws its insight from this experiential foundation. In any case Schachter's and Singer's study does demonstrate that the subjects' experiences are visible through the cohort's behaviors. It illustrates the relation of reflection between behavior and experience and it demonstrates that this relation of reflection *makes a difference*. The other's behavior reflects my experience, which means that it *re-figures* it. The mirroring of experience through behavior is not an identification of one's experience with the other's behavior. It is rather a *deepening* of one's experience through that behavior. The other's behavior is the way in which my experience *matters*. It is the depth of my experience, just as my behavior is the depth of the other's experience.

Imaginal Understanding: Psychological Life as Story

The recovery of behavior and experience as realities of reflection demonstrates that my experience is visible through the other's behavior and that the other's behavior is made visible (observable) in some particular fashion through my experience. The question which now arises concerns the way in which one's experience makes the other's behavior visible. This is the second implication to be considered in this chapter. It is an issue about the mode and form of psychological understanding. As always I begin with an example.

SUNDAY MORNING

When I was a boy there was an old man who on Sunday mornings would walk with his wife in the park close to my home. The woman too was old. I would see them every Sunday on my way to the bakery. They would walk slowly, the man gently resting one arm on hers for support, using the other to steady himself with a cane. He was somewhat stooped as I remember, and although he always wore a cap I knew that his hair was snowy white. The woman's hair was more grey, and she stood straighter than he did. They would rarely talk from what I could see, but I could tell even at a distance that they shared something very close with each other without words. Occasionally she would reach over and take hold of his hand, a touch that seemed even to me as a small boy full of warmth and care. Half way around the park they would come to a bench and together they would sit down, first he and then she. She would help him and when he was settled she would take her place beside him. Then they would sit there and simply look at the world of Sunday morning. On my return from the bakery they were always gone.

I have not thought of this incident in many years, but I now remember well how it affected me as a small boy. I remember thinking how much sadness they seemed to carry and yet also how much peace they seemed to have. The world seemed so special to them, so important, as if nothing else really mattered on Sunday morning. As I watched them I would imagine who they were and where they had come from. They had been immigrants, I supposed, and had come to America to struggle in a lifetime of work. She would have been a domestic or maybe a store clerk, and he would have been a laborer. I was sure they had children, a schoolteacher, a lawyer, and maybe a policeman. But they were all gone now, married, and living far away from these two old people. Maybe they telephoned on Sundays. I thought she would like that. Maybe that was why they would leave the park.

One Sunday, however, the old man and woman were not there, and for several Sundays thereafter I did not see them. But finally on another Sunday I saw him. He came into the park, more slowly than usual, and alone. And I remember that as I watched him make his way slowly toward the bench and pass it I knew that his wife had died. I never went that way again, and I never saw the old man after that final Sunday morning.

Today after so many years I recognize that I *understood* those two old people through a *story*. I understood them through a story of old age, of the course of life, and of dying. On those Sunday mornings a tale was spun between me and those two old people, and around that tale, among others, a little boy began to change. Was my understanding *in fact* correct? Had she *in fact* died? Were they in fact immigrants? To this day I do not know the answers to these questions, and while I suppose I could have talked to them, the most important feature of those Sunday mornings would not have changed. Our conversation would have *continued* the story and perhaps it would have corrected and even changed it into another story. *But it would not have changed the story into a fact.* It could not without changing what mattered most about those Sunday mornings. *The story mattered.* It moved an eight-year-old boy toward a vision of life as biography. No empirical facts, however many he might have collected about those people, could have been more psychologically real.

STORY: IMAGINAL, NOT FICTIONAL

Psychological understanding proceeds by way of story, a point of view which Hillman advocates in persuasive fashion.[35] Story, not fact, defines human psychological life, and in this sense psychological experience as story is to be distinguished from a factual account of experience. A factual account about experience is not wrong. It is only that it is not psychological. Even in daily life we live and recognize this difference between a factual account of another person and a story about him. It is the story we remember and not the facts, and when so-called hard facts are given they also are remembered and become memorable when woven into a tale. Factualness is not antithetical to psychological life, but it is secondary to the dimension of story. The fact is the matter which matters in another way. Story is the form of psychological life and psychological understanding.

But if story is the form of psychological life and understanding then is psychological life a fiction? Is the move away from psychological life as fact necessarily a move toward psychological life as fiction? It would initially seem to be so, since stories are usually regarded as unreal. But we have learned already to be critical about the meaning of real and unreal when dealing with psychological life, and hence a more cautious reply to the question is required. The reply has two parts.

First, the story of Sunday Morning itself illustrates an incident which is so dramatically real that it is remembered to this day as transformative of a human life. What would be gained by reducing the significance of this incident to a fiction? What would be gained by negating this reality and calling it un-real? Nothing! Or at best one would gain the comfort of an old familiar dichotomy. The real would be narrowly defined again in empirical, factual terms, while all else would be unreal. But with this gain everything which matters psychologically would be lost. We would protect the real at the cost of the psychological, and more importantly we would miss the significance of the story. The story would become untrue, and maybe even a lie. It would no longer count. The thing which mattered most about those Sunday mornings to the eight-year-old boy would suddenly not matter. What was so dramatically real would be unreal. Could he accept it? Would anyone be able to accept this reversal? I seriously doubt it, because in terms of his, and our, psychological experience the story does count. It does matter. It is not a fact but neither is it a piece of fiction.

Second, even the etymology of the word *story* does not tie it to fiction, or for that matter to questions of fact. Its Indo-European root, *weid*, is neutral with respect to this division. This root form means simply *to see*, which is related to the Frankish form *witan* which means *to show the way*, or *to guide*. Moreover, as a suffix, *weid-to*, the root of *story* is found in the Old English *wis*, which means *wise*, as well as in the Old English *wisdom*, which means *learning* and which still appears as our own word *wisdom*. And in Old French this root appears in the term *guise* which means *manner* or *guise*. Moreover, in the suffixed *weid-os*, *story* is related to the Greek *eidos* meaning *form* or *shape*.[36] In terms of its own story, then, a story is primarily a way of seeing, a guide, something which shows the way. It is the manner, guide, or appearance of things, the way in which things and human events appear. It is the form and shape of things and human events, their *eidos* or what is essential to them. It is a kind of wisdom, a psychological wisdom which is the ability to hear the story through the facts.

Psychological life and psychological understanding are, therefore, no more matters of fiction than they are matters of fact. In the form of story they cut through this dichotomy. The consequence of course is that the *mode* of understanding psychological life is neither empirical nor rational, if we take *rational* here in the sense of a system of ideas which someone like a *critic* may apply to a work of fiction. No, the mode of psychological understanding seems closer to the *reader's* approach to the story. A reader understands a story and the story matters precisely to the extent that it portrays a *believable* world into which one can enter and within which one can dwell. How could one read, for example, James Agee's *A Death in the Family* if at the very outset of the reading one approached the work with the word fiction on one's lips? The word would bar one's entrance into the world which Agee portrays, and such a reader would learn little, if anything, about the meaning of father, about time and life, about the joy of living and the sadness of dying. That word would prohibit the reader's participation in that world. With the word fiction in one's ears one could never hear, for example, those words about the nostalgic sense of home which Jay, the father of the family, speaks to himself in the darkness of the night after comforting his young son Rufus who was afraid of the dark:

How far we all come. How far we all come away from ourselves. So far, so much between, you can never go home again. You can go home, it's good to go home, but you never really get all the way home again in your life. And what's it all for? All I tried to be, all I ever wanted and went away for, what's it all for?

Just one way, you do get back home. You have a boy or a girl of your own and now and then you remember, and you know how they feel, and it's almost the same as if you were your own self again, as young as you could remember.[37]

These are not words of fiction, any more than they are statements of fact. And yet the reader is moved by them, and through them one *understands* something about the meaning of home which perhaps one never understood before: a home is found only because it has been lost.

The reader understands, and this understanding is one which awakens one's imaginal life.[38] This same kind of understanding describes that eight-year-old boy on that final Sunday morning. The experience lived and remembered as a story intensified the boy's experience of the two old people and of himself. Through his imagining them, the way in which they appeared to him was deepened, and through their appearance in his life as *figures* of age, and maybe of wisdom, his own life was also deepened. Those two old people on Sunday morning entangled that boy in a drama of age and of death, and in that drama they figured as characters in a tale. In the way they looked, in the manner of their walk, in their slowness and silence, they introduced into the active, noisy, and busy world of an eight-year-old boy a moment of disruption. Through the ending which they enacted before his eyes they awakened a sense of his own beginning.

Nothing of this experience was or is empirically understandable as a fact. And yet it mattered. It was not a fiction. It mattered *imaginally*, as the mirror *image*, that reality of *reflection*, matters. Poets and painters, novelists and children are granted this domain of the imaginal. All of them have their excuse: they are not realists. But as adults more is expected of us, and we expect more of ourselves. We are expected to distrust the imaginal—to discount the reflection—or at least to keep it in its proper place: poems, paintings, novels, and our childhood games. This expectation, however, demands too much, for an imaginal understanding of others and ourselves is the texture of human life. It precedes poetry and painting. It is their condition. And it somehow survives the maturing process. It is not just a childish phenomenon. On the contrary, imaginal life is the mode of psychological life and understanding, the mode of a human existence which has not completely fallen asleep to the psychological. If we are to awaken to psychological life, then we must recover the place which the imaginal—the image, the reflection—has in our lives. We must recover that domain of reality and that mode of understanding which lie between the divisions of fact and fiction, the empirically real and the rationally ideal.

I am sitting in my office, looking out the window, thinking of this final paragraph, when suddenly I realize that for the last few minutes I have been watching a young woman cross the campus mall. It is a warm day and she is tired. Classes are finished, but she must still go to work for several hours, and later this evening there is an assignment to be completed. After that, however, there will be some time for friends and conversation. All of this is visible in her walk, in the style of her posture, in the manner in which she slowly passes by the things which compose her landscape. That girl, who is a stranger to me, is nevertheless known to me, and her behavior is visible and observable through my experience which imaginally weaves around the manner of her behavior a story. It is a rare occasion when we do not see in this way, imaginally. It is rare and perhaps even impossible, because "everyone thinks of his life and all lives as something that can in every sense of the word be told as a 'story.'"[39] Stories imaginally understood belong to the character of human psychological life as much as facts empirically understood belong to the character of scientific life and ideas rationally understood to the life of philosophy. One's own life and the life of an other *make sense* psychologically as a story. They do not make sense because we know all the facts or because we have a rational idea of them. A *psychological* discipline needs to appreciate this difference.[40]

THE ECLIPSE OF IMAGINAL UNDERSTANDING IN THE MODERN AGE OF SCIENCE: A HISTORICAL EXAMPLE

The remarks made in the previous section might lead one to suspect that the recovery of psychological life means a *separation* among psychological, scientific, and philosophical modes of understanding. They may appear to suggest a *separation* among story, fact, and idea. Such an interpretation would be erroneous because my intention is to emphasize a *difference* and not a separation. Certainly one can adopt a philosophical or scientific understanding of psychological life. The history of psychology as a science bears witness to the latter, while the long past of psychology's confusion with philosophy attests to the former. In much the same manner one can treat story as fact or fiction. There are stories which we readily accept as empirically real and those which we automatically consign to the realm of fiction. But on the other hand one can be psychological about science and/or philosophy; one can hear the story in the facts of science and in the systems of ideas built by philosophy. The intention is neither to replace one mode of understanding with another nor to reduce any one of these perspectives on the world to a particular one. For example, hearing the story of science psychologically is not a reduction of science to the psychological, a form of psychologism. Rather it is a glimpsing of one way in which psychological life appears. It leaves science as science but sees through it the reflection, the appearance, of psychological life. Conversely, to glimpse psychological life scientifically requires that we avoid the error of scientism: the reduction of psychological life to the mode of science. This error would not leave psychological life psychological. The task then is to see the proper character of each of these perspectives. The task is to appreciate these respective modes of understanding in their differences. Such a task is never easy, and it is made all the more difficult in light of the modern history of scientific-philosophic thought since the sixteenth century. Since that time psychological life has lost its own place. Understanding itself as a separate field of study, it has actually uncritically bound itself to the scientific mode of life and understanding. It has thereby forgotten that science is one way in which psychological life can appear. Psychological life has forgotten its own *indirect* character which its long past of confusion reveals. The eclipse of the imaginal mode of understanding in the age of science illustrates this point. The work of Ernest Becker, especially *The Structure of Evil*, tells the story of this eclipse in a comprehensive fashion.[41] I will focus, however, on only one figure in this story, the eighteenth-century Italian historian, philosopher, and jurist Giambattista Vico. The obscure fate of his work in his own life, and for some hundred years thereafter, reflects the fate of psychological life and understanding in the age of science.

Vico's major work, *The New Science*, was first published in 1725, when Vico was already 57 years old. A second and greatly altered version appeared in 1730, and in 1744, the year of his death, that version was again reprinted with some additions. The work attracted little attention in his lifetime precisely because it proclaimed the autonomy of historical studies and heralded their superiority over the scientific study of nature. In this proclamation Vico set himself against an age which was steeped in the Cartesian ideal of knowledge. Vico emphasized history to an age which was resolutely a-historical in its thinking. Descartes, after all, did banish history and such allied studies to the realm of amusing distractions, with which one might idle away an hour or two but which were not objects of serious study and meditation. True knowledge, certain knowledge, was to be found in the realm of clear and distinct ideas and in the principles and rules deduced in orderly fashion from them. Mathematics and the physical sciences were the epitome of this kind of knowledge. Mathematical knowledge was the norm, the paradigm of all knowledge, and measured against this norm historical knowledge was anything but a true science. As Descartes contemptuously remarked, the continuous efforts of historians to reconstruct the last years of the Roman Republic could give us at best no better information than Cicero's servant girl might have possessed. In such a climate is it any wonder that the fate of Vico's "New Science" was obscurity? The appearance of another "new science" slightly earlier, the science of psychology modeled on the natural sciences, was already a sign of the impoverished historical imagination. In this regard Vico's "failure" is only the other side of the coin of modern psychology's "success."

Of all the many insights in Vico's creative work, the one which matters here is the emphasis which he placed on the method of historical studies. That method can be called *fantasia*,[42] by which is meant a capacity for imaginative insight, an ability to reconstruct imaginatively other worlds and times. Without this capacity for an imaginal understanding,

Vico felt that mere knowledge of empirical facts was of no avail. Indeed, this latter kind of knowledge characterized for Vico the physical sciences of nature, and while such knowledge afforded an understanding of nature, it was an approach insufficient for historical studies. One could, for example, study a tree and gain thereby a knowledge of what a tree looks like and how it is affected by external conditions. But one could never penetrate in this study to what it is like to *be* a tree in the way in which one could do this with other people. Historical studies, then, were for Vico more than matters of empirical fact. They involved matters concerned with the imaginative recovery of the facts.

Vico, however, was equally certain that such an imaginal understanding did not *create* the historian's object of study. In this regard Vico's most famous formula for the method of all human knowledge was the covertibility of the true and the made: *verum et factum convertuntur.*[43] The true (*verum*) and the made (*factum*) are convertible. The truth is what is made. It is true, of course, that people do make their history, in much the same way as they make their civil institutions and their language. But this making has an element of the unmade within it, or perhaps it is more accurate to say the *already made*, and to the extent that history contains elements merely found by us it does not offer the kind of truth (*verum*) which is gained from that which we freely create. What then does offer this kind of truth? Mathematics, and particularly algebra and geometry, were regarded by Vico in this fashion. In them the true and the made are virtually one. Vico's point, however, was that mathematics achieves this certainty precisely because it is a *fiction.* It is most certain precisely to the degree that it is distant from the world in which we live. The consequence of Vico's formula then was a double one. On the one hand history was less certain than mathematics, but on the other hand it was for all its uncertainty a study which bears upon the world in which we live. History, unlike mathematics, offers us a world which is not fictional.

These few remarks certainly indicate that for Vico the nature of historical studies was characterized neither by the *discovery* of empirical facts, which more or less characterizes the physical sciences of nature, nor by the *creation* of fictional realities, which more or less characterizes the mathematical sciences. Historical reality was neither fact nor fiction, and if Vico did not state the point precisely in this fashion, his effort to situate historical studies between fact and fiction cannot be missed in his work. His defense of the historical imagination as the method of historical studies is nothing less than a plea for another perspective on reality, a perspective which is needed when we confront the problem of understanding others. Such an understanding, as Vico brilliantly saw in the age of science, is never of the order of facts or of fictions. On the contrary, when I understand others it is because I can *imagine* them, because I am able to imagine their past, or the situation they are in, or their motives, because in short I can imagine what it is *like* to be the other. One's understanding of the other, then, was not for Vico an inductive conclusion drawn from a series of facts nor a deduction from firmly established a priori principles. Rather it was an *achievement* gained through what can be called the making of a *story*, the achievement which we call hi*story*.

Vico's concerns about *historical reality* expressed over 250 years ago are equally true of *psychological experience*. In both cases we are faced with a reality which is neither fact nor fiction, and with a mode of understanding which must be imaginal. The problem of history which Vico so passionately defined and defended in the early eighteenth century is still the problem of psychology today, the problem of securing this reality on its own grounds. One can only wonder about the fate of psychological life had it been founded on the vision of this obscure Neapolitan jurist rather than on a Cartesian vision.

Reflections on Unconsciousness as the Absence of Reflections

The recovery of self and other as realities of reflection has led to a reconsideration of the notions of behavior and experience, and to a revisioning of psychological life and understanding as an imaginal story. The third implication of the recovery concerns the psychoanalytic notion of the unconscious. A recovery of psychological life as a reality of reflection helps us to reformulate unconsciousness as an absence of reflections. The immediate gain is that unconsciousness is situated back in the world between us. It is recovered from its interiority as a subterranean layer of instinctual desires buried deeply within each of us. An index of time or of historicity is attached to unconsciousness. Unconscious life, like psychological life in general, changes. It appears in different ways in different historical and cultural settings.

Insofar as a relation of reflection characterizes my relation to an other, it is correct to say that one's *presence* to oneself is also an *absence*. The two moments of reflection, the moment of "being given back by" and the moment of "bending back upon," suggest a dialogue of absence and presence, and this presence to oneself through the other, this presence by virtue of an absence, indicates a kind of *natural unconsciousness* at the heart of the relationship between us. If "man is [a] mirror for man,"[44] then the mirror as this dialogue of absence and presence is an index of how one is already possessed by others and the world. It is an index of that unknown life which one already lives amidst things and with others.

But the figure reflected through the mirror of the other may be recovered. I can recover the figure in the story when I see the mirror reflection, just as I can ask the other to clarify for me the reflection which I glimpse of myself through the other's behavior. This natural unconsciousness, the presence to oneself by virtue of an absence, knows no resistance other than the forgetfulness of habitual and uncritical ways of living and thinking. The Freudian unconscious, however, is discovered through and characterized by resistance. Becoming conscious is a task, and any notion of recovery is marked by effort, work, and labor. Initially, therefore, it seems that the notion of psychological life as a reality of reflection cannot help in reformulating the notion of the unconscious. To be of help, psychological life as a reality of reflection must be able to address itself to the *repressed* unconscious.

In order to see how the repressed unconscious can be reunderstood from the perspective proposed here, consider this brief illustration.[45] One day as I gaze in a mirror I see no reflection. Literature and folklore inform us about the meaning of this strange event. To gaze in a mirror and see no reflection would mean that I am a vampire, that legendary creature who casts no reflections, a creature who is neither living nor dead, a creature who has no place in the world. Freud's neurotics, I would seriously suggest, are very much like this vampire.[46] They too find no reflection of this or that experience in the mirror of others and/or the world. Whether it is the experience of one's sexuality or aggression or whatever, there is no reflection. The first moment of reflection, this moment of finding oneself through the other, disappears. The repressed unconscious is the absence of this first moment of reflection. Repression is not an intra-psychic event, a play of interior forces, but the absence of a relation of reflection between me and you, the absence of a relation of reflection between a subject and the world.

As a failure of the first moment of reflection, repression character-izes a style of living in which a subject faces a world which offers no mirrors for this or that particular experience of human life. To illustrate this point consider a moment in the history of psychoanalysis itself. It is September 1897, and Freud and the beginning science of psychoanalysis are thrown into a crisis because the stories of sexual seduction of the child by the parent are not *factual* events. It is a decisive moment because when Freud reasons that psychology is not a discipline of real events but of fictional ones—the child has not been seduced by the parent; on the contrary, the child has *wished* to be the seducer—, he also transforms psychoanalysis from a science which finds psychological life in time and in the world to a science which now discovers psychological experience in natural and universal conditions which are older than time and prior to any world. The positive move which is made from psychology as a science of factual events in an empirical world is offset by the negative move which is made away from the world altogether toward psychology as a discipline of universal fictions. One month later, in October 1897, he introduces the name of this fiction in a letter to Wilhelm Fliess. Oe-dipus appears, and with him Freud encloses the wish within a universal drama of incest and taboos. The child's wish, or actually the patient's imagination of the wishful child, is not an index of relations with others. On the contrary it has become a symbol of everyone's internal dilemma.

Leaving aside here the question of the accuracy of Freud's interpre-tation of Sophocles' play, my concern is with *why* Freud reads it as he

does. Part of the answer is to be found in the Cartesian ground of
Freud's thinking, a ground which already predisposes him toward a view
of psychological life as an individual and interior rather than relational
phenomenon, and toward a notion of reality defined primarily in empirical terms. Hence, *either the parent actually* seduced the child, *or the
child wished* to seduce the parent, and between these two alternatives
there is nothing to choose. One *or* the other is guilty, and either something really happened or was only imagined to happen—if not the factual deed of the parent, then the fictional wish within the child. Freud
hears his patients' stories with a Cartesian ear, and he reads Oedipus with
a Cartesian eye. One might even say that Freud is a Descartes of the
depths. Within this context it is not possible for him to hear his patients'
stories as descriptions of the parent-child relations of his time. He cannot hear their tales as descriptions of how relationships between people
in that age concealed more than they revealed the sexual dimension of
human life. Or perhaps it is better to say that with his Cartesian ear he
could not hear these stories as descriptions of how those relations *reflected* a false innocence masking human desire. Freud did not discover a
universal unconsciousness of aggression and desire. On the contrary he
recovered the unconscious side of Cartesian consciousness. His work bears
witness to the way the life of passion finds no reflection in the Cartesian
dream of reason. Freud recovered the blind spot of the Enlightenment
vision.

The stories of sexual trauma which Freud's patients tell him do not
express real, actual events, as Freud discovered, but neither do they express a forbidden, repressed, instinctual wish as Freud imagined. Rather
they describe a way of being in the world with others which finds no
reflections in that world. They reveal a world in which the relations
between individuals, as well as with the things of that world—the styles
of dress, of furniture, of architecture for example[47]—, cover over more
than they reveal the living human body. These stories reveal an age which
in offering no mirrors for the reflection of an authentic sexuality reflect
in its place a way of living one's sexuality, and one's passions, as only a
hidden and forbidden wish of a helpless child.

Unconsciousness in the Freudian sense of the repressed can be viewed, therefore, as a failure in this first moment of reflection. But what is absent for reflection in the first moment is also unavailable for reflection in the second moment. An experience which is not given back by the world is not available for bending back upon. An experience which finds no reflection in the world and through others slips away from the world and is buried beneath it. This is where Freud's work begins, with the *maintenance* of repression, and herein lies the vision of a *vertical* depth in psychoanalytic psychology. It is also where the strength of psychoanalysis lies. His patients' stories do reveal that a passion which finds no place in the world does reappear either as a fantasy above life or as a symptom from below. Freud's Cartesian heritage, however, leads him to extend this vision of the maintenance of repression back toward its *origins*, and consequently these origins are destined to be found *within* the individual rather than between the individual and others. Any notion of a *lateral depth*, of the depth of reflection, is lost, and consequently what is *below* life takes on a priority over what is within life and in the world.

Ironically, however, the *practice* of psychoanalysis betrays the *theory* of repression. Indeed the practice strongly supports the notion that the origins and maintenance of repression are respectively the failure of the first and second moments of reflection. Freud recommends, for example, that the analyst be like a perfect reflecting mirror to the patient. Does not this recommendation suggest that the task of the analyst is to bring to reflection in its first moment what has slipped away so that the second moment of reflection can occur? Indeed, does not the recommendation acknowledge that what is recovered for reflection in the mirror of analysis becomes available for reflection as *expression?*

Psychoanalysis was originally called "the talking cure," and this notion of the two moments of reflection allows us to bring psychoanalytic theory more in line with its practice, and to see repression as the other side of expression. Repression, the failure of expression, is overcome by expression. As the failure of expression, repression originates in the absence of reflection in its first moment. It is the consequence of a kind of dialogue in which words and gestures hide more than reveal what they mean and mean only what they hide. And as the failure of expression, repression is maintained in the second moment in a conspiracy of silence, in a conspiracy of at least two in which there are no words and no gestures to say what is hidden.

What is constituted in partnership, however, is also overcome in partnership, albeit of a different style, the style of analytic conversation. The analyst now expresses what is hidden. The analyst's interpretations are addressed to what has slipped away. The process of repression is reversed, and through this second moment of reflection, through the conversation, the first moment of reflection begins to emerge. The analyst's words become the outline of the figure who has disappeared, and through those words, and through the analyst's behavior, the patient's experience of that figure begins to find its reflection.

I have suggested in these remarks how the notion of reflection revisions the Freudian unconscious. In conclusion I would add this final point. Insofar as psychological life is essentially a reality of reflection and unconsciousness is precisely the absence of reflection, unconsciousness can be nothing less than an index of the absence of the psychological. It is *not* the terrain of what is most genuinely psychological. Stated in another way, the unconscious is an *un-image-able* (unimaginable) existence. It is a way of living this or that experience not as a reflection but as a literal fact or as a fantastic idea.

Reflection and Interiority

The discussion of psychological life as a reality of reflection in the previous chapter and in this one attempts to reverse the interiorization of psychological life which is so characteristic of modern psychology as a science. Psychological experience is visible through the world of things and through the behavior of others. The self is a reality of reflection.

The reversal of this notion of *interiorization* may seem to suggest, however, the dismissal of the notion of *interiority*. But such is not the case. Interiority is not the equivalent of interiorization, and the recovery of self as a reality of reflection changes our understanding of interiority without discounting it. It moves our understanding of self from a substantive agent of action occupying an inside space on this side of the world toward self as a temporal reality and as a style of relation with others and the world.

"I am *thinking* of the Cartesian *cogito*, *wanting* to finish this work, *feeling* the coolness of the paper under my hand, and *perceiving* the trees of the boulevard through the window."[48] So writes Merleau-Ponty, and it is clear from these remarks that the moment of *thinking*, that moment of reflection in which, as a subject, one bends back upon one-self, is also a moment of *perceiving* the world, that moment of reflection in which through one's body one is in relation to the world and to a task at hand. These two moments of reflection are never actually separable from one another. Every act of reflection in the sense of bending back upon oneself presumes an already given relation of reflection or mirror-ing between a subject and the world. Consider, for example, the I who you are at this very moment! Imagine it! Is it given apart from a moment of reflection which is a mirroring? Does one ever catch a glimpse of the I who one is apart from a network of relationships with the world and others? At this very moment when I am recalling the I who I am, the clock is ticking in the next room, the dog is barking outside, my child is stirring in a fitful sleep, and the meeting with a friend earlier in the day is remembered. These "items" are not distractions, non-meaningful distur-bances which are unrelated to my effort to recover the I who I am. On the contrary they are like the noise of the typewriter and the smell of cooking which have everything to do with the man who thinks of his love and reads Spinoza.[49]

Two moments of reflection characterize the meaning of self, and in this regard *interiority* refers to a *temporal* moment and not to a region of retreat away from the world. Interiority is a moment of reflection and not a space inside the subject. Interiority is not a withdrawal from the world, but a way of being with the world. The I is caught up in a circuit of reflections and the self who one is, one's sense of identity, is the history of both of these moments of reflection. In the moment of interiority one encounters a self which does not pre-exist time but which is time, as an old face is the history of a person's relations with the world. In the moment of interiority one encounters a self which is one's history.

The two moments of reflection are also two styles of reflection. Each moment is *figured* in a different way. We all immediately recognize, for example, the difference between a person of action and a person of thought, the doer and the thinker. They are two different styles, two different figures. This difference, however, is not one between the outside and the inside. The latter figure, the thinker, is not one who dwells inside and away from the world but one who lives with others in the world in a different fashion. Conversely, the doer is not an empty husk or shell devoid of interiority. We may regard each of these figures in this fashion, but such thoughts express a cultural valuation which transforms a figure or a type into a stereotype. Such musings are not a proto-philosophy of the inside and the outside. These different styles of existence, these two different ways of conducting oneself with others in the world, do not invite a philosophy of the "inner man." Indeed, in the language of Merleau-Ponty, "Truth does not 'inhabit' only 'the inner man,' or more accurately, there is no inner man, man is in the world, and only in the world does he know himself." And, he adds, "When I return to myself from an excursion into the realm of dogmatic common sense or of science, I find, not a source of intrinsic truth, but a subject *destined* to be in the world."[50] A recovery of psychological life as a reality of reflection bears witness to this destiny. One can return to oneself because one lives in the world with others.

Conclusion

An infant before the mirror, an anxious little girl, Sartre's vision of hell and Harvey's vision of the heart, the experimental subjects of Schachter and Singer, and even Freud's neurotic patients all illustrate a relation of reflection between self and other. They all illustrate how the behavior of the other reflects one's experience and how one's experience makes the other's behavior observable, that is, imaginally understandable, not as a fact or a fiction but as a story. But the other whose behavior reflects my experience is embodied, just as I who reflect the other's experience am embodied. We must recover, therefore, how the human body is a reality of reflection. We must recover how the human body is a psychological body. We must recover how, like things, the matter of the body matters in another way.

IV

REFLECTIONS OF THE PSYCHOLOGICAL WORLD: BODY

Introduction

In the previous chapter we saw how one's experience is the way in which the other's behavior is brought from darkness into visibility. Self and other were recovered as realities of reflection, and insofar as self and other, I and you, are ways of experiencing-behaving the world, experience and behavior were also recovered in this fashion. You and I, however, are each embodied. Experience is embodied and behavior is an embodied action. The previous chapter concluded, therefore, with a recognition of the necessity to recover the body psychologically, as a reality of reflection. This is the task of the present chapter.

The immediate question, however, is, how one begins this work of recovery. If we stay within the context of what has already been presented about psychological life, the suggestion of an answer is already available. The point which matters here is the appearance of psychological life as story.

Recall, for example, the story of the wine bottle in Chapter 2. Two accounts of the event were offered there. One account was given in terms of the science of psychology. It was primarily logical, conceptual, and useful within a scheme of factual knowledge. It was an account which appealed to mind. The other account, which was given in terms of the loneliness and disappointment of an evening reflected through an unopened bottle of wine, was not nearly as logical. It worked in a differ-

ent way. It was a moving account in the sense that it could arrest the
forward momentum of a listener's life in order to move her or him into
another place, a remembered or imagined place of loneliness and disappointment. It was, in this sense, disruptive, moving the listener out of the
on-going habitual routine of life to this other place. But to be moved in
this way, to be moved in a disruptive fashion, to be disturbed out of the
ordinary course of one's life, is a descriptive way of speaking about emotions. The etymology of the word *emotion* tells us as much. It means to
move out or to move away.[1] When we are moved by something we are
stirred emotionally, and when we are emotional about something we are
moved. We may say, then, that this second account was primarily emotional in character and when we recognize that daily life senses an inti-
mate connection between emotions and the human heart, we can add
that this second account appealed to the human heart.[2]

I am not defending here either a dichotomy of mind and heart or
one of logic and emotions. Nor do I intend to suggest that the pursuit
and/or appeal of science is unemotional. The latter view is a stereotype
without much regard for the truth. I am only suggesting that there is an
important and recognizable difference between mind and heart as attitudes which portray ways of experiencing the world. To put this point
another way, there is a recognizable difference between an understanding
which proceeds from mind and the understanding of the human heart. I
can, for example, understand your grief at the loss of your friend when I
know the circumstances surrounding this loss. But certainly my understanding of your grief is changed when it moves my heart. At that
moment I understand you and you yourself feel understood by me. Pascal already spoke of this difference when he wrote, "Le coeur a ses raisons,
que la raison ne connait point" (The heart has its reasons, which reason
does not know).[3]

The appearance of psychological life as a story suggests therefore
that the recovery of the psychological body can begin with the human
heart. Indeed it may even be the case that the human heart is preeminently the embodiment of psychological life. To be psychological it is
perhaps necessary to see life and to live it through the heart. Moreover,
this incarnation of psychological life in a *specific* way is not as unwar-

ranted as it may seem. Scientific psychology, for example, finds psychological life in the brain, and depth psychology has a distinct proclivity towards the mucous membranous regions of the body. These two traditions understand, therefore, that psychological life is incarnated and that this incarnation has an index of specificity about it. My suggestion accords with these two notions. Nevertheless it also differs from them. Unlike the tradition of scientific psychology, this incarnation of psychological life is not meant in a literal way. Psychological life is not *in* the heart as opposed to the brain. On the contrary it is lived *through* the heart. To say it another way, the heart is neither the condition nor the cause of psychological life, but a reflection of it. It is a reality of reflection, as this chapter intends to show. As such this incarnation also differs from the tradition of depth psychology which *tends* to reduce the incarnation of psychological life to a symbolic meaning which is added to the order of material reality. In other words, the body remains only a material reality caught up in the order of forces to which there is added the order of meanings.[4] In contrast to this view, the suggestion offered here already begins with the heart as a material reality which nevertheless also matters in another way, as a reality of reflection.

The task of recovering the psychological body can be illustrated, therefore, with the heart, and through this task we may gain anew an opportunity to see the distinctiveness of psychological life. As a matter of the human heart we may be able to appreciate how psychological life radically differs from the inquisitive eye of science and the questioning mind of philosophy. Through this difference we may be able to appreciate again that psychological life has a distinct style of embodiment, a unique posture, attitude, or point of view.

The Everyday Heart as a Psychological Reality

To begin the recovery of the human heart as a psychological reality it is necessary initially to locate this heart. The first question, therefore, must be: where is the psychological heart?

Initially we are tempted to say in reply to this question that the heart has a fixed location in the chest. Everyday language, however, defeats this reply and bears witness to the wandering character of the human heart. My heart, for example, may rise up in my throat or sink to my stomach. My heart can be in my mouth or I can wear it on my sleeve. This heart about which language speaks appears, therefore, to be a vagrant heart, a heart which is not fixed in a literal way.

But surely these ways of speaking are not to be taken seriously. They are after all only figures of speech. They are metaphors which do not really matter. The truth of the heart is that it lies in the chest and that its movement is restricted to the rhythmic motion of systole and diastole. This is the empirical truth which can be easily demonstrated. And yet what is obviously empirically true in this fashion does not negate this other movement of the heart. This other movement is what we live, and language bears witness to this vital reality. The heart which is in my mouth is a metaphor. But it is a metaphor which matters as attested to by the conduct of my life.

Consider an example of how the heart matters in this way. I have a friend. He is downcast, listless, without appetite or ambition. He weeps often and is lately slow to speak. When I ask him to tell me what troubles him he can say only that he has a *broken heart.* Certainly from the point of view of empirical reality this phrase is just as strange as the heart which is worn on one's sleeve. And yet I have no difficulty in understanding him. This phrase, a broken heart, makes immediate sense to me and through it I am able to make sense of his condition. He has suffered a loss. A relationship which mattered to him has been broken. It is a metaphorical way of speaking which matters, as my conduct with him reveals. I console him. I listen to his grief. I do not consult a cardiologist, nor do I dismiss his reply as only a metaphor and implore him to tell me the truth.

In an earlier age there was a greater receptivity to a bodily organ which wanders. The womb wandered, and this wandering womb was the classical understanding of hysteria. Few of us would believe that today even after Freud, who recovered this ancient notion by showing us that hysteria is a sexuality in search of its place in the world. Few of us would believe it because we do not cultivate an appreciation of how this metaphorical speaking of the body imagines a world. The broken heart is a world of experience and the human heart, as we already can anticipate, inhabits many worlds. We can cultivate this notion with some additional examples which are offered by the etymology of the word *heart*. In addition a return to etymology allows us to hear the originary ways in which the heart speaks in human life.

Heart springs from the Indo-European root *kerd* which in Latin becomes *cord* and in English appears in such familiar words as *cordial, concord, discord, record,* and *courage*. In addition the word *heart* also echoes in our word *belief* through the Latin term *credere* which is connected to another Indo-European root for heart, *kerddhe*.[5] Already, therefore, we hear how the experiences of harmony and disharmony, cordiality and courtesy, memory, courage, and belief are originally matters of the human heart. Indeed one needs only to say it to realize that we have always known that these experiences concern the heart. We have always known it but in a lived, forgetful way. We have always known, for example, that discord and strife between us can break our hearts, and that the harmony of friendship between us can set them again at rest. In much the same way we have also always realized that memory is essentially a matter of the heart and not the mind or the brain.[6] It is true, of course, that we can remember information, that we retain the past and can recall it. But it is also true that such remembering is not the memory of the heart, the remembering which is most essentially human. To see this difference we need only recognize that we share with animals this ability to retain the past and to recall it, while the memory of the heart is specifically human. My cat, for example, remembers the time when I arrive home in the evening and he is there to greet me. But my cat does not celebrate his birthday nor the day he first arrived in my house. Among all the creatures of this earth only humans remember with celebration. Only we remember in this heartfelt way those moments like marriage, birth, and death which touch the human heart. We are the only ones whose memories are and can be anniversaries.

The human heart is a rich world of experience and its etymology tells us that manners too are a matter of the human heart. The cordial, courteous person is often seen as one who has a warm and a big heart: the kind of person who for example, will greet a stranger at the door in such a manner that, if ushered across the threshold, the stranger will be transformed into a guest. This may be done with a word and/or a gesture, but however it may be done, each of us who has crossed so many thresholds will recognize those words and gestures spoken and performed with heart. How recognizably different is the manner of such greetings from that style which offers no courtesy at the threshold. If someone knocks at my door and I shout from the distance of another room, "Come in, it is open," I am not revealing my trust in humanity as much as I am revealing my indifference. Anyone and everyone can cross my threshold, and your visit is of no special importance to me. Am I not saying in this way that you do not matter to me? Is not my lack of manners which is revealed in this instance by indifference a clear statement that you, even as only a representative of my fellow humans, do not have a place at the heart of my life? And, perhaps even more seriously, is it not possible that this thoughtless indifference to my manners is indicative of the loss of heart? I am suggesting here that the decline of manners may be coincidental with a loss of heart. Let me illustrate this suggestion with a story.

Before going to work one morning I stopped to have a cup of coffee in a small restaurant and to read a brief article. The article was by Hannah Arendt, a summary of her book *Thinking*.[7] I remember that I was struck by her thought, particularly by her observations about evil. She had written *Eichmann in Jerusalem*, and what had impressed her about this man was the great disparity between the monstrosity of the crimes and the doer of those deeds. This man, Eichmann, was not maliciously cunning. Nor was he stupidly ignorant. On the contrary, he was simply thoughtless and it was this figure of thoughtlessness who haunted the beginning of her article.

I began then to think about thoughtlessness, and under the influence of Arendt's work I saw how thoughtlessness is the condition of modern humanity. We are an educated society. We are knowledgeable about many things and are taught many facts and taught how to think. But we are thoughtless and particularly thoughtless about what we have been taught and told.

It was time to leave. As I approached the door, an old man and his wife were about to enter the restaurant. He reached the door before I did, and he opened it for his wife. I stepped aside to let her enter, and as she passed me she smiled and said, "Thank you." I nodded my head in acknowledgment, and then an extraordinary thing happened. I had intended to let the old man enter after his wife and before I exited, but the old man waited at the door and held it open for me. He smiled, and with a broad, sweeping gesture of his arm he ushered me through the door.

An ordinary event which was however extraordinary because this gesture of courtesy was performed so thoughtfully. Only two words had been spoken and the entire incident lasted less than ten seconds, but in that time and space a world of manners, style, and grace had briefly appeared. This wave of an arm by an old man waiting at an open door was not an empty, formal ritual. Enacted with an eloquence and a carefulness which seemed for a moment to have come from an older world, his gesture gave visible expression to what I had been thinking about before my exit. That gesture threw the world of today into relief, and figured against that gesture the present world seemed poorer in many ways. Such thoughtful gestures of courtesy seemed so absent today, or very rare, and I thought for a moment that perhaps this is why our world is in danger today. It is not for want of the great things. It is for want of such simple gestures performed with heart.

The world today may not be in danger for want of these simple things. Perhaps this story claims too much. But if we take this story as illustrative of a style of manner which springs from the heart, it is not difficult to say that such things do seem to be in decline. If we can accept the old man's gesture with his arm, which actually exposes the heart, as an action which embodies the human heart, then we do seem to be witnesses today to an eclipse of such gestures performed with style and grace. And if this eclipse is true, is it any wonder that today hearts are failing in such great number? It is not simply what we eat or what we do or what we say to each other, but also the *manner* in which we eat and work and relate to each other which matters to the heart. Norbert Elias has shown in fine detail the change in our manner of doing these things between the fifteenth and nineteenth centuries. Numerous forms of conduct like the eating of meat or the blowing of one's nose are considered in his extensive work. For our purposes, however, what is important is the decline of that style of manners called courtesy which he notes. He writes that "In the course of the seventeenth century . . . the concept *courtoisie* (courtesy) gradually goes out of fashion in France."[8] Courtesy or cordiality declines in the same age when the human heart is in transition. Later in this chapter we will see this transition in detail. Here I want to note only that in part this transition is from a full heart to an empty one. There is an emptying of the heart, a loss of heart, in the seventeenth century which is thematic of English medicine and English letters. Should we be surprised? In seventeenth-century France a form of manners whose origins connect it to the heart is in decline. In seventeenth-century England the human heart is being emptied of its blood and its beliefs. Are not these two historical changes related? Do they not support our proposal that a decline of manners (specifically cordiality, courtesy) coincides with a loss of heart?

We have seen in these remarks some examples of how the human heart is a reality of reflection. The worlds of harmony, discord, and manners, for example, are reflections of the human heart. They are matters which are at the heart of daily life and which concern the everyday heart of human life. But the everyday heart of life, that heart which we live, is not the heart which we know, the heart of science, and we have seen that it is a struggle to accept the reality of this living heart which is reflected through so many worlds of experience. To speak of fickle hearts and constant hearts, light hearts and heavy ones, warm hearts and hearts that are so cold that they have turned to stone is to be deceived by language. A soft heart is a medical condition and a heartless individual a medical impossibility. Measured against the scientific heart we simply cannot accept these hearts as anything but metaphors. At best they are figures of speech, poetic illusions, and we are not prepared to accept them as ways of *figuring* the rich depths of human experience, as ways of narrating the many *stories* of human life. Try as we may, then, we are not convinced that these hearts are real. The real heart is the one which pumps in my chest. The pumping heart which is at the heart of science is the one in which we believe.

If we are to change this vision, then we must do more than show how this everyday heart in its metaphorical speaking matters in the conduct of our lives. We must do more than recover the everyday heart as a reality of reflection. Specifically we must recover the scientific heart in the same way. We must show, in other words, how the pumping heart is also the reflection of a world, how it too is a psychological reality. If we can do this, then we will have demonstrated that the everyday heart, this heart which as a reality of reflection is psychological, matters as much as the scientific heart. We will have shown the *reality* of the psychological heart by showing the *psychological* character of the empirical heart. A dualism between the objective, empirical, real heart of science and the subjective, psychological, unreal heart of everyday life will have been replaced by a difference. The everyday heart and the scientific heart will be seen as reflections of different worlds, as different appearances of human psychological life.

To achieve this intention I will begin with a historical example which concerns the courage of the human heart. We have already seen that courage is a matter of the human heart. The origins of the word *heart* have suggested this connection. At the beginnings of modernity, however, courage becomes also a matter of the scientific heart. In the same example, then, we will find two experiences of courage, two different worlds of the courageous human heart.

Of Courage and the Human Heart

In 1628 the English physician William Harvey published *An Anatomical Disquisition on the Motion of the Heart and Blood in Animals.* Near the end of that work Harvey considers some conditions which impede the flow of blood in the body. A tightly bandaged arm, for example, slows the blood's motion, and its movement is even further impeded if conditions like alarm or fainting intervene. Explaining that the blood flows slowly from a puncture under any of these conditions, Harvey concludes that a contrary state of affairs occurs when one rids oneself of one's fear and recovers one's courage. In that moment of courage "... the pulsific power is increased, [and] the arteries begin again to beat with greater force . . ."[9]

This is a remarkable statement which offers a vision of courage in terms of the pumping heart. It is remarkable because of its contrast with another vision of courage which appears earlier in the work.

The avowed purpose of Harvey's text is to demonstrate that the singular function of the heart is to pump blood continuously in one direction throughout the body. This is a bold intention because for centuries most men have believed with Galen that the course of the blood in the body is like the ebb and flow of the tides. The blood surges back and forth in the veins. It does not circulate in a single direction. Harvey's vision is, therefore, a daring one, and in espousing it he stands against this tradition. He sees what others before him have not seen, and thus we are not surprised to find in the beginning of his work a confession of fear regarding its publication: "And as this book alone declares the blood to course and revolve by a new route, very different from the ancient and beaten pathway trodden for so many ages, and illustrated by such a host of learned and distinguished men, I was greatly afraid lest I might be charged with presumption . . ."[10] His fear in fact has been so great that for more than nine years he has withheld his views. But during this time he has lectured at the Royal College of Physicians in London, and now in 1628 their requests, and even their entreaties, have persuaded him to publish his position. Harvey has taken a stand against tradition, and his colleagues have stood by him. The book which we read today, the book about which we are now speaking, is the work of a man who has overcome his fear. It is a courageous work, and his confession is another statement about the courage of the human heart.

This experience of courage clearly involves others and even requires them. In taking a stand against tradition, Harvey is supported by others. He does not stand completely alone. The courageous heart which speaks here is a social heart, a heart which, as Harvey himself says, is surrounded by "faithful witnesses," a heart which others "stand by and bear me out with your testimony."[11] The courage of this heart is nourished by faith and by belief. It pulses with the continuing belief and support of a community. This courageous heart expands through the witnessing gaze of colleagues. It is a heart whose life blood circulates among friends. This courage of which Harvey speaks is not found inside the body but through this world of supporting colleagues, and the blood of this courageous heart does not flow through the veins or the arteries of the anatomical body but through the words which compose the text. This courageous heart reveals itself through the work and not in the body.

Harvey's text lies at the foundation of modern thought about the body. It offers the modern vision of the heart, the heart as a pump. But this same work also offers a different vision of the heart, the heart as it is courageously lived through the world. The development of modern science, medicine, psychology, and philosophy has all but erased this difference which throbs at the origins of the modern heart. This difference has been eclipsed by a separation of these hearts or by a reduction of one to the other. In the separation the pumping heart has been regarded as real, factual, empirical, and/or literal, while the courageous heart has been ignored as unreal, fictional, psychological, and/or metaphorical. In the reduction the courageous heart, this vital reality of human life, has simply become a matter of a pumping organ and arterial pressure.[12] The irony, of course, is that Harvey's work inaugurates these two positions. The very same work which reveals this difference is also the one which will allow its concealment. In the text Harvey's heart roars out with the courage of a lion. The work itself, however, will help to undo this leonine vision. The heart which acts with a unique boldness and daring in this work will be undone by a heart whose action is mechanical, repetitive, and the same for everyone. Today when we so naturally take our psychological vision of humanity from the context provided by the sciences of physics and physiology, can we continue to forget with impunity the initial daring and courage of that vision? Can we continue to forget the courageous heart with which the text is written in favor of the pumping heart whose courage is written about in the text? It is obvious that we cannot forget, because neither the separation nor the reduction which spring from this forgetfulness does justice to either heart. The courageous heart is no more unreal (in the sense here of something which does not matter) nor reducible to a pumping organ than the pumping heart is only and exclusively real (in the sense of something which matters because it is material). A heart which was really and only a pump could no more have written this work than a courageous heart which failed to pump blood could have written it.

Two visions of the courageous heart are present in Harvey's work and each one is the reflection of a different world. One of the visions is the reflection of the world of the interior body, a world of tightly bandaged arms, of measurements and calculations. The other is the reflection of a social world, of a community of colleagues which supports a daring vision. This difference is not yet the dichotomy which it will later become. It is not yet a dualism between the empirically real and the psychologically unreal. It cannot be because the presence of the vision of the courageous heart offsets any tendency to literalize the vision of the pumping heart. But if we are to capitalize on this opportunity to recover the pumping heart as the reflection of a world, we must show in more detail the world which actually does reflect this heart.

The Scientific Heart as a Psychological Reality

INTRODUCTION

> First of all, the auricle contracts, and in the course of its contraction throws the blood . . . into the ventricle, which being filled, the heart raises itself straightaway, makes all its fibres tense, contracts the ventricles, and performs a beat, by which beat it immediately sends the blood supplied to it by the auricle into the arteries; the right ventricle sending its charge into the lungs by the vessel which is called vena arteriosa . . .; the left ventricle sending its charge into the aorta, and through this by the arteries to the body at large.
>
> These two *motions*, one of the ventricles, another of the auricles, take place consecutively, but in such a manner that there is a kind of harmony or rhythm preserved between them . . . *Nor is this for any other reason than it is in a piece of machinery.*[13]

With these words written in 1628, the movements of the human heart are understood to be like the motions of a machine. With these words, written by a man who was destined to become in 1630 "Physician in Ordinary" to Charles I, the king to whom this book is dedicated with ill-fated irony, the heart begins to pump the blood in an endless, repetitive, circular course throughout the body. In Harvey's hands, a phrase which must be understood literally, as well as figuratively, the human heart begins to change. Why does this change occur in the early years of the seventeenth century? More specifically, why does it occur on April 17, 1616, some twelve years before the publication of the text, when Harvey in his role of Lumleian lecturer at the Royal College of Physicians first makes public his new theory of the heart's motion?

Already some one hundred years before Harvey, the valves of the veins had been seen and described by the master anatomist of Paris, Sylvius of Louvilly, and in 1574 they were seen again by Harvey's teacher Fabricius, who published his views in 1603 in a small book entitled *De Vanaruum Ostiolis*. But neither of these men saw through the structure of the arrangement of these venous valves that the venous blood can flow only toward the heart, that it cannot back up, and that the arterial blood can stream only away from the heart. Neither of them could see through the disposition of these valves the action of a pumping heart. The work of Sylvius of Louvilly fell into oblivion, and as late as 1603 Fabricius still saw through these venous valves the image of Galen's heart. The venous blood still flowed for him in an outward direction from the liver, and the heart, far from a machine whose sole function is to propel the blood through the body, is still "*a living organ*, the center of animal heat, . . . the agent which brings about the transformation of substances: air into the vital spirits, venous blood into arterial blood."[14] But by 1616, just thirteen years after the publication of Fabricius, Harvey is seeing this same heart differently. He sees through those very same venous valves a heart whose one action is "the transmission of the blood and its distribution, by means of the arteries, to the very extremities of the body."[15] For Harvey the important thing about the blood's movement is not that "it might be generated anew but that it is displaced."[16] Generation belongs to the older Galenic tradition. The blood's movement in space is a new concern which places the Harveian heart in the same tradition as the Copernican earth and the falling bodies of Galileo. By 1616, therefore, the heart which moved as recently as 1603 as a living organism now has the motion of a pump. What could not be seen in 1603 is seen in 1616.

In that brief period human existence and the world has changed. How, again, are we to understand this change?

An answer may be found in an event which occurs in 1610. In that year Galileo turns his telescope toward the moon and *confirms* the Copernican vision. But this confirmation is more than a piece of empirical evidence. It is also and more importantly psychological confirmation. With his telescope Galileo *sees* the new earth of Copernicus *through* the moon. It is the decayed surface of the moon which *reflects* the Copernican earth. Through the telescopic observation of the moon the Copernican earth becomes *a psychological reality.* As a *reflection* this new earth becomes an "image-able" reality, an imaginable reality, a believable reality. One can now not only see this new earth with one's eyes, one can also believe in it with one's heart. One can now believably imagine a moving earth.

The Copernican earth appears in 1543, the same year that the living human body becomes defined from the side of the corpse. That corpse which lies on Vesalius' dissecting table inhabits the Copernican earth. The moving earth and the human corpse belong together. One is the reflection of the other. Hence Galileo's telescope also makes the corpse a believable reality, a new psychological reality. And Harvey's mechanical heart animates that corpse. The body which becomes a corpse in the sixteenth century (1543) is resurrected in the seventeenth century (1610-1628). A new kind of life begins to "dwell" on the *moving* earth.

Before 1610, in 1603, the heart cannot move like a pump because it is not yet a psychological reality. The moving earth is not yet a new world. After 1610, in 1616, the heart must move like a pump to keep pace with a moving earth. Moreover, lest this psychological relation of reflection between these events seems too improbable, consider one other curious feature of the early years of the seventeenth century. Hugh Kearney in his book, *Science and Change, 1500-1700*, tells us that logarithms were invented between 1610 and 1620. This is correct but incomplete, because as van den Berg points out it was Michael Stifel who first developed this mathematics of faster motion in his *Arithmetica Integra* in 1544. We should notice the date which is one year after the Copernicus-Vesalius connection. Stifel, however, "shut his eyes" to his discovery because according to van den Berg the world of Stifel did not yet reflect this reality. "This means," van den Berg writes, "that the things around Stifel must still have been characterized by such a slowness that the faster calculus method, the faster bridging of distances, in short the speed of movement, did not fit those things."[17] This is exactly the point made above. Before 1610, in 1544, the moving earth was not yet a world. Before 1610, in 1544, the moving earth was not yet psychologically real. But between 1610 and 1620 the world has changed, allowing this new mathematics to appear. Logarithms belong as much to the pumping heart and the moving earth as does the human corpse.

What cannot happen in 1603 happens in 1616 because in that interval human existence changes. In that interval the earlier stirrings of modern science in the previous two centuries become a world. A resurrected corpse animated by a mechanical heart and occupying a moving earth becomes psychologically real. An answer to the question of why the pumping heart appears in the seventeenth century (1610-1628) can now be given: it appears because at that time the pumping heart becomes a psychological reality reflected through a new earth and a new body.

Like the courageous heart, the pumping heart is the reflection of a world. Like the courageous heart, it too is a psychological reality. Harvey's work, however, is not understood in this fashion either by himself, his contemporaries, or his successors. On the contrary, the subsequent history of the pumping heart is the history of a medical, empirical science. It is a successful history and these remarks are not addressed to its validity or its results. Nevertheless it is a history which *covers over* the very psychological character of this heart and the human life which springs from this heart, and modern scientific psychology is nourished in the soil of this history. Moving this heart, and the body which belongs to this heart, from the realm of science, where it is properly speaking an empirical fact, to the realm of psychology, where it is properly speaking a metaphor, modern scientific psychology forgets this transfer and hence misses the metaphor. The factual meaning of the pumping heart in the realm of science is simply carried over to the psychological domain without an acknowledgment that a transfer of meaning has occurred. The pumping heart makes a *literal* appearance in psychology, and the physiological body of which this heart is a part becomes the support upon which the interiorization of psychological life in modern times is justified. *In* the physiological body the *interiorization* of modern psychological life, a theme which was demonstrated in the first chapter, finds a *literal* expression. The first example of this tendency already appears in Harvey's text in the suggestion that courage is an increase in pulsific power, and *in principle* this example is no different from the most recent and more sophisticated attempts to find memory, for example, *in* the electrochemical workings of the brain.[18] In over three hundred years the details have changed and methodological sophistication has increased, but the founding principle has remained the same. Today as yesterday, therefore, the science of psychology *obscures* psychological life. It obscures the metaphorical character of psychological life and how psychological life is visible as a world. To recover these features we must show how the pumping heart is not just a mechanical organ inside the body. We must recover this heart as a way of envisioning human life. We must deepen the world of the Harveian heart.

REFLECTIONS OF A DIVIDED HEART

The pumping heart which Harvey sees is a divided heart.[19] There is a "right heart" from which the blood flows into the lungs by way of the pulmonary artery, and a "left heart" which, receiving blood from the lungs, propels it throughout the body. The right heart receives venous blood, a blood which is impure, while the left heart contains arterial blood, a blood which has been purified by the lungs. But I speak somewhat loosely here, because there are not two bloods any more than there are two hearts, a right one and a left one. On the contrary, there is *one heart* which is *divided within itself*, and *one blood* which exists in two different states. Walter Pagel rightly claims that this *unitarian* idea about the blood is completely new with Harvey, and the point is that Harvey unifies the blood by dividing the heart.[20] The difference between what is pure and impure, between the arterial and venous blood, is erased by the divided heart. What was a matter of *differences* yields to a created *unity*, a unity which is created by a *division*.

To appreciate Harvey's achievement we need to realize that in the older Galenic tradition there were two bloods separated through their *differences.* The addition of vital spirits supplied by the lungs and heart transformed venous blood into arterial blood, and for Galen this process was a "continuous transformation of substances."[21] The Galenic body possessed so to speak a miraculous power of transubstantiation. Within this tradition moreover there were even *two hearts,* the liver being a kind of proto-heart in which venous blood was made. Harvey's vision changes all this, and in his hands and eyes the human heart divides. It divides in the early seventeenth century when the *differences* in blood and else-where have become so problematic they are to be made the same. It *divides* in the seventeenth century when a *unity* is created by making the differences invisible, by moving the differences *inside.* In the seventeenth century the differences between what is "pure" and "impure," "right" and "sinister," like that between Puritan and Catholic, became a matter of the divided heart. A body which in an earlier age possessed the miraculous power of transubstantiation, as symbolized for example in the Eucharistic body of Christ, becomes in the seventeenth century a divided body, as symbolized in the mechanical heart. If the Galenic body seems to echo an earlier, Medieval, Christian world, a world of miracles and the transformative powers of nature, then the Harveian body echoes the newer, modern world of the Reformation. The division which Luther inaugurates in 1517 fractures the heart of the Christian world. It divides the "Christian" heart. Harvey's vision of the divided heart is the corporeal reflection of that change. We might wonder, then, if modern medicine and modern psychology, based as they are in this divided heart, are the heritage of the Reformation. We may wonder if *modern* psychology is a "Protestant" enterprise, not however in the sense of any religious idea but rather in the sense of Protestant, and Christian, as reflections of a world. Recall that Melanchthon, friend of Luther, is credited by some with coining the word *psychology* in the sixteenth century.

Regardless of the merits of these remarks, it remains true that the human heart unmistakably divides in the seventeenth century. We must understand what this reality means in more specific detail. And we must understand how Harvey divides the human heart.

How Harvey divides the heart is no mystery. He tells us in the very first chapter of his work. Confessing how confused he was by the dizzying and rapid motion of the heart, Harvey tells us that his vision became clear when he looked at the *dying* heart. Through vivisection Harvey brings the animal heart close to death, and it is through death that he sees a new living heart. Looking at death he *turns away from* life, and turning away from life he sees a divided heart. We may say then that Harvey *sees* by *not seeing*. By not looking at the living heart he sees a divided heart. Harvey divides the heart in the seventeenth century when *he does not see* what others before him have seen. The divided heart is the consequence of a special kind of vision.

But what specifically does Harvey *not* see? Before Harvey, and with very few exceptions which made no impact, the septum which is between the right and left sides of the heart has tiny, obscure but nevertheless visible pores. Anatomists see it and even as late as 1648 Jean Riolan, Dean of the Paris Faculty of Medicine, opponent of Harvey and defender of a modified Galenist perspective, sees these holes in the heart. We are not surprised. Riolan looks with Galen's eyes, and he sees a different heart. Indeed he says against Harvey that the septum closes up in a *dead and dying body*, and in this respect Riolan *unknowingly* understood more of Harvey's *way of seeing* than he could have realized. We should not be too quick, moreover, to dismiss his view as an error. We should not be too quick to discount the idea that before the seventeenth century there were holes in the septum of the heart. He sees in a different way. He lives in a different world. Within his world death has not yet parted company with life. Within his world life has not yet been defined from the side of death. The questions which are raised by withholding judgment on these matters needs to be considered.

Before Harvey there are tiny holes in the septum of the heart, and it is these holes which Harvey does not see. His failure to see these holes makes of the septum a wall. In the seventeenth century a wall appears in the human heart. Harvey himself says it this way: "Still less is that opinion to be tolerated which . . . supposes . . . that there are numerous pores in the septum cordis . . . But, in faith, no such pores can be demonstrated, neither in fact do any such exist. For the septum of the heart is of a denser and more compact structure than any portion of the body, except the bones and the sinews."[22] The intraventricular pores of the heart close up in the seventeenth century. In the seventeenth century a wall appears within the human heart. Do these statements mean that the septum was porous before the seventeenth century? Were there holes in the human heart in the sixteenth, tenth, or first century? Did Galen or Hippocrates, or Jean Riolan, have such holes in their hearts?

We are easily ready, I think, to say "No!" to these questions, but such a quick answer too easily obscures *how* we speak and *how* we hear the questions. These questions are not simply matters of scientific debate. They also reflect matters which concern human psychological life. If we hear the questions *only* with a scientific ear then they must receive a negative reply. Anatomical science does deny that these holes ever existed. It does claim that Harvey discovered the truth about the heart. It does presume that Galen and Hippocrates and Riolan had holes in their heads rather than their hearts. But if we hear these questions with a psychological ear, then they must receive a different reply. Listening psychologically, we must say, "Yes! There were holes in the heart before the seventeenth century."

How we speak and *how* we listen is a *difference* which *matters*. In the seventeenth century the intraventricular holes close up in the human heart. This is a psychological way of speaking which asks us to hear that people of another age and time had a different kind of heart, that their hearts *mattered* in a different way. The holes in the heart were never really there, and Harvey corrects an error. This is a scientific, empirical way of speaking which asks us to hear how people of an earlier age and time suffered from a false vision. The psychological style of speaking and listening affirms that human existence, including bodily existence, changes. It affirms the changing character of human life, a point of view which is cogently argued in van den Berg's book, *The Changing Nature of Man*.[23] The scientific style affirms that human existence, particularly in its essential materiality, does not change. What is *error* for one perspective is a transformation in human existence, a *different* existence, for the other.

The scientific and psychological style of speaking and listening are two perspectives through which these questions appear, and the point is not which perspective is right or which one is wrong. On the contrary, the point is to be able to see the perspective within which one is. If Harvey cut open the chest of Jean Riolan in 1648, he would see no holes in the heart. This man, Jean Riolan, who sees holes in the heart, this man who lives in a different world, would have no holes in his heart. But Riolan would still not be convinced, and Harvey's vision would still not prove that there never were holes in the heart. It would not convince because Harvey sees with a different eye, a scientific eye, because Harvey lives in a different world. To be convinced, Riolan would have to become a modern man. He would have to live in a different world. His life would have to change. To be convinced, Riolan would first have to allow the heart to matter in another way, because this matter of the heart is not simply a question of empirical observation. It is a question of historical vision, of a seeing eye which inhabits a believable world, and Riolan's believing eye is no less real or trustworthy than that of Harvey which is also our own. We find it difficult even to entertain these questions about the pre-Harveian heart, because the heart which we see today, this pumping heart, is one in which we believe. We believe in it so much in fact that it seems quite natural and unquestionable to project it back in time as the real heart, as the heart as it has always been, a heart with no holes in the septum, a heart with a wall within it.

What seems so natural in this way is, however, actually quite unnatural because it presumes that our access to the past is without a point of view, that this access is only a retreat along the line on which we have traveled to the present. In fact, however, this is never the case. The past which I remember is in light of a future which I more or less intend. The discovery of the past is in light of the creation of a future. Hence when Harvey sees a wall in the heart, he is in fact sketching a future style of existence which has become our life today. It is safer, however, to think that he is simply discovering the ways things have always been, that he is simply discovering the past. This is the way of science, and of ordinary human life. When modern cosmology, for example, tells us that the universe began with the big bang, it is committing (condemning?) us to a destiny as much as it is discovering our heritage. Vision has consequences. The heritage which we believe lies behind us is also a destiny which lies before us.[24]

When we commit ourselves to a scientific truth we also commit ourselves to a psychological style of life. The heart with holes in the septum and the heart without such holes are two different historical styles of existence, two different psychological worlds. If we remember this aspect of the questions which we have been considering, then we cannot forget that the divided heart which Harvey sees is a *historical, psychological vision.* We cannot then forget that the heart which he sees is also a way of seeing, a means by which human life is envisioned in a new way.

The divided heart which Harvey sees in the seventeenth century announces a new style of psychological life. Human life is now seen through death. Human life is now envisioned from the side of the corpse. The significance of this shift becomes more explicit in investigating *what* this divided heart means.

Harvey's text is dedicated to Charles I, who ascended the English throne in 1625. The dedication should be noted:

> The heart of animals is the foundation of their life, the sovereign of everything within them, the sun of the microcosm, that upon which all growth depends, from which all power proceeds. The King, in like manner, is the foundation of his kingdom, the sun of the world around him, the heart of the republic, the fountain whence all power, all grace doth flow. What I have here written of the motions of the heart I am more emboldened to present to your Majesty, . . . because . . . many things in a King are after the pattern of the heart. The knowledge of his heart, therefore, will not be useless to a Prince . . .[25]

In light of what was to come, King Charles I might have done well to refuse this dedication.

Of Scottish heritage, Charles, like his father James I (1603-1625), ruled a land in which differences between King and Parliament were becoming increasingly strained. The historian C. V. Wedgwood has written that there were administrative, economic, and religious differences in this period, and that the last one "seemed to the men of the seventeenth century far more significant than either of the others."[26] In the span of less than one hundred years, England had passed through the reigns of Henry VIII (1509-1547) and Elizabeth I (1558-1603), and in that time it had witnessed Henry's excommunication by the Pope in 1533, the restoration of Catholicism under Mary I in 1555, and the re-establishment of Protestantism under Elizabeth in 1588. Her rule, however, did not settle the differences, and by the time of Charles I the established Anglican Church, through which Charles tried to *unify* all factions "under a benign but rigid control,"[27] found itself amidst opposing forces. On one hand there were the Presbyterians, who accepted the idea of unity but not the king's view of the church. On the other hand, there were the Independents, who asserted the individual's right to choose for himself. In popular speech both of these groups were classed together and known as Puritans, but while they shared the name they differed as much from each other as each differed from the established church of the king. When Charles finally attempted to impose his policy of unification in Scotland, rebellion began. His attempt to unify differences ended in the division of his kingdom, with the king's army on one side and the forces of Parliament on the other. History has named this division the English Civil War (1642-1648).

The king is the heart of his kingdom. So says William Harvey in the dedication of his work. Harvey's attempt to unify the blood divides the heart. Charles' attempt to unify his kingdom divides its heart. Charles I might have benefited from a reading of Harvey's text. When one recalls that the work was published in 1628 and that the Civil War began in 1642, one cannot help but wonder if the king would have learned more from reading this work than he did from his friends and political advisers. But he would have had to read it as more than a work in physiology. He would have had to have read it psychologically to learn that *an intolerance of differences results in a divided heart.* Moreover, he would have had to know how to read in Latin because Harvey's text did not appear in English translation until 1653, some four years after Charles lost his head. Why Harvey chose to publish his work in Latin and with a foreign publisher is something of a question, but the fact makes one wonder if he saw more in the divided heart than he fully knew. In any case, Harvey explicitly repudiates in a later publication of 1649 the central position which the heart occupies in the earlier publication. The privileged place of the heart now belongs to the blood. Harvey writes, for example, that he does not think that the heart is "the framer of the blood" nor that the blood has "force, virtue, motion or heat, as the gift of the heart."[28] What lies between the lines of *De Motu Cordis* in 1628 becomes explicit in 1649. "Harvey dethroned the heart in the same year as the English Republic was proclaimed."[29]

What does the divided heart of the seventeenth century mean? It means that human life has changed in such a way that what was formerly a matter of visible differences to be lived with in the world and among people has now become an interior matter of the heart. This shift in psychological life is revealed through the mutual *reflections* of the scientific and political events of the time. The gathering of these reflections is a way of *deepening* the significance of these events as a story of human experience. It is a way of recovering the psychological dimension of these events. Seen through the political events of his age, for example, the physiological work of Harvey is de-realized. Its event character is now seen through this reflection; and, mirrored in this fashion, the literal character of the event is recovered as a metaphor. From a fact in physiology which can be seen, it becomes a way of seeing the political events of the age. Or, vice versa, the political events become a way of envisioning this new heart. The king as the foundation of his kingdom is "like" the heart which is the foundation of life, Harvey says. The division of a dying kingdom is "like" the division which is seen in the dying heart. Hence I have offered in these remarks a psychological perspective, and not either an argument of historical causality or an exercise in the history of ideas. The political events of an age and the physiological work of the time are not merely parallel lines running alongside each other. Nor are they isolated events one of which determines the other. They are reflections of each other through which the psychological life of an age can be seen. Therefore, even if the political events did shape Harvey's work, this *influence* which may be of *historical* concern, is not properly speaking a *psychological* one. The psychological concern is not with the *influence* of one event *on* the other, a concern which would move psychological studies into the causal styles of thinking more proper to the sciences and perhaps history, but with the *deepening* of one event *through* the other. History is past psychology, but psychology is not merely a history of the past. Psychological life is historical, but the historical events as events do not explain psychological life. On the contrary, historical events, like this appearance of the divided heart, are psychological matters. Through the events, and not in them, psychological life shows itself. *Through the events psychological life matters.* This is the way psychological life counts and the way in which as a reflection it is real.

REFLECTIONS OF A DEMOCRATIC HEART

Harvey sees the divided heart in a dying animal. The dying kingdom of Charles I reflects the divided heart of his reign. In the seventeenth century the life of kingship and the human body are envisioned in a new way. That intolerance of differences which leads to a divided heart ushers in the reign of the corpse. Death is enthroned. Life is reflected through death, and in death we are all equal and the same. The dying, divided heart of William Harvey is also a heart of false equality, a heart of created unity. It is the heart of everyone. It is the democratic heart.

Harvey's intention, which he makes clear in the introduction to his work, is "to discuss the motion, action, and use of the heart," and for this purpose he makes use of "a variety of animals." Indeed, in order to find his place in the dizzying confusion of the heart's motion he studies the slower-moving cold-blooded hearts of "toads, frogs, serpents, small fishes, crabs, shrimps, snails and shell-fish," as well as the hearts of warm-blooded animals "such as the dog and the hog."[30] Amidst this variety he finds the heart's pumping motion. In the midst of all these differences he envisions all these hearts as the same. The pumping heart is a democratic vision, and despite the visible differences which appear among these animals this vision establishes *an identity on the inside.* The animal's heart and the human heart are the same, and from the point of view of this identity the differences become invisible. The pumping heart creates an equality. In terms of the pump we are all equal and the same: dogs are the equal of men, and men are the equal of women.

Recall that in his dedication Harvey advises that the king may learn many things from this work. But what could a king learn from the previous passage? Perhaps with an interest in physiology he could learn how Harvey overcame his difficulties in order to see the heart as a pump. But perhaps with an interest in his kingdom he could also learn that a king is like other people. We do not know if Charles I learned any physiology. We do not even know if Charles I ever read Harvey's book. But we do know that Charles I suffered the lesson of equality implicit in Harvey's new physiology. In fact we even know the date when Charles I suffered his lesson in a rather painful way. Charles I was beheaded in 1649 by the Parliamentary forces of Cromwell, and his dying words on that occasion present an ironic counterpart to the words written by Harvey in 1628. As he mounted the scaffold and surveyed his subjects one last time, Charles I, a king to the end, said: "A subject and a sovereign are clean different things."[31]

A pumping heart can beat only in a democratic world, in a world which is blind to differences, in a world of created and false equality. The eighteenth century is such a world, for it is at this time according to van den Berg that "a compulsion towards the equality of men"[32] begins to appear. The *eighteenth* century and not the seventeenth! Are these remarks on Harvey wrong? Van den Berg's evidence is persuasive. A false equality does manifest itself in eighteenth-century life. I wish to claim, however, only that the *whisperings* of this equality begin in the seventeenth-century human heart. In Harvey's work we can find perhaps the earliest expression of this theme. The literature of the double which begins to appear in the 1790s—van den Berg cites Ludwig Tieck's novels *Ryno* (1791) and *William Lovell* (1792) as opening this theme—may be the *voice* of this democratic and divided heart. The demons who haunt our dreams and our literature since the eighteenth century may be the *shadows* of those differences denied by the human heart. And in fact van den Berg suggests as much himself. In Tieck's novels the double is a being who "dwells in the heart of his hero."[33] When the obvious differences of daily life must surrender to a created and false equality these differences must retreat inside. Harvey's work has already created a place for that retreat.

Harvey questions the action and the use of the heart in his work, and through the questioning he finds a *common* heart. Despite, therefore, the avowed central place which the heart holds in this work, it is a central place which we all now share. Moreover, this central place of the heart is not above being questioned. In his fourth chapter Harvey writes that "it seems very questionable whether or not we are to say that life begins with the palpitation or beating of the heart."[34] Compare these words with those quoted earlier from the dedication. The heart may *not* be the foundation of life, and indeed in 1649, a date whose significance we now more fully appreciate, it is no longer the heart which rules the body. On the contrary, the heart is now explicitly in the *service* of the blood. The heart is no longer the center of life, the giver of warmth, the source of all power. It is an ordinary pump. This vision of 1628 is more explicitly confirmed in 1649. The sovereignty of the heart which is already in question in 1628 is deposed by 1649. If it is still a monarch then it is a monarch bound in service to its kingdom. The heart now holds first place only within a constitutional monarchy of the body.

This questioning of the heart occurs at the same time that Parliament is questioning the king. In 1628 the *Petition of Rights* appears. It is a document in which some of the most basic features of modern democratic government are first explicitly stated, a document which directly challenges the absolute sovereignty of the king. This document contrasts sharply with the vision of kingship announced only thirty years earlier by James I. *The Trew Law of Free Monarchies* which appeared in 1598 insisted that the power of the king derives from God. One could still do that in 1598. The heart had a different world then, and the world had a different heart. Harvey's vulgarization of the heart is the psychology of a new age.

Charles I, the son of James I, is perhaps the first modern witness of the new psychology of false equality which appears through the pumping heart. I said witness, but perhaps I should have said victim. But whichever term is chosen, it seems evident that the divided heart is the reflection of a psychological existence which denies apparent differences and creates a false equality. Harvey's physiological vision reflects a psychological style. We are the inheritors of that vision and of that style.

Modern depth psychology, which van den Berg characterizes as "a pass-ing cultural phenomenon,"[35] bears witness to how our differences have become our symptoms. Today it is only our symptoms which unfortu-nately make us different. The democratically divided heart which Harvey sees in the seventeenth century finds a continuing reflection in the cul-tural phenomenon of depth psychology. The heart of neurosis is a pump-ing heart, a divided heart which is blind to differences. It is a heart which shows how differences which are denied in the name of a false equality become an interior matter of the human heart.

REFLECTIONS OF AN EMPTY HEART

In daily life we are of the opinion that "when the heart strikes the breast and the pulse is felt without, the heart is dilated in its ventricles and is filled with blood . . ."[36] These words appear in the second chapter of Harvey's text, and they state unequivocally that in everyday life we believe that the vigorously felt pulsing of the blood belongs to an *ex-pansive* heart. A full heart, we believe, beats at the center of a vigorous and worldly life.

Common experience, however, is deceived in this matter and Harvey tells us that "the very opposite of the opinions commonly received, ap-pears to be true."[37] When we most believe that the heart is expansive, full, and open, it is constricted, empty, and closed. The heart enlivened within one's breast, like the quickening pulse of life felt throughout one's body, betrays an *empty heart*. The systole and not the diastole is the basic motion of the heart, and emptiness, not fullness, characterizes its primary state. In ordinary life we are deceived because what we believe to be an opening of the heart is a closing, and what we believe to be an abun-dance at the heart of life is a only a void. The active heart is a con-stricted, empty, hard, cold, and tense heart, despite what we may other-wise believe. The full heart, the expansive heart is soft and passive, also in spite of what we may believe. Paul Hazard characterizes the late seven-teenth century as an age in which "men craved to know . . . what they were to believe . . ."[38] In the same period in which Harvey sees an empty heart men are no longer certain of what they are to believe. This mutual occurrence is no accident. The empty heart belongs to a psychological age which doubts its most unquestioned beliefs.

De Motu Cordis describes an empty heart, and on the literal level of physiology Harvey's words are not difficult to understand. Neither for Harvey nor for physiology do these words pose a question or raise a problem. This is as it should be for physiology. The expanding or contracting heart is merely the action of a muscle, and the empty heart or the full heart is only a matter of the blood. But Harvey's physiology is also the reflection of a world. This heart reflects a style of existence and a change in the human style of existence. Expansion and contraction are not only neutral, empirical terms. This rhythm of the heart beats in accordance with a new rhythm in human life, and *empty* and *full* refer to more than the mere presence or absence of blood. Harvey's text not only defines a contracting, physiological organ drained of blood. It also describes a way of living in which an expansive movement toward the world leaves behind, and indeed even requires, an empty, doubtful, and divided heart. The human heart becomes empty in the seventeenth century. Human existence becomes empty and lonely in the expansiveness of the seventeenth century.

Harvey writes his work in an age of expansion, magnificence, and exaggeration. It is the age of the baroque, and in this "infinite world movement and force are of primary importance."[39] A sense of expansive movement is so characteristic of the age that even buildings begin to move. The more static forms of High Renaissance architecture give way to the dynamic and vital forms of baroque space. It is a space whose "energetic forms . . . resemble pulsating organisms."[40] The Italian architect Francesco Borromini, for example, makes use of the undulating wall which gives his buildings a sense of expansive-contracting movement. The Church of San Carlino al Quirinale in Rome illustrates this point (Figure 5). The facade of this church, which dates from 1665-1667, breathes, giving the viewer an experience of the stone as a pulsing organism. The same pulsating character can be seen in Borromini's Chapel of Sant' Ivo (Figure 6), begun in 1642. The lower curve of the facade sweeps inward, while the drumlike structure immediately above it expands outward in contrasting fashion. Pilasters rib the drum and appear to "restrain the

Figure 5. Church of San Carlino al Quirinale, Rome. Photo from Archivi Alinari, Florence, courtesy of Art Resource.

Figure 6. Chapel of Sant'Ivo, Palazzo della Sapienza, Rome. Photo from Archivi Alinari, Florence, courtesy of Art Resource.

forces that seem to push the bulging form outward";[41] their presence emphasizes the powerful outward thrust of a drum, which is offset by the concave movement of the lower part of the facade. Viewed in its totality with the surrounding earlier walls which frame the court, the building actually does pulse and throb with a vital energy. This pulsating feature of baroque architectural style is not, however, only carved in stone. It is also a characteristic feature of the philosophy of architecture which appears at this time. In 1665 the architect Guarino Guarini writes a book entitled *Placita Philosophica* (*Philosophy of Place*) where he insists that this pulsating movement is a basic property of nature. "The spontaneous action of dilation and contraction is not governed by any principle, but is present through the whole living being."[42] Baroque space, and particularly baroque sacred space, beats with the rhythm of the pulsing human heart.

But the pulsating heart is an empty heart. Is baroque space also an empty space? Is the space of the baroque world which seems to define so confidently a movement toward the world also a space which defines the emptiness of a heart which doubts its beliefs?

Baroque *elation* hides an *uneasiness* of the human heart. It hides an incipient loss of faith, a disillusionment with human concerns. Writing of baroque literature, Miroslav Hanak says that it betrays a "titanic struggle between reason and faith," a never-ending struggle between the exuberance of flesh and the asceticism of spirit. There is, he says, a "baroque pessimism," and he illustrates his point with numerous examples. John Webster's *White Devil* (1612) and his *Duchess of Malfi* (1614), for example, both "bring into relief the vanity of all human endeavor rather than the glory of man's grand, even if unsuccessful, designs." The confident belief in human effort begins to fade as a sense of the hollow emptiness of human endeavors begins to appear. The tragically comic exploits of Cervantes' knight-errant Quixote first appear in 1605. Quixote is looking for values which have been lost, but his search appears futile, vain, empty, and foolish. An "atmosphere of futility" marks the age according to Hanak, particularly after the death of Elizabeth I in 1603, and "Shakespeare [too] seems to be caught up in [this] common atmosphere of resignation."[43] One sees it portrayed, for example, in the figure of Hamlet. As noted by A. C. Harwood, the words which Hamlet speaks to Rosencrantz and Guildenstern betray "not only a personal disillusionment, but a world disillusionment." Hamlet pre-figures a new type of consciousness, "the spectator consciousness."[44] It is a style of life which is marked by a withdrawal from the world, a retreat. One is no longer quite sure how to act or what to do. Hesitation born of doubt and despair interrupts the confident flow of action.

Another poet of the age also expresses this despair of the empty heart. The *Anniversary Poems* of John Donne, first published in 1612, deal with the "decay of Nature and the degeneration of man."[45] This theme is even clearer in the full title of the *First Anniversary*. It reads: *An Anatomie of the World. Wherein, By Occasion of the untimely death of Mistris Elizabeth Drury, the frailtie and the decay of this Whole World is represented.* Death, frailty, decay, degeneration—these are the themes which occupy the poet's mind. They do not make happy thoughts, for Donne, like others of his age, sees the ending of a world. Marjorie Hope Nicolson says that the lines of the poem echo the sentiments of one for whom the "traditional values of royalty, aristocracy, family were facing disruption." They reflect a world in which the "individual was no longer content to play his allotted role in an established scheme."[46] It is our *place* in the world which is now in question, and it now seems as if we have no place. No, that is not quite correct. Rather our place is now defined by ourselves. Each of us occupies a unique, lonely place. Donne says it better in this way:

> For every man alone thinkes he has got
> To be a Phoenix, and that then can bee
> None of that kinde, of which he is, but hee.[47]

In our *thoughts* each of us is an individual. But in our thinking each of us stands alone. Thinking, singular, solitary, individual, each one is one of a kind. Unique, we are all individuals. Unique, we are all alone. Unique, we are all strangely equal in our loneliness. We are all equal and equally alone.

Hanak captures this mood of solitary emptiness. "Never before or since," he writes, "has man been so obsessed with reaching the absolute through such desperately elated interiorization of his existence."[48] His words are worth our attention. An interior *desperate elation* marks the age of the baroque. The exuberance which characterizes an outward, vigorous movement toward the world betrays a quiet inner despair, the loneliness of an empty heart. It is to this word that the Harveian heart belongs, and through its poets one can faintly hear amid the magnificent splendor of the age the sigh of the empty heart.

But it is not only the poetry of the age which reflects a "baroque pessimism." The theme of emptiness is also reflected in other human endeavors. In 1609 and 1619, for example, Johannes Kepler published two important works, *Astronomia Nova* and *Harmonice Mundi*. For the science of astronomy their significance lies in the three laws of planetary motion which fittingly crown the Copernican achievement. For human life their significance lies in a different and changed style of existence. The heavens now no longer contain those transparent crystalline spheres which daily wheel about our corruptible home, the earth. They no longer contain those spheres which in ascending order of purity, from the moon through the sun, planets, fixed stars, and primum mobile, reach toward the purest regions of all, God's heavenly abode. Kepler's mathematical laws, a work of sure genius, shatter those spheres and empty the heavens. His "music of the spheres" is a hymn to mathematical harmony and regularity. In abandoning the traditional belief in the spheres, Kepler envisions "the planets as moving through immense empty spaces."[49] With Kepler the heavens, like the human heart, also become empty of all except matter in motion in the early seventeenth century. Later in that century Pascal will experience the loneliness of those heavens when he looks toward them and sees only an immense and empty void.

An empty heaven requires an empty earth, and in the mid-seventeenth century Otto von Guericke performs a dramatic experiment at Magdeburg, Germany, which in one respect empties the earth. In 1654 he succeeds in emptying two semi-spheres of air, and two teams of horses, one team attached to each side of the sphere, are unable to pull the semi-spheres apart. Von Guericke creates a vacuum. It is an astonishing and significant achievement, for with it he divides the older Aristotelian word from the newer Galilean one. The older Aristotelian tradition denied the existence of a vacuum, and on the basis of this denial it constructed its physics of the earth and its astronomy of the heavens. The new Galilean tradition not only affirms its existence but places the vacuum in a central position. Galileo's laws of falling bodies presume it. Von Guericke's vacuum belongs to this new world, and in this change the "theory of plenitude, by which each nook and cranny of the created universe was believed to be occupied by something,"[50] is destroyed. There is *nothing* in the space of the earth and *nothing* in the endless depths of the heavens except the fortuitous flux and reflux of atoms moving in empty space. What we believe to be full is in reality empty. The fullness of creation begins to disappear in this void. Should we be surprised, therefore, to find Pierre Bayle in 1682 vehemently opposing any *miraculous* interpretation of heavenly comets? There is no place for such *beliefs* in a universe whose heart is nourished by reasoned doubt. Belief in the miraculous is drained away with the emptying of the heart, and modern psychology is the discipline of this empty heart. Or perhaps it is better to say here that insofar as modern psychology is born in this change from a believing heart to a doubting mind it is a discipline without heart. According to the etymology of the word, this means a discipline without courage and belief. How much of psychology today is so trivial? How much does it protect itself behind the accumulation of meaningless data?

In the first quarter of the seventeenth century Harvey sees an empty heart. It is a heart which is drained of blood in an age which feels drained of its beliefs. It is a heart of troubled belief. In the last decade of this same century John Locke places this heart at the foundation of a psychology of human desire. "The Uneasiness a man finds in himself," Locke writes in 1690, "is what we call desire . . . . [and] the chief, if not the only spur to human industry and action is uneasiness."[51] An interior uneasiness in place of belief becomes the spur to human action. Lack and privation are the springs of a human response. With Harvey the heart is empty when we feel most active. With Locke we now act because the heart is empty. The circle is closed. Between Harvey and Locke, between the beginning and the end of the seventeenth century, a world of waning and troubled belief becomes a world of restless and uneasy desire. We are the inheritors of that psychological style of human life.

This discussion of the empty heart began in the moving space of the baroque cathedral, and it is fitting it should end there. The emptiness of the human heart is not only a matter of blood but also of belief. What better place to conclude these remarks than in the space of belief, the space of the church. The baroque church pulses with the same rhythm as the pumping heart. Is it an empty heart which beats within the walls of these cathedrals?[52]

On December 27, 1673, in a small cloister in mid-France, Paray-le-Monial, a Visitation sister by the name of Margaret Mary Alacoque kneels in adoration before the altar of the convent chapel. She is twenty-six years old, and that day she experiences the first of her Great Apparitions. On this first occasion she sees the Sacred Heart of Christ. Her description of that experience deserves our attention:

> One day, when I was before the Blessed Sacrament, and having at the time more leisure than usual, I felt myself wholly invested with the presence of God. Thus I lost all thought of myself, and the place where I was . . . surrendering my heart to the power of His love. My sovereign Master granted me to repose for a long time upon His divine breast, where He uncovered to me the marvels of His love, and the inexplicable secrets of His Sacred Heart, which He had hitherto concealed from me. He opened for me for the first time His divine Heart.[53]

These words describe the *opening* of another heart. But this heart which opens in 1673 is not the same heart which opened in 1628. It is, on the contrary, the heart which has been forgotten with the appearance of the pumping heart. The words which are spoken to her on this same occasion betray this forgotten heart: "My divine Heart is so full of love for men . . . that it is unable to contain within Itself the flames of Its burning love."[54] This heart which appears in 1673 is a full heart. It is a heart which speaks with the fullness of love. The other heart, which appeared in 1628, is an empty heart. It is a heart drained of blood *and* belief. Forty-five years after Harvey's work a heart which is once again full appears. Can it be a coincidence? That seems quite unlikely, and in any case to speak of a coincidence is to say nothing at all. It is an admission of our ignorance. Rather we can say that in the seventeenth century the *fullness* of the heart begins to matter when the *emptiness* of the human heart becomes a theme. The appearance of this heart which is filled with love is an acknowledgment that one cannot live with an empty heart, with a heart without belief. The human heart is, as we earlier saw, essentially nourished by belief. It is the "organ" of belief, and to forget this aspect of the heart is to invite its reappearance in another fashion. If not as symptom, then as a vision of life the fullness of the heart appears. A second apparition attests to how this fullness of the heart cannot be so easily forgotten.

In late 1673 or early 1674, Margaret Mary sees the Cross implanted in the Sacred Heart. A cross of suffering rather than a wall of division marks the heart, and this heart suffers "in order . . . to *touch* the *unfeeling* hearts of men."[55] These are the words which Margaret Mary hears, and they testify to how the human heart has grown empty, hard, and cold. Unfeeling, the human heart is untouched by others, and unfeeling it is empty of its love and its beliefs. Men now "'entertain only coldness towards me,'"[56] the Sacred Heart says, and in this coldness the human heart has forgotten how it swells with life through its beliefs, how it expands with life through its love. Can we ask for any more? Can we still doubt that when the human heart is emptied, the fullness of the human heart will begin to speak for itself in another way? The space of human psychological life changes in the seventeenth century. It is a dynamic but empty space. The sacred heart which Margaret Mary sees in the same century is a reflection of that emptiness, a reflection which *in its reversal* testifies to the troubling appearance of the empty heart.

It would be a mistake however to suppose that these appearances of the Sacred Heart refer *directly* to the Harveian heart. There is no *direct* link between this small convent in mid-France in 1673 and a laboratory in London in 1628. There is no *direct* link between any of the events presented in this discussion. Such a view would *reduce* one event to the other, the event of 1673, for example, to the one of 1628, or 1628 to 1673. Theology would become psychology, or psychology theology.

On the contrary the relations are *indirect*, psychological and not causal. They are *reflections* of each other which indicate on one hand that human psychological existence appears through the things which we do, through the churches we build, the sciences of the heavens and the earth we create, the literature we write, and the ways in which we worship our God. On the other hand, these relations indicate the changing character of our psychological life. In the seventeenth century a new psychological existence emerges. The pumping heart is a reflection of that psychological life which is our own life in the modern world.

CONTEMPORARY REFLECTIONS OF THE PUMPING HEART

The pumping heart is a scientific, medical, empirical reality, and the history of medical science has impressively developed the validity of this vision. No one would contend against it. But it is necessary to recognize and to remember that this vision of the heart reflects the see-er, that this vision of the heart is a way of seeing. It is necessary to remember that this vision of the heart is also a vision of humanity, that through this heart which we see we spy ourselves. The pumping heart, this scientific, medical, empirical reality is also a psychological reality. In speaking of the heart as a pump we speak also of ourselves, of our own psychological style of life.

The pumping heart is a divided heart. It is an empty heart. It is a heart which is equal for all. Division, emptiness, equality, these are terms which belong to the empirical heart. But they are also terms which reflect a world. Specifically, these terms in relation to the heart reflect the baroque world. Baroque, then, is more than a period in history. It is a way of living the world which continues today in our image of the heart and the psychological style of life which belongs to that heart. This baroque heart is at the heart of our modern world.

The Harveian heart belongs to a divided world. It reflects an existence whose tolerance of and blindness to differences become matters of the heart. When there is opposition at the very heart of a human life, when one's psychological life is predicated on the denial of differences, on the pretense of equality, a wall appears in the human heart. Charles I was perhaps the first victim of this new style of life, of a life which is lived with a divided heart. And he was perhaps also the first figure in modern times to embody his life in this fashion. Insisting on the clear differences between subjects and kind, he nevertheless tried to supress the differences among the religious factions in his kingdom. We might say, then, that the divided heart beats within the chest of the "kingly figure." It is the heart, we might say, which lies at the heart of life of those monarchical kinds of figures who are intolerant of differences. Set upon one course of action, incapable, or unresponsive to change, imposing and impatient of attitude, do we not find something of this "kingly," "monarchical" kind of figure in the Type A individual who today runs the greatest risk of a failing heart?[57] Do not these individuals more than others *real-ize* the heart as a pump because these individuals more than others live a psychological style of life in which the heart appears as a pump? Indeed, is not the more recent medical attention to this relation between heart disease and life style an implicit acknowledgment of the psychological sense of the heart? Is it not a support for the claim advanced here that the pumping heart in its original appearance is a psychological reality?

The "kingly" figure, however, is not the only embodiment of the divided heart. The divided heart as a psychological style of life is also *figured* in other ways. Pascal, who belongs to the same age as Harvey, expresses another style in the following words:

> There is internal war in man between reason and the passions.
> If he had only reason without passions . . .
> If he had only passion without reason . . .
> But having both, he cannot be without strife, being unable to
>   be at peace with the one without being at war with the
>   other. Thus he is always divided against, and opposed to
>   himself.[58]

These are the words of another type of division of the heart. Reason and passion! The division of the heart which belongs to the Cartesian dream of reason! The blind heart divorced from the reasoning mind!

This heart is not one which belongs to the "kingly" figure as much as it is the modern heart of neurosis. Mind without passion, passion without mind, it is this heart which is echoed in these words. These words presage those figures who will disclose in a small consulting room in Vienna the forbidden secrets of a divided heart. Neurosis and the divided heart reflect the same world.[59]

The divided heart intolerant of differences is a heart which is equal and the same for all. The heart which Harvey sees in the seventeenth century reflects a democratic vision. It is a heart which belongs to a democratic world. The differences which appear among people now becomes matters of the inside. Differences which once were publicly visible become private matters of the heart. An equality which no one can ever see, much less live, becomes a new style of belief. The pumping heart reflects a falsely democratic world.

Since 1950 heart disease, which is the realization of the pumping heart, its most conspicuous manner of appearance, has been "the leading cause of premature death among U.S. adults between the ages of 24 and 65."[60] This is an astonishing fact. In the most technologically advanced country in the world, more people die prematurely of heart attacks than almost anywhere else, and in the last thirty years these numbers have increased. Much has been made of the role of diet, tobacco, alcohol, and coffee as contributing factors, and no doubt they play their part. Much also has been made of our harried life style and lack of exercise. But in addition to the cholesterol we consume, the cigarettes we smoke, and the alcohol we drink, perhaps we should also pay attention to those things which we profess to believe. "All men are created equal." This is the foundation of our democratic way of life, and in the face of obvious differences, which have become increasingly apparent on the world scale with the emergence of Third World countries since the end of the Second World War, we try to live out this belief. We profess in theory an equality which is impossible to carry out in practice. We profess an equality which while true as an abstraction is falsified in the face of obvious differences. We profess an impossible equality. We espouse an illusory vision. The heart of today lives in this strange world, where the threat of war, for example, has become identical to living in peace. Situ-

ated within this context, are these facts about heart disease still so astonishing? Do we not *open* our hearts toward this vision of it as a pump in
an atmosphere which believes that beneath the appearance of visible
differences we are all the same? And do we not continue in this fashion
the very same conditions of equalizing vision which allowed Harvey in
his opening of the heart to see it as a pump?

A divided heart, a falsely equal heart, an empty heart! This emptiness of the heart is also our style of psychological life today. James
Lynch, in a recent book entitled *The Broken Heart: The Medical Consequences of Loneliness*, describes that style of life when the human heart
now emptied of its nourishing beliefs breaks. Citing a work by Victor
Fuchs entitled *Who Shall Live?* Lynch points out that in the neighbor-
ing states of Utah and Nevada, which are statistically equivalent in such
areas as income and educational levels, Nevada's death rate by heart disease significantly exceeds that of Utah. Nevada in fact has one of the
highest rates and Utah one of the lowest in the United States. According to Fuchs, one factor which may account for this difference is that
Utah is an extremely religious state, whereas Nevadans have allowed their
state to become one of the "divorce capitals" of the nation. While
religion does not prevent heart disease, any more than divorce causes it,
nevertheless the issue of divorce may very well be a psychological difference which matters. Divorce is the end of a relationship in which one
once believed, and we have already seen how a heart emptied of its beliefs defines a pumping heart. The medical reality of Harvey's empty
heart finds its psychological reflection in a life which has been severed
from its relations. As Lynch puts it in the introduction to his book,
"human relationships *do* matter"[61] to the human heart. I would certainly agree! But I would add here for the sake of psychological clarity
that the human heart is a matter of human relationships. It is not that
human *psychological* relationships matter to a *material*, physical organ
of the body. Rather this physical organ of the body is the material of
psychological life. The human heart is first and foremost a psychological reality. Human relationships *are* the *matter* of the human heart.[62]

In its origins and in its continuing appearance today, the human heart
which science knows is a way of living the heart. It is the reflection of a

world. It is a particular historical way in which the material heart matters psychologically. But the heart which Harvey originally saw in the seventeenth century is a muscle. It is a bundle of tissues, nerves, chambers, ducts, veins, valves, and arteries. There is a septum in this heart. It has weight, size, color, and form. A surgeon opens a chest, and this is the heart which he sees. A heart transplant is performed, and this is the heart which is exchanged. How can we speak, then, of human relationships as the *matter* of the heart? Are not these valves, ducts, veins, arteries, etc., immutably present? Are not human relationships merely an addition to this immutable reality? It is easy to think so, but the historical fact is that the way in which this material organ was seen in the seventeenth century is not how it was always seen. The historical fact is that *the material changed.* An earlier age saw the material heart in a different fashion. People of another age had a different heart.

We see differently "and" the heart changes. If we are to realize the full significance of this recovery of the human heart, and by implication the human body, as a psychological reality, then we must understand this conjunction between the seeing and the seen, this creative confusion between the what and the how of experience. This task concerns the approach I have taken in this work.

The Recovery of Psychological Life and the Practice of Phenomenology

It is a dark evening, and my car is the only one on this deserted country road. I am preoccupied with the events of the day, thinking about the things I have not yet done and those which I still must do when I arrive home. Thinking of these things, I have more or less given my eyes over to the task of searching the road. They are there on the road before me, guiding the car through my hands and feet before I do. Suddenly my foot presses the brake and the car jerks to a halt. It takes a moment for the one who was considering the events of the day to rejoin his eyes on the road. But when I do it is easy to see why my foot pressed the brake so suddenly. There in front of me at a distance which is already too close looms a dark and sinister-looking shape. That is what I saw;

that is what my eyes saw while I was thinking of the day.

I wait, and as I wait that shape in the distance begins to change. What was only a moment before a dark and sinister shape now appears to be the twisted and gnarled trunk of a tree which has fallen across the road. I blink my eyes and I move my head slightly forward to get a better look. But the light is dim and I still cannot quite make out what I am seeing. Cautiously and not without some misgiving I leave my car and approach the object in the road. Now at this distance I am sure. Yes, there is no doubt about it. Lying across the road is a fallen, twisted tree trunk. I certainly will not be able to drive my car around it. I will have to turn around and take another way home.

This is a simple example which illustrates an ordinary experience which is possible for anyone. But what the example signifies is quite another matter. We can begin to appreciate its significance by raising a question. What is the reality which is there on the road to be seen?

The answer to this question seems obvious. It is a fallen, twisted tree trunk which is on the road. That is a fact, and with this knowledge of the facts I am convinced that the dark sinister shape which I saw earlier was a mistake. A moment ago I was in error about what I saw and this later experience proves it. What I see now corrects what I saw before. The fact replaces an illusion.

We should not however be so ready to accept this answer which seems so obvious, because it discounts the earlier experience too readily. To be more precise this obvious answer commits a retrospective fallacy. It replaces an earlier experience with a later one, and in this process it establishes an illusion where none originally existed. At the moment when I saw the dark and sinister shape, I was not seeing an illusion. The dark and sinister shape was there before me on the road, and the conduct of my foot proves it. If I do not want to deny that earlier experience, I cannot dismiss that first appearance as unreal.

But if we refuse this obvious reply, then how can we understand this experience? Are we saying that the reality of what we see changes from moment to moment?

Certainly we have to admit that that thing on the road is a matter of time. What I see changes, and its changing face is the presence of time.

But in addition to the temporality of the experience, there is another aspect which cannot be ignored. In addition to saying that *what* I saw changed I must also admit that *who* was looking changed. The figure who sees the dark and sinister shape is one who is distracted and preoccupied by the events of the day. He is a figure who has abandoned the car to his body. In contrast, the figure who sees the twisted, fallen tree trunk is a cautious, hesitant, probing individual. He is embodied in a different fashion. *What* appears is not separable from *how* it is experienced and this how is a matter of *who* looks. The reality of what is experienced is not therefore simply a matter of time.

To appreciate this point consider what might happen when I return to my car to recommence my journey home. Initially I may feel embarrassed by my earlier fear. How silly of me, I might think, to have reacted so emotionally. Confident now with this later knowledge and engaged in scolding myself for being so foolish, my eyes again catch one more glimpse of that object on the road as I turn my car around to go home. And again out of the corner of my eye I may see that dark and sinister figure. A momentary lapse is enough to restore that first figure, and in *that* moment I will not be able to suppress an anxious feeling. Despite what I have just recently seen, despite what I know, I cannot deny that I am only too ready to leave this place.

What is seen is in relation to *how* one looks (*who* is looking). *What* is experienced and *how* it is experienced are essentially correlated. The example which we have just given illustrates this point, and in principle it is no different from the phenomenon of the changing heart. We see differently, and the heart changes. I look in a different fashion, and that thing on the road changes. If we want to remain faithful to experience as it is given, if we wish to remain close to the reality of things as they appear, then we must suspend that attitude which would sanctify one moment of experience—the appearance of the tree trunk—and deify one figure—the one who sees this appearance. But this suspension amounts to a temporary bracketing of the factual status of things, not because the world and its things are in doubt but in order to regain the way things come into being. It amounts to a bracketing of that attitude which in its uncritical allegiance to this factual status of things already dismisses all other appearances as illusions. Indeed, in the final analysis this decision to put the factual status of things temporarily out of play amounts to the practice of phenomenology.

But what is phenomenology?[63] The question as it stands is obviously too broad for this work, and in any case the intention of this work has not been to answer this question. On the contrary the purpose of this work has been to present a psychological psychology, and within this context the approach of phenomenology has been indispensable.[64] In one sense, therefore, the work itself addresses the question, but obviously only in an indirect fashion. It is possible, however, to offer a more direct way, even if it is only in an illustrative manner. The example has led to this question, and the manner in which I dealt with the example is already a reply.

Phenomenology is that approach which allows us to take the appearance of what appears precisely as it appears prior to any judgment about the factuality or illusory status of what appears. If we recall here the first appearance of the thing on the road as it appeared, the thing as a dark and sinister shape, then the difference between this approach and the factual attitude is clear. In the factual attitude my commitment is precisely to the factual status of what appears, which means to the thing as a material, substantial reality, and in light of this commitment the sinister shape is unreal and my experience is understood as being based upon an illusion. Within this attitude this explanation is certainly correct, but this explanation which accords with a *scientific* psychology does not proceed toward an understanding of the experience. The explanation, illusion, cuts short the story of the experience. It leaves the experience too quickly. Phenomenology, on the other hand, lingers with the experience and allows an understanding of it to emerge. The panic which was felt when that dark and sinister shape appeared is taken as it was experienced, and when it is accepted in this fashion, a psychological account can be given. The story of the experience and the figure who belongs to it can be recovered, and in this sense phenomenology is the indispensable approach for a *psychological* psychology.

The difference, therefore, between a factual and a phenomenological approach is that in place of *error* the latter approach sees a *differ-*

ence between the two experiences, and in this respect this approach remains closer to the truth of each experience. My conduct in relation to the dark and sinister figure demonstrates that this reality is as believable as the later one, and phenomenology, unlike the factual attitude, does not demand that I dismiss this reality as unbelievable. Of course nothing which has been said here denies that it is the later appearance which establishes the earlier one as a difference, just as, for example, the world of being awake establishes the world of dreaming as a difference. The point for phenomenology is the *difference*. The later appearance is not an indictment against the earlier one, any more than the world of being awake is an indictment against the dream. On the contrary, *because* phenomenology begins with a temporary suspension of the reality of things and events, the difference can be explored, and this suspension, which allows for example the experience of the dark and sinister figure or the experience of dreaming to be interrogated on its own terms, can occur because phenomenology believes in the world's reality and not because it doubts it. It is because we are already so tied to the truth of the world as it is given in our waking life that we can temporarily loosen these ties. If the world of things and events were ever really in doubt, the practice of phenomenology could never begin.

In response to our question, therefore, we may suggest that phenomenology is a practice of fidelity to experience as it takes place. With respect to the phenomenon of the changing heart, this practice means that we do not have to measure the significance of the heart for people of an earlier age against the vision of the heart which we have today. It means that we are free to approach the heart of an earlier age on its own terms and hence more readily disposed to approach our own vision of the heart today not only as a fact, but also as a vision, as a way of seeing.

Method and the Recovery of Psychological Life: From Reflection to Metaphor

We have seen that the approach taken in this chapter, and in this work, acknowledges the essential co-relation between the what and the how of experience. What something is, is inseparable from how it is envisioned, and if at one level this issue of how is an issue of who is figuring the experience, it is also at another level an issue of method. In these remarks, I want to discuss the method used in recovering the heart as a psychological reality.

Initially we must acknowledge that at the beginning of the chapter the question of how to view the heart had already been prescribed because what the heart is had already been indicated. Psychological life had been presented as a reality of reflection, and hence the human heart already had appeared in this way. The task of the chapter, then, was to deepen this experience. The task was to recover the specific reflections of the heart. How was this done?

With respect to the everyday heart we began with language, and in several descriptions of the heart we heard the heart as a way of speaking. These whispers of the heart, like all language, were references to a world, and we took up these words as mirrors though which the many worlds of the heart appeared. It was not the saying themselves in their literal meanings which mattered. The heart was not *in* the words. It was, on the contrary, *through* the words that the heart appeared.

Essentially, therefore, the work of this chapter was a work of mirroring, and this mirror work became more explicit with the recovery of the scientific heart. A text in physiology was brought face to face, for example, with the political events of the age, and in this mutual facing each event was deepened, re-figured, and de-realized through the other. A physiological fact, the division of the heart, was seen through the political divisions of the age, and in this fashion that fact was de-literalized. It was not the factual status which mattered (recall here the previous remarks on the phenomenological approach), but the story which appeared when that fact was imagined in this other way, *as if* it were a political event, which mattered. The fact became a way of telling a story, an image through which another meaning appeared. The division within the heart, which on the factual level of physiology meant that there were no holes in the septum cordis, became the vehicle for a story about the consequences for social life of an intolerance of differences.

But we did not see Harvey's physiological text only through the political events of the age. The architecture, poetry, literature, science, and theology of the age also re-figured his work. The mirror work was multiple, and in this respect this work of mirroring was like a nonrepresentational painting in which something appears between or among the images. For example, as in Picasso's classic *Seated Woman (Nude)*, where the figure is not in any of the lines but appears in the interplay or reflections among them, the psychological story of the scientific heart was not already in any of these events but emerged in the reflections between or among them. For example, the *psychological* significance of the emptiness of the heart was realized only when this aspect of Harvey's text was mirrored through, among other things, baroque sacred space. *Before* this mirroring the emptiness of the heart which Harvey described referred to a literal, empirical fact. It referred to the systolic moment of the heart, when it is momentarily drained of blood. But *after* the mirroring this emptiness of the heart took on a deeper significance. Mirrored through baroque sacred space this emptiness was understood to describe a heart drained of its beliefs, the emptiness of a nonbelieving heart in a new age of reasoned doubt. Was this sense of emptiness already present in the Harveian text? It hardly seems possible. Was it already present in the baroque cathedral? To be sure, the appearance of the Sacred Heart spoke explicitly to the eclipse of faith, but did this eclipse extend beyond the domain of the church? Was it already seen to be a matter of the human heart in the broader context of daily, worldly belief? Again it hardly seems to be the case. The emptiness of the human heart as a psychological story was not, therefore, already in Harvey's text, nor in the baroque cathedral. It was not already in either of these vents as a condition for this work of mirroring. It was, on the contrary, a consequence of this work, a third term as it were which appeared between these two events.

Earlier I suggested that this work of mirroring was like a non-representational painting in which an image appears which is not in any of the lines, shapes, or colors but in the mutual interplay among them. Another illustration is possible, however, and it is one which is closer to the direction of this text. A metaphor too generates a third meaning which is not already contained in the two terms of the metaphor. When Nietzsche speculates, for example, that "truth is a woman"[65] the metaphor announces a meaning which is not given in either term. A perspective on truth is offered which envisions it in a feminine way. It may suggest, for example, that truth is elusive, or charming, or seductive, if one has this image of a woman. Or it may suggest that truth is too often taken for granted. Is the elusiveness of truth or its taken for granted character already present without this mirror of the woman? It seems doubtful, and in any case these visions of truth become manifest through these reflections. On the other hand, consider what happens to woman when she is mirrored through the image of truth. Is she not alluded to in a way which offers a perspective not present before this reflection? Women and truth! Does not this work of metaphoring invite the imagination to consider again the relation of man to truth, and of man to woman? Are we not invited by the metaphor toward new discoveries? · The meaning which the work of metaphoring achieves is not to be found, therefore, in the meanings of the terms which compose the metaphor. On the contrary a metaphor seems to work by bringing together two terms or two realities which in their mutual facing generate or reflect a third term, another meaning, a different reality. I think that Ortega y Gasset intends this sense of metaphor when he ways that a metaphor "creates imaginary reefs among the real things."[66] What are these imaginary reefs if not the reflections of reality, the reflections generated in the mutual facing of things?

The work of mirroring which describes our psychological method may be viewed, therefore, as a work of metaphoring. Psychological method is a work of de-literalizing, of de-realization. In this work it is not the factual status of things or events which matters but the story which is reflected through them. We see, therefore, that method follows on the way in which psychological life appears. As a reality of reflection, psychological life de-realizes the material through which it appears. Its appearance demands that it be taken in a non-literal fashion. The work which we do remains faithful to the work which is already done with the appearance of psychological life.

But if method follows on the appearance of psychological life, which is after all only the other side of saying that what appears is in relation to how it is envisioned, then we have another way of speaking about the appearance of psychological life. In other words, insofar as the relation between the what and how of experience, the subject matter and the method, turns out to be reciprocal so that what is experienced is inseparable from how it is envisioned and how one looks already follows what appears, the characterization of psychological life can be expressed in terms of either the what or the how of its experience. We can continue to say that *psychological life is a reality of reflection*, and in this respect we will be following the direction already established in the first three chapters. But on the other hand and in light of this fourth chapter we can begin to say that *psychological life is a metaphorical reality*, and in this respect anticipate the direction to be taken in the final chapter. In either case, however, the development of this work has actually proceeded along this line from reflection to metaphor. From the initial appearance of psychological life as a reality of reflection, we were led through things and others to the recovery of the body in this way, and this latter effort raised the question of method, which in turn has led us to this notion of psychological life as a metaphorical reality. In the final chapter we will test this suggestion in detail. We will consider there some specific ways in which psychological life is a metaphorical reality. Before we do this, however, we should conclude this chapter with this last suggestion clearly in view. Let us return to the heart with this suggestion.

Conclusion: The Psychological Heart as a Metaphorical Reality

We see differently, and the heart changes. This phenomenon of the changing heart is the reality which we have considered in this chapter, and it has been suggested that the Harveian heart, the heart which is a pump, this heart which is divided, empty, and equal, is as much a way of seeing as it is a reality to be seen. The heart which is a pump was not there before Harvey and the age in which he lived saw it and spoke it. It was not there before the Harveian way of seeing and speaking about it appeared. It *is* not there except in relation to this way of seeing and speaking. For the heart to be seen as a pump the see-er already has to have a democratic eye and a divided and empty existence, and to look in this fashion is to see a heart which is the equal of every other heart, whose septum is nonporous, and whose primary systolic rhythm means the emptying of the human heart. In this regard the heart which appears as a pump is more than an empirical fact in the world simply waiting to be discovered. The pumping heart is not the consequence of a causal observation.

But this way of seeing and speaking in relation to which the pumping heart appears does not create reality. If this way of looking entails more than the passively recording eye, it also involves less than the actively creating mind. The Harveian heart is no more a thought in the mind than it is a thing in the world. If it is not there before Harvey and his age envision it, it is nevertheless there when one looks and speaks in a specific way. A style of vision encounters something to be seen. The eye which is a style of seeing finds its support in a world which is seen.

We have in the story of the Harveian heart, therefore, a reality which is neither a discovery nor a creation, neither a fact nor an idea, neither in the world nor of the mind. This heart which is recovered psychologically is neither a thing nor a thought. It is an elusive reality, and the work of Harvey which bequeaths to us the heart which we know today is an allusion to what is elusive. If we ask now what such a reality is, knowing that it is neither fact nor idea, thing nor thought, empirical nor mental, we can suggest that it is metaphorical. This psychological reality which *alludes* to what it is, which shows itself indirectly, is a metaphorical reality, since a metaphor too is a mode of indirection which escapes these dichotomies, or lies between them. The heart which we have recovered psychologically as a reality of reflection matters metaphorically. Psychological life, which is neither thing nor thought, fact nor idea, empirical nor mental, is a metaphorical reality.

V

THE METAPHORICAL CHARACTER OF PSYCHOLOGICAL LIFE

Introduction: From Reflection to Metaphor

The science of psychology is the modern historical appearance of psychological life. This distinction between the science of psychology and psychological life, which emerged from the acknowledged difference between the short history of psychology as a science and the long past of confusion of psychological experience with other human endeavors, initiated this work. The distinction has been valuable because it has enabled us to recover the positive sense of confusion which reveals psychological life as a reality of reflection. Psychological life is always in the middle of things, and since the sixteenth century it has been reflected through a physics of nature and a physiology of the body. On the other hand, this distinction has allowed us to see that scientific psychology conceals psychological life *in* the reflections *through* which it appears. More specifically, the short history of psychology as a science demonstrates how the *difference* between psychological experience and the material conditions through which it appears—a physics of the world and a science of the body—is forgotten in favor of an *identity* between them. *In* the density of matter, scientific psychology finds the stimuli which trigger the responses of psychological life, and *in* the darkness of the body it discovers the physiological foundations which allow them.

But modern scientific psychology not only conceals psychological life, it also remains unaware of this concealment. Indeed the distinction between the science of psychology and psychological life is absent, and

as a consequence psychology believes that it sees *in* the mirror of phys-
ics/physiology the literal facts of psychological life. The mirror becomes a mask which not only conceals the character of psychological life
as a reality of reflection, but also conceals this concealment.

I would be remiss however if I did not add here that this tendency
toward concealment is not a fault which exclusively characterizes modern scientific psychology. It is not only that the science of psychology
conceals psychological life, it is also that psychological life conceals itself in the science of psychology. Concealment is an aspect of psychological life as a reality of reflection. It is an intrinsic feature of its confusion. The particular materials through which psychological life appears
are and *are not* what it is, and this manner of concealment, this way of
being elusive, is how psychological life *matters*. As a reality of reflection,
psychological life matters by not being literally what it is.

The work of this text, therefore, has been one of de-literalization.
The recovery of psychological life as psychological has been a work of
metaphoring. This has been the method called for by the appearance of
psychological life as a reality of reflection, and this appearance has led to
the suggestion that psychological life is a metaphorical reality. In this
concluding chapter I want to support this suggestion. More specifically
I want to illustrate how psychological life in its texture, structure and
function is a metaphorical reality. The task has two specific meanings.

First, the reader should not expect to find in this chapter an elaborate treatment of metaphor, since my purpose is to illustrate how psychological life is a metaphorical reality. It is not a psychology or philosophy of metaphor which is at issue here but the appearance of psychological life as metaphorical. To be sure this task requires a knowledge
of what is a metaphor and a valid use of this knowledge. My assumptions, therefore, about what is a metaphor must be explicit if my illustrations of psychological life as metaphorical are to be believed. I intend
to do this by discussing those approaches to metaphor which inform my
illustrations.

Second, in proposing that psychological life is a metaphorical reality I am not offering a new metaphor for psychology. It is only too
apparent that psychology does not need another metaphor. If any-

thing, my proposal addresses itself to the rich abundance of metaphor which characterizes the birth, development, and present condition of psychology and asks that we draw the obvious conclusion: psychology abounds in metaphors because psychological life matters metaphorically.

The Metaphorical Texture of Psychological Life

In his book *The Changing Nature of Man*, J. H. van den Berg cites a passage from the diary of Jean Cocteau, French playwright and critic. The passage describes an event which happened to Cocteau when he visited his childhood home. The story which it tells is worthy of our attention.

Finding himself one day in his childhood neighborhood, Cocteau returned to the house where he had spent his youth. Entering the back yard, he was noticing how things had changed when he was interrupted by a man who inquired about his reasons for being there. Unable to persuade the man of his intentions, Cocteau was forced to leave. Disappointed and not wishing to forget his past too soon, Cocteau recalled how as a child he had walked near the houses and had trailed his finger along the wall. Repeating this action, Cocteau hoped to remember the past. The results, however, were disappointing. The memories which came were thin and pale. Suddenly, however, he recalled that as a child his hand trailed along the wall at a different level. He was smaller at that time. Bending down and closing his eyes, Cocteau again moved his finger along the wall. The result was astonishing. He writes: "Just as the needle picks up the melody from a record, I obtained the melody of my past with my hand. I found everything: my cape, the leather of my satchel, the names of my friends and of my teachers, certain expressions I had used, the sound of my granfather's voice, the smell of his beard, the smell of my sister's dresses and of my mother's gown."[1]

Certainly, Cocteau's experience, which reminds one so much of the work of Marcel Proust, is not an extraordinary occurrence. Each of us at one time or another has had the past enlivened in a similar way, and if we are not as gifted as Cocteau in describing it, we nevertheless are able to understand his experience. But while the experience is not remarkable, it does raise an important issue. If one listens to Cocteau's account, then there is no doubt that for him his experience is given through the wall. His experience is a place, and it *takes place* over there through the wall. His experience occurs there, and that wall is its place. Standing on the street and trying to command the past, Cocteau fails. When he bends down, closes his eyes, and trails his finger along the wall, the past returns. Cocteau adopts an attitude, a posture, toward the past. He embodies the past again, and the wall which he touches opens up the past. Cocteau enters the past again through the wall. That wall is his memory.

The wall is a memory! Cocteau's account makes this claim, and our lives bear witness to its validity. We surround ourselves with mementoes and souvenirs, with those things which give our experiences their place. Such things embody a past. We believe it. But just as much as we believe this claim, we are taught that it cannot be true. Things are only things, bits of extended matter. The wall is only brick and stone, a dense, indifferent material reality. Cocteau, therefore, may say what he wishes, but we know better. We know the wall cannot be the memory. We know the memory belongs to Cocteau.

The memory belongs to Cocteau! It comes from him and/or is produced by him. It is his memory. It belongs to him, which means it resides inside him.

How does memory reside inside Cocteau? Here the answer is rather easy. The memory is in Cocteau either as an *idea* which is then projected onto the wall, or as an empirical *factual* event which occurs in his brain. This easiness, however, is deceptive, because with it we bypass too easily the way in which this answer ignores experience. Cocteau neither speaks about nor experiences projected ideas or neurological patterns in his brain. He experiences his childhood taking place over there through the wall, and he describes his finger in touch with its face. To speak what we know, to say that the memory is Cocteau's idea, is to dismiss the wall as only a screen which receives the projections. Or to say that the memory is those physiological events which occur in his brain is to dismiss the wall as a stimulus which triggers those events.[2] In either case, as a stimulus or a screen, the wall does not matter. Or it is better to say here that in either case the wall is allowed to matter in only one way, as the so-called real wall of brick and stone. This real wall, the wall whose reality is identified with its materiality, is saved if the experience is explained as either a physiological fact or a subjective idea. This reality of the wall is saved if psychology situates its explanation between the bricklayer's wall, which is everybody's wall, and the anatomist's body, with or without mind, which is everybody's body. The wall is saved, however, at the price of Cocteau's experience. We are taught to save walls by forgetting experience.

Such a teaching, according to van den Berg, belongs to the "unfriendly science" of psychology, and he rightly contests its view that "Memories are within us, without our inner life" by reaffirming what we first experience and believe. The "memories are within the wall," he writes, and this is the "real and true reality."[3] In spite of what we are taught, therefore, we remain confronted with that wall which insists that its reality is as a memory. It is an insistence which is logically, scientifically, and literally absurd. But it is also an insistence which is psychologically sound. A respect for psychological experience leads us back to the wall. The memories are there within it. Of this we are sure and are assured by Cocteau. He describes his experience in this fashion, and a brief look at his behavior confirms it.

Cocteau initially stands on the street trying to recall his past. Probably he is motionless in this effort of concentration, but at one point he begins to move toward the wall. He no longer stands back from it in an attitude of detached contemplation. On the contrary, he intentionally moves toward the wall to touch it with his finger. He *traces* his finger along the wall, and from his diary account we know that in that moment he recovers his memory. Motionless just a moment ago, it seems as if Cocteau has been called by the wall to touch that place. This call seems irresistible. Would it not also seem this way to any of us? Indeed has not each of us at one time or another felt a similar temptation, in the presence of an old keepsake of one of our children for example? The toy which he once used and which I have accidently found again always solicits more than a distant gaze. It *moves* me in both senses of the term. I am touched by it and I touch it, and in touching it I am in touch with him, my child, again. Cocteau behaves in the same fashion and his *behavior* leaves no doubt that his memory is "in" the wall. The question, however, is how a memory is *within* a wall. Is it within the wall in the same way that the science of psychology says it is within the brain? Is the memory hidden somewhere in the cracks of the wall as it is supposedly hidden in the folds of the brain? Does it lie among the particles of sand which compose the wall?

Obviously an affirmative answer to any of these questions is not possible, and yet Cocteau's specific analogy of the needle and the record shows how difficult it is to understand the way in which the memory does lie within the wall. Our understanding is advanced, however, by another return to Cocteau's behavior.

Cocteau *touches* the wall with his finger. His hand does not break the wall. The finger which *traces* the line of his memory is a care-ful one; it is a finger filled with care and one which seems to know the fragility of the occasion. His finger, we might say, grazes the wall; it does not penetrate it. His finger touches the wall in a way which acknowledges that the memory which is "in" the wall will not be found among the grains of sand. Indeed it is easy to imagine in Cocteau's behavior a moment of hesitation at the boundary of the wall, as if to say that there is a doubt that the memory is there, and Cocteau's behavior confirms this imagined hesitation. *He closes his eyes.* When he touches the wall, he closes his eyes. Touching hand and closed eyes are in coordination. His eyes betray the hesitant touch, and this hand and eye behavior reveal that the memory *is not* the wall. Touching hand and closed eyes reveal that the memory is not in the wall in any literal way. A scrutinizing eye does not guide a hand searching for something which can be seen.

Cocteau's behavior leaves no doubt that his memory is "in" the wall. His memory is not an idea in his mind nor an event in his brain. But his behavior also leaves no doubt that his memory is not "in" the wall. Cocteau closes his eyes, and he sees in this way. His closed eyes are a way of seeing. If the memory is within the wall, then it is there in this particular way. It is there as a way of seeing. It is not there as something to be seen. We may say then that Cocteau's memories are "in" the wall in the same way that the mirror reflection is "in" the mirror. That wall mirrors Cocteau's experience. Cocteau sees *through* the wall the memory of his child-

[margin handwritten note: he need to see the wall like we need to see out a mirror in a mirror reflection]

hood.

A wall on a street in Paris is a reality through which another reality is given, the memory of one's childhood. Who can believe it? Anyone can who is seeing psychologically, if the wall is allowed to matter as a psychological reality. No one can who refuses to break or to suspend the "prejudice of the real."[4] If one's eye remains fixed with a literal vision, if it remains the apparatus described by anatomy and physiology to which there necessarily corresponds the wall as only a physical reality, then one must dismiss Cocteau's experience as a subjective idea or explain it away with scientific facts. But between the idea and the fact psychological experience is lost, because it is neither an idea nor a fact. The Cocteau example illustrates this point. We are convinced that his memory is given through the wall, but we are also puzzled in this domain which belongs neither to the fact nor to the idea. Fidelity to psychological experience on its own terms leads us beyond these alternatives of fact and idea, thing and thought, empirical and mental reality toward a metaphorical reality. But a second and third example are needed.

DANTE'S LAKE OF ICE AND HÖLDERLIN'S JOYOUS WAVES

Douglas Berggren has written two illuminating articles entitled "The Use and Abuse of Metaphor." The examples which I use here and much of my discussion are drawn from him. The first example concerns the poet Dante's description of "a lake of ice at the bottom of Hell."[5] In what sense, we may ask, is this description true?

In answer to this question, Berggren initially considers the position of the literary critic Northrop Frye, who insists that the truth of Dante's description does not depend on whether or not a lake of ice *actually* exists in Hell, or even whether Hell exists. Dante's description is not a factual account and to treat it as such is to miss the metaphorical character of the claim. Berggren agrees with Frye on this point, and in further support of this position he cites Paul Weiss, who says that "any metaphor is implicitly akin to a counterfactual statement."[6]

According to Berggren, however, Frye's next step goes too far because it implies that the lake of ice is an idea insofar as it emphasizes that "the final direction of meaning is *inward*."[7] Berggren objects here that such a step would destroy any sense at all of the truth value of Dante's vision. The metaphor as only an idea, as only a pure mental creation, would lack support from the side of the world. It would show us nothing. It would leave us blind with respect to the human condition. But Dante's metaphor is a way of seeing, and through it we do see something of the cold loneliness of a human life when it exists in a state of selfish isolation. Berggren concludes, therefore, that while Frye's position is helpful, it nevertheless leaves unanswered the sense in which a metaphor presents a valid reality which is neither factual nor rational.

At this point Berggren offers another example. He considers the German poet Hölderlin's reference to the "joyous undulation of the waves" at Lake Constance. Hölderlin looks at the moving waves and through them he sees joy. Rejecting the argument which would convert the poet's experience into a projection of emotions onto a neutral factual reality, Berggren says that these waves are a "textural reality."[8] He argues that these waves "are not inner feelings, emotional reactions, or mere projections,"[9] and he states that to regard them as such is not only "irrelevant from a phenomenological point of view; it is also based on the faulty supposition that objects are initially apprehended in a completely sterilized or immaculate manner."[10] The joyous waves are an experienced reality, and to regard them as Hölderlin's emotional idea is to deny their validity as a perceptible reality. These waves are not simply contaminated or polluted by Hölderlin's emotions of joy. Nevertheless, Berggren adds again that "no purely immaculate perceiver would detect them," because this joy is not merely a fact to be seen. He concludes, therefore, that "while textural perception is not independent of the senses,"[11] it is not reducible to or identical with the empirical facts of sensation. And in all of this Berggren is affirming the validity of a textural reality which belongs neither to the inwardness of thought nor the outwardness of things. He is affirming the metaphorical validity of textural reality.

Cocteau's experience is like these joyous waves of Hölderlin and/or like Dante's lake of ice at the pit of Hell. None of these experiences are either facts or ideas, and no one of them makes either an empirical or logical claim of truth. Nevertheless each of them does make a claim of truth, and if we are to appreciate this claim, if we are to appreciate the reality of each of these experiences on its own terms, then we must acknowledge the validity of metaphor. Each example opens up the world in a metaphorical way. Each one involves us with a metaphorical reality. *Metaphorical textures are psychological* (and poetic) *matters.*[12] If we are to appreciate psychological life on its own terms and the claim of truth which it makes upon us, then we must appreciate how the reality of metaphor lies between empirical and mental reality.

METAPHORS, THINGS, AND THOUGHTS

A metaphor, the literary critic Howard Nemerov says, "stands somewhat as a mediating term between a thing and a thought."[13] It claims, in other words, neither the eye nor the mind. A metaphor is no more a matter of what the eye sees than it is a matter of what the mind thinks. It is no more a question of perception than it is a question of conception. A metaphor neither discovers a fact which is already there, nor creates an idea out of nothing. On the contrary, *a metaphor embodies mind and minds the body.* It brings mind to eye and incarnates mind. With a metaphor eye is deepened through mind and mind now matters through eye. Nemerov illustrates this point with a vivid example:

> While I am thinking about metaphor, a flock of purple finches arrives on the lawn. Since I haven't seen these birds for some years, I am only fairly sure of their being in fact purple finches, so I get down Peterson's *Field Guide* and read his description: "Male: About size of House Sparrow, rosy-red, brightest on head and rump." That checks quite well, but his next remark — "a sparrow dipped in raspberry juice" — is decisive: it fits. I look out the window again, and now I *know* that I am seeing purple finches.
>
> That's very simple. So simple, indeed, that I hesitate to look any further into the matter, for as soon as I do I shall see that its simplicity is not altogether ucanny. Why should I be made certain of what a purple finch is by being led to contemplate a sparrow dipped in raspberry juice? Have I ever dipped a sparrow in raspberry juice?

Has anyone? And yet there it is, quite certain and quite right. Peterson and I and the finches are in agreement.[14]

This simple example secures the reality of metaphor. A purple finch is a sparrow dipped in raspberry juice and it is through the metaphor that Nemerov sees this reality. But please notice that he sees something which is not factually there to be seen. Through a sparrow dipped in raspberry juice he sees the purple finches, even though the finches are neither sparrows nor dripping with juice. Should Nemerov leave his house and enter his garden, should he capture one of those birds, no juicy sparrow would be discovered among them. A purple finch is not such a juicy sparrow. That much is *factually* true. And yet when Nemerov looks he sees the purple finch which *is* a raspberry-dipped sparrow. This way of seeing and of speaking is more than Peterson's or Nemerov's idea. Peterson, Nemerov and the birds all agree: these purple finches which are sparrows dipped in juice are no mere fiction. A reality which is neither fact nor fiction, thing nor thought, is opened up by the metaphor. And indeed as Nemerov himself states, the metaphor is the decisive moment.

Nemerov looks with a metaphorical eye and think how much he would miss if he insisted on an empirical vision. Think of what would be lost if Nemerov in a sudden burst of empirical frenzy insisted that the finches are not empirically, literally, or factually sparrows dipped in juice. He would be proving an empirical fact but at the point of becoming blind. Nemerov could no longer see the purple finches.

Cocteau's experience is essentially no different, and to insist in this case on either a scientific-empirical or a philosophical-logical explanation of it would destroy the experience. I do not doubt that it is factually true and empirically verifiable that Cocteau's experience is a neurological event. Nor do I doubt that Cocteau's behavior is evidence of mindful activity. But between mind and brain the memory-wall is lost. Between these categories of science and philosophy, between fact and idea, Cocteau's experience as he behaved it and as he described it is lost. We hear Cocteau and we understand him because he has told a story. It is a story about age, about the memory of lost youth, and about the things of the world, these metaphorical pre-things, which anchor and preserve a human life. For the sake of science, do we wish to lose this story? For the sake of being empirically minded, do we want to lose the poetry of experience? Story makes experience believable, and experience makes a believable story. The metaphorical texture of psychological life opens up this domain of the story.

The Metaphorical Structure of Psychological Life

In the *Poetics* Aristotle defines a metaphor as "the application of an alien name by transference either from genus to species, or from species to genus, or from species to species, or by analogy, that is, proportion."[15] This definition inspires what Cyril Dwiggins calls the "transfer tradition"[16] of metaphor. It is a tradition which presumes that the transfer of meaning is based on a similarity or a likeness between things. It is a tradition which emphasizes resemblance as the core of metaphor. As such, therefore, this tradition, which offers perhaps the most common conception of metaphor, reduces metaphor to a factual datum. Metaphor becomes a special case of simile: the likeness or resemblance which a metaphor hides is nevertheless at its base. A is *like* B, even though I may say A *is* B. A literal likeness between A and B is the condition for metaphor, and the likeness about which it speaks is all that it means. A metaphor, then, is essentially a comparison which tells us that and maybe how one reality is like another.

From the viewpoint of this tradition, the wall through which Cocteau remembers his childhood cannot be a metaphorical object, because there is no way, obvious or otherwise, in which a wall is like a memory or a memory is like a wall. In spite of its metaphorical texture, therefore, it is not structured as a metaphor. In this psychological experience, the comparative structure of metaphor has no place.

Max Black and I. A. Richards, among others, however, have criticized this comparison theory of metaphor. Black rejects the comparison theory on the grounds that it loses the metaphor because it substitutes a literal meaning for the non-literal one.[17] Richards complains that speaking of one thing as though it were another or like another misunderstands a metaphor, because it implies that a literal translation of the

metaphorical claim can always and easily be made.[18] Both criticisms, therefore, focus on the literal bias of this comparison theory. The comparative structure of metaphor undoes its metaphorical character.

Dwiggins makes another objection. Not only is the comparison theory
of metaphor questionable, it is not even supported in the *Poetics* of
Aristotle. He claims that "a close reading of *Poetics* 21 makes it impossible to interpret Aristotle's conception of 'transference' as a comparison
of objects or a covert assertion of literal likeness."[19] Considering Aristotle's
first three types of metaphor, he notes that the important point is
"Aristotle's *unwillingness* to say anything like 'We transfer a name from
one object to another in order to express the similarity we perceive between the two.'" "If this is what *metaphora* is all about," Dwiggins says,
"why not say so plainly . . .?"[20] Dwiggins' extensive discussion of Aristotle's
fourth type of metaphor, the proportional metaphor, makes it clear
that Aristotle does not say so plainly because similarity is not what metaphor is all about.

This fourth type of metaphor exists when the terms of the metaphor, A-B-C-D, are structured in such a fashion that "the second term is
to the first as the fourth to the third." Thus a proportional metaphor
exists when B is related to A as D is related to C. "We may then use the
fourth for the second, or the second for the fourth."[21] Aristotle's example is "As old age is to life, so evening is to day." The metaphor, then,
may be "Old age is the evening of life." And the metaphor works, according to Dwiggins, not because there is a direct resemblance between
old age and evening, but because a relationship between old age and life
"parallels" a relationship between evening and the day.[22] In place of any
theory of resemblance at the heart of Aristotle's theory of metaphor,
Dwiggins suggests that a metaphor offers a relation in which one reality
parallels another. But what precisely is the meaning of this parallel?

An example used by Dwiggins suggests an answer to this question.
His example is provided by Winston Churchill, who called Mussolini
"that utensil." The meaning of the metaphor is clear. Mussolini is to
Hitler as a tool is to its user. In the briefest possible way, the metaphor
describes its subject. Vividly and immediately the listener understands
the character of Mussolini. But this understanding is not based upon any

resemblance between Mussolini and a utensil, and indeed if such resemblance is established, as it was by the political cartoons of the day, it is in fact incidental to the metaphor. On the contrary, the understanding seems to be based upon a *vision* or *a way of seeing* which one relationship sets up for the other. The tool in relation to its user is a *reflection* of the relation between Hitler and Mussolini. Dwiggins' parallel, we might say, turns out to be a way of seeing one reality through another, a relation of reflection. A metaphor, then, is not essentially a way of seeing how one reality is *like* another. It is a way of seeing one reality *through* another. Its resemblance, if we should call it that, is the resemblance which a reflection bears to the reality of which it is a reflection. It is not a real (factual) resemblance but a resemblance where likeness is a difference.

A concern for the metaphorical structure of psychological life moves metaphor toward reflection, and in this respect this present chapter and this book turn back upon themselves since they began with a movement from reflection to metaphor. Psychological life and metaphor, it seems, converge on this theme of reflection. Indeed, if psychological life as a reality of reflection is a metaphor, it is because a metaphor is essentially a reality of reflection. This convergence should not be a surprise. As we have already seen, a reflection deepens and re-figures reality, and a metaphor is, if anything, a deepening of the reality which it reflects by re-figuring the context in which it appears. One's understanding of old age, for example, is deepened when it is figured by the context of the waning day.

This convergence, moreover, is not only unsurprising but also helpful, because it *specifies* the structure of metaphor as a paradox of identity-difference. As a reflection a metaphor does have a likeness pole, but only insofar as there is a pole of difference. A metaphor says not only that X is like Y, but also that it is unlike Y. Indeed it indicates that X is Y because it is not Y. The remarks which follow develop this theme of paradox, and insofar as they do they also indicate that the metaphorical structure of psychological life is the paradox of identity-difference. Cocteau's memory is the wall because his memory is not the wall.

PARADOX

In his recent book, *The Rule of Metaphor*, Paul Ricoeur writes that the "is not" of metaphor is "implied in the impossibility of the literal interpretation, [and] present as a filigree in the metaphorical 'is.'"[23] And I. A. Richards in his now-classic distinction between the vehicle and the tenor of metaphor points out that the "peculiar modification of the tenor which the vehicle brings about is even more the work of their unlikenesses than of their likenesses."[24] A metaphor, therefore, may impress the hearer with the likeness which it imagines, but it is the *difference which makes the metaphor.* I do not mean here a real, factual, empirical difference, but *the difference which a metaphor makes* in the sense of the reflection of reality which it allows. The Harveian *metaphor* of "the heart as a pump," for example, *makes a difference* in terms of the histories of medicine and science. But this metaphor can make a difference because of the difference which makes the metaphor. The heart is a pump precisely because it is not a pump, and this difference, which does not matter *before* the metaphor, now matters in the most essential way. The difference which before the metaphor is merely factual becomes the matter of a metaphor.

One of the more interesting presentations of the paradoxical structure of metaphor is the one which is offered by Douglas Berggren.[25] He situates this theme within a dialectical movement from mythic ambiguity through literal nonsense or absurdity toward metaphorical tension, and he indicates that disruption is the condition which sets this dialectic in motion. It is an interesting argument because this development of metaphor from myth through the literal reflects the historical path of psychological life suggested in this work. This work recovers psychological life as a metaphorical reality from its literal appearance in scientific psychology, and James Hillman's works[26] present the older appearance of psychological life as myth, even while they critically examine that appearance from a metaphorical perspective. In addition Berggren's emphasis on disruption reflects what will be discussed later under the metaphorical function of psychological life.

The present relevance of Berggren's argument is, however, in relation to the theme of structure, and within this context the example of justice can be used to illustrate this point. In the mythic stage of experience, I may believe naïvely in the inevitable triumph of justice — that murderers will eventually be punished, for example, because murder is believed to be wrong — and I may therefore conduct my relations with others according to this belief. But then one day I may suffer an injustice which shakes my naïve belief: a close friend may, in all good conscience, inadvertently frame me for a murder I did not commit, and the courts of justice, acting in accordance with those very tenets of justice I believe in, may mistakenly convict me and condemn me to a life of imprisoned solitude. *Justice*, which I uphold as the paragon of the good, now metes out *injustice*, which I abhor as evil. At this point I am faced with a conflict between what I believe in and what has happened. A contradiction has been thrown up before me between my belief that justice is good and my experience which demonstrates that the actions of justice are, in this case at least, evil. According to Berggren's argument, I am forced by this impasse to recognize that a solution to the contradiction is *literally* impossible, and it is at this point that experience and language become metaphorical. The impossibility of a literal solution gives rise to a metaphorical style of experience and expression. Contradiction becomes paradox. The tension between the belief and the occurrence becomes the core of the experience. The blindness of justice is understood in another fashion. The sword of justice cuts two ways. Now I no longer naïvely and literally believe that the blindness promises impartiality. On the contrary, it becomes the source of my being unfairly wronged and unjustly jailed. But insofar as the blindness of justice has become a metaphor, I have not simply moved from naïve hope to a naïve despair. I have not simply changed one myth — the literal, naïve belief in impartiality — for another — the literal, and equally naïve belief in no justice at all. Rather, *the metaphor* in denying that the blindness is a literal being-in-the-dark affirms another truth. It affirms the limited vision of justice, its *human* imperfection.

This may be small solace to one who wishes to maintain the earlier belief. The move from myth to metaphor seems to offer little comfort. It appears, however, that Berggren accepts this consequence which seems to find confirmation in daily life. If we extend the sense of mythic experience to include those myths of everyday life by which we live, the myths embodied in our habits, customs, and routines, then the pain experienced by their contradiction by events seems hardly lessened by the move to metaphor. And yet the metaphor which embraces both sides, which "lowers" the belief to accord with events and "raises" events to be touched by the belief, is therapeutic when compared with the pain of literal contradiction. What may be experienced as a painful loss from the viewpoint of the mythic stage of belief and experience is a therapeutic gain from the viewpoint of the literal contradiction of one's belief and experiences.

We are not, however, directly concerned with the therapeutic value of metaphor.[27] It is the issue of a metaphor's structure which concerns us, and Berggren's work affirms the paradoxical character of this structure. A metaphor, he says, is the transition from "the naïve thesis of mythic ambiguity, through the reflective antithesis of literal nonsense or absurdity, to the more sophisticated tensional principle of identity-in-difference."[28] The dialectical story of metaphor which Berggren tells affirms, therefore, this identity-in-difference paradox of metaphor, and in this regard he stands between two inadequate traditions. According to Ricoeur, who discusses these two traditions, the first one is inadequate because in its naïveté it affirms only the identity aspect and thereby "ignores the implicit 'is not.'" The second one is inadequate because "under the critical pressure of the 'is not,' [it] loses the 'is' by reducing it to the 'as-if' of a reflective judgment." In the first instance, a metaphor becomes almost a literal definition. In the second, metaphor becomes only a comparison. Moreover, Ricoeur also situates "metaphorical truth" in the same way.[29] The paradox of identity-difference is not only the structure of metaphor, but also the realization of its truth.

There are, of course, others who defend the paradoxical structure of metaphor, but it is perhaps more illuminating at this point to offer two examples. They are poems. The first one is from the Chinese *Tao Teh Ching* of Lao Tse.

We put thirty spokes together and call it a wheel;
But it is on the space where there is nothing that the utility of
   the wheel depends.
We turn clay to make a vessel;
But it is on the space where there is nothing that the utility of
   the vessel depends.
We pierce doors and windows to make a house;
And it is on these spaces where there is nothing that the utility
      of the house depends.
Therefore just as we take advantage of what is, we should recognize
   the utility of what is not.[30]

The second poem is by Wallace Stevens. It is entitled "Thirteen
Ways of Looking at a Blackbird."

   I
Among twenty snowy mountains,
The only moving thing
Was the eye of the blackbird.
   II
I was of three minds,
Like a tree
In which there are three blackbirds.
   III
The black bird whirled in the autumn winds.
It was a small part of the pantomime.
   IV
A man and a woman
Are one.
A man and a woman and a blackbird
Are one.
   V
I do not know which to prefer,
The beauty of inflections
Or the beauty of innuendoes,

The blackbirds whistling
Or just after.
VI
Icicles filled the long window
with barbaric glass.
The shadow of the blackbird
Crossed it, to and fro.
The mood
Traced in the shadow
An indecipherable cause.
VII
O thin men of Haddam,
Why do you imagine golden birds?
Do you not see how the blackbird
Walks around the feet
Of the women about you?
VIII
I know noble accents
And lucid, inescapable rhythms;
But I know, too,
That the blackbird is involved
In what I know.
IX
When the blackbird flew out of sight,
It marked the edge
Of one of many circles.
X
At the sight of blackbirds
Flying in a green light,
Even the bawds of euphony
Would cry out sharply.
XI
He rode over Connecticut
In a glass coach.
Once, a fear pierced him,

In that he mistook
The shadow of his equipage
For blackbirds.
XII
The river is moving.
The blackbird must be flying.
XIII
It was evening all afternoon.
It was snowing
And it was going to snow.
The blackbird sat
In the cedar-limbs.[31]

Two poems! One emphasizes the essential usefulness of what is not for what is, and the other makes the same point in another fashion. In each of thirteen separate stanzas the blackbird appears. Is it the same blackbird across the thirteen different stanzas, or is it thirteen different blackbirds? Is the blackbird the bird which appears in the first stanza, the fourth, the tenth? Or is it each of these appearances even while it is not any one of them?

To the first question the poem certainly does not allow a choice of either alternative. To the second question it answers with a positive reply to the third. The blackbird is and is not the bird which appears in each stanza. The poem embraces the tension of identity-difference. The eye of the blackbird which is the only moving thing among twenty snowy mountains is the same as and different from the blackbird which sits in the cedar-limbs when it is evening all afternoon.

Stevens' blackbird, like Cocteau's wall, is a metaphorical object. Each one is as much what it is not as it is what it is. But if Stevens' poem affirms the paradoxical structure of the metaphorical object, then it does so by tying this structure to the perspectival character of experience. There are thirteen ways of looking at a blackbird, the title says, and in each stanza the blackbird *is seen* in a different way and *one sees* differently. The poem awakens the reader to the reciprocal relation between the perspectival character of experience and the paradoxical character of what is experienced. Through the immediate juxtaposition of the thirteen stanzas, each one of which loosens the preceding identification of the blackbird, the reader is no longer able to forget the differences which haunt the habitual things of everyday perceptual life. Through the vehicle of each stanza the reader remembers that a blackbird, like a chair or a tree, is a way of seeing as much as it is a something to be seen. The poem is a work of therapy and education for the experiencing eye.

Stevens' poem, however, does even more than indicate that the metaphorical object is paradoxical because metaphorical experience is perspectival. It also suggests that each *perspective* is a *figure*. Read the stanzas again! Does not each one allude to a see-er? If each stanza offers a way of looking at a blackbird, a perspective, then does not each stanza also suggest the figure of a see-er who sees in this way? I grant the shadowy presence of the figure. But in spite of its elusiveness, it seems beyond doubt that the thirteen visions are also thirteen "visionaries." Stevens is not one see-er in that poem. Neither is the reader. Indeed, neither Stevens nor the reader is any more singular than the blackbird. On the contrary, a metaphor enlarges the self as much as the object. It de-literalizes the ego as much as the thing. It re-figures the person as much as the world.

The poem by Stevens *suggests* these points. It does not make them explicitly. Psychological experience, however, does make explicit this connection between paradox, perspective, and figure. Cocteau's experience, the wall which is a memory, prescribes a look, a way of seeing, a perspective, and it is clear that this wall is and is not a memory. But in the telling of the experience the presence of the figure is also clear. It is one who bends down, closes his eyes, and trails his finger along the wall. *As such* he enters his childhood again. He enters it by *embodying* or *figuring* his experience in an explicit way. What is implicit in linguistic metaphor — paradox, perspective, figure — becomes explicit in psychological experience as metaphorical. A second example, presented below, illustrates this point and presents again the metaphorical structure of psychological life.

FIGURING THE PERSPECTIVE

A metaphor is a perspective, suggests Kenneth Burke,[32] and indeed every metaphor says as much about a way of seeing as it does about what is seen. The utensil which Mussolini is says as much about the speaker Churchill in relation to Mussolini as it does about Mussolini. A metaphor, we might say, looks both ways: toward the speaker and the spoken.

The figure, however, is rarely and not necessarily specified. And yet I take seriously here the classification of metaphor as a "figure of speech." That phrase, a "figure of speech," has psychological value. It preserves the figure who gives concrete body to the metaphor as a figure of speech. Psychological experience recovers what the linguistic treatment of metaphor tends to forget. It recovers and preserves the figure, as this second example illustrates.

A Walk in the Park

Imagine a park, a sunny, soft, Sunday afternoon, and mid-Spring. It is a day to be outdoors, a day when the green of the grass mirrors the blue of the sky. Now add to this scene two young people, a man and a woman. They are strolling together, hand in hand. Nearing a giant oak tree whose full branches spread a cover of shade over the grass, they stop to eye the carving they have made in the tree. Their names are inscribed in its bark and this tree is their memory of that occasion.

A few yards distant from the tree and the couple, another young man stands looking at the tree. In front of him there is an easel and a box of paints. He is an artist. Looking at the tree, he also turns away from it from time to time in order to place on canvas what he sees.

Two other people now enter the scene. They are an older man and his young son, a boy of eight years. The father is a botanist and a teacher, and as he and his son amble through the park he points to the trees and gives each of them its scientific name. In front of the giant oak he stops and names it. "It belongs to the genus *Quercus*," he says, and then he goes on to explain the parts which compose the tree. It is a learned story which consumes the father, although the son seems uninterested.

Two young lovers, a painter, a botanist father and his young son in a park on a warm, Sunday afternoon! A scene of quiet contentment. The tranquility is, however, soon to be broken, for another man now appears. He is tall and rather muscular. Approaching the tree, he is carrying something in his hand. As he gets closer to the tree everyone is able to see it. A noise has attracted their attention. The tall, muscular man is carrying a chainsaw. He is a lumberjack. He has come to cut down the tree.

With this last arrival it is not difficult to imagine that a disagreement will erupt among the characters in this story. The painter will surely protest the destruction of this beautiful tree, while the two lovers will resist this threat to the memory of their love. The painter will even shout at the lumberjack. He will tell him that this tree is a work of art and as evidence he will invite him to look at his painting. The two lovers, on the other hand, will insist that the tree is their love, a part of their life together, and in support of their view they will point out to him the names that are carved on the tree. The lumberjack, however, will remain unmoved, and in answer to both of them he will say that this tree is a million yellow pencils. "The tree," he will insist, "is worth a lot of bucks," and in support of his position he will produce a contract from the Yellow Pencil Company which proves the value of his words. Arguing in this fashion, each will remain unmoved by the others. Each will insist that the tree which he or she sees is *the* tree, while the views of the others are only their feelings. At this point the botanist will interrupt and waving his doctoral diploma which he has just removed from his hip pocket, he will proceed to lecture to the group about the real reality of the tree. For a moment they will listen, but eventually they will be unconvinced by this scholarly demonstration, and the botanist will become only another participant in the disagreement. The argument will continue and each one will think that all the others are either blind or mad or lying.

It will not suffice, however, to end the story without stopping the argument. Thus we may imagine its ending through mutual exhaustion. Or, with equal plausibility, we may imagine a victory for power. The argument ends, then, with the fall of the tree. But another ending, which is also plausible and which suits better this scene of Sunday afternoon, involves the little boy. As the characters continue their disagreement, we can imagine that little boy, who was as bored by their argument as he was by his father's earlier lecture, slipping away from the crowd and climbing the tree. From atop his high perch he now looks down upon the gathering, and with sounds reminiscent of a diving fighter plane he begins to bombard the group with the leaves and acorns he has picked from the tree. The tree has become his airplane, and if not out of a memory of their own childhood days of warm, sunny Sunday afternoons in the park, then at least out of irritation at this pesty little boy, we can imagine an end to the story.

A Brief Reflection

Certainly I grant to the reader the fantastic nature of the story. A lumberjack in a park on a Sunday afternoon preparing to cut down a tree transforms what could be an ordinary scene into something which seems more like a dream. The point, however, has nothing to do with the actual occurrence of the event. The tree which each one sees is a multiple reality. More accurately, the tree which each one sees and about which each one speaks is a metaphorical reality.

There is a disagreement among the characters in the story because each of them sees a different tree. The tree which is a painting for one is a profit for another. The tree which is a future profit for one is a memory of the past for another.

The disagreement, however, would be impossible if this tree was only these differences. No one of the characters regards his or her experience of the tree as private, interior, or subjective, and the occurrence of the argument is evidence that no one regards the experiences of the others in this way. They argue about the tree because each one takes seriously the ways in which each of the others sees the tree. Indeed, if each one did not regard the arguments of the others in this fashion, then each one could readily and easily dismiss those arguments. The arguments of the others would have no bearing on the tree. They would be illusions. Thus, in spite of what each one may think of the others' viewpoints — they are blind or mad or lying — their action together bears witness to what they actually believe. The argument is about the tree. The *different* trees which each one sees and experiences are nevertheless the *same* tree.

The story clearly illustrates, therefore, the paradoxical character of metaphorical reality. In addition it also illustrates the perspectival character of metaphorical experience. The *tree* which each one sees is understandable in relation to or as a reflection of the *see-er*. The tree is a million pencils for profit when one sees it in a particular fashion, when one is within the perspective of the lumberjack. Conversely it is an object of science when the see-er is within the perspective of the botanist. Of course, this point does not mean that the perspective creates the tree which is seen. It means only that without a perspective, a way of seeing, there is no tree. The price of being a thing, Merleau-Ponty suggests, is that it be seen from somewhere[33], and this somewhere is always more than a physical place. It is a way of being in place, a psychological style. In addition, as George Herbert Mead points out, the individual is in the perspective, not the perspective in the individual.[34] The paradoxical character of this metaphorical object finds its counterpart, then, in the perspectival character of metaphorical vision.

Both of these points, however, simply dramatize what has been already indicated in the discussion of metaphor, and if the story went only this far its value would consist only in being another example. The story, however, does make an additional point. It explicates the point about the figure. Each way of seeing the tree, each perspective, is a figure, a type. There is the sensitive artist, the pedantic botanist, the playful but irritating young son, the muscular but insensitive lumberjack, and the tender lovers. Each perspective is embodied. Each perspective is *figured* in a concrete way. If you compare this story, then, with the poem by Wallace Stevens, the value of it becomes clear. The figure which is always implicit in the linguistic metaphor is explicit in psychological experience as metaphorical. Stated in another fashion: the story indicates that the metaphorical structure of psychological life is always a *figured* reality. Figure moves metaphor psychologically! It is not only through a perspective that we enter the world; it is also, and most importantly psychologically, as a figure that we enter the world.

A CLOSING EXAMPLE

Ortega y Gasset perhaps more than any other thinker in recent times has drawn our attention to the vital presence of metaphor in human life. "Compare what the earth means for a peasant and for an astronomer," he advises. For the peasant "it is enough to *tread* the planet's reddish skin and *scratch* it with his plow; his earth is a *path*, some *furrows* and a *field of grain*." On the other hand, "the astronomer must *determine exactly the place* which the globe occupies at every instant within the *enormous supposition of sidereal space*, *the point of view of exactitude* obliges him to convert it into a *mathematical abstraction*, into a case of universal gravitation."[35] For each one the same earth opens in a different way. The peasant knows the earth through his crops and in his hands. The astronomer knows the earth through his numbers and in his mind. Thus, Ortega writes that "each 'thing' is . . . *many things* [and that] it has no being 'in itself', but gradually acquires one in the different vital *functions* which it assumes." Functions! What are they? They are the enactment of one's perspective, the figuring of it, its embodiment. They are this *treading* and this *scratching* of the earth; they are this *exact determination of its place*. Paradox, perspective, and figure all coalesce in Ortega's thought, and this confluence is "the thematic use of the metaphor."[36] But Ortega, who so beautifully illustrates the metaphorical character of experience and the world, is bothered by a question: "When will we become open to the conviction that the definitive being of the world is . . . not any particular thing, but a perspective?"[37] The answer, it seems, is when we become open to the psychological character of experience and the world. The answer, in other words, is when we become more fully open to the psychological character of metaphor, and/or the metaphorical character of psychological life. Two steps have already been taken in this direction in the discussions of the metaphorical texture and structure of psychological life. One additional step now needs to be made.

The Metaphorical Function of Psychological Life

Psychological experience is textured and structured metaphorically. But does psychological experience function metaphorically? Let us begin with an example of psychological experience to see what can be learned of its functioning. Then we can ask about the function of metaphor.

PSYCHOLOGICAL EXPERIENCE AND DISRUPTION

The example, illustrated in Figure 7, is taken from an article by Gaetano Kanizsa entitled "Subjective Contours," where it is used to demonstrate how "subjective contours have the same functional effects as real contours." The figure on the left is the Ponzo illusion, and "although both vertical lines are the same length, the effect of the subjective triangle is to make the line at the left appear to be longer." For the Poggendorf illusion, which is the figure on the right, "the subjective surface gives rise to an apparent displacement of the slanted line."[38] Since both figures lend themselves equally well to the present discussion, my remarks are confined to the figure on the left, the Ponzo illusion.

The Ponzo figure is called an illusion because in spite of what we see the two vertical lines are the same length. The left line, which appears to be longer, is not the least bit longer than the line on the right. Measure them with a ruler. They are the same. The ruler confirms that our eyes are deceived. The ruler-guided eye "sees" better than the living eye. The ruler removes the illusion.

But if the ruler removes the illusion, then what is the cause of the illusion? It is the *subjective* triangle. The white triangle which we see among the black incomplete circles *stretches* the left line. It *transforms* the measured lines. It *distorts* this measured reality. That experienced triangle *disrupts* the expected, habitual, and certain length of the line. This triangle, however, is not really there. In fact it is as much of an illusion as the *longer* left line. It only appears to be present; it has no basis in *physical* reality. Nothing registers on the *physiological* eye. The

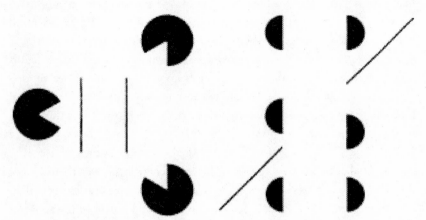

Figure 7. Left, the Ponzo illusion; *right,* the Poggendorf illusion. From "Subjective Contours," by Gaetano Kanizsa. Copyright © 1976 by Scientific American, Inc. All rights reserved.

triangle is only a psychological experience. It is a subjective reality. Nevertheless, this psychological reality disrupts those two real (measured) lines. The subjective triangle, the psychological triangle, has an experienced effect, and that is Kanizsa's point. What is *subjective* nevertheless affects what is *real.* What is *not real* nevertheless transforms what is *real.* What is *psychological* nevertheless disrupts what is *real.*

Everyone, it seems, should agree with this conclusion because the evidence is right there before our eyes. The left line is stretched beyond its fixed, measured reality. But should we so readily agree with the conclusion, especially when the argument that supports it should be questioned? Kanizsa's way of speaking betrays a "metaphysics of opposition" between the real and the psychological. Throughout the article reality is unquestionably located between physics and physiology. The lines which are "really" the same length are the measured lines as they are quantitatively known, and it is the optical system, the neutral eye, the disembodied eye of anatomy and physiology, which "sees" these lines. Within this context of reality by prescription, the figure as it is experienced is unreal. Between this physics of the line and this physiology of the eye, the figure as it is experienced is (only) psychological. In fact we may say that the Ponzo illusion is composed of two parts, or has two dimensions. There is the real dimension, which includes the two vertical lines of a fixed length and the three incomplete dark circles. And there is the unreal, psychological dimension, which includes a left line which is longer than the right one, and a white triangle which is situated among the three dark circles. But is the figure composed of these two parts? Does the figure support this metaphysics of opposition? Or is this metaphysical vision *imposed* upon the figure?

Look at the figure again. The triangle is no more subjective than the two vertical lines and/or the three black circles. It is over there before the see-er as much as the lines and circles are there. It is no less real than any other part of the figure. It is no more psychological in the sense of belonging only to the subject than the rest of the figure. Everyone sees the triangle, and of this experience there is no doubt. In fact, a doubt can arise — the triangle can be called subjective, and the figure can be called an illusion — only if the definition of reality is prescribed in advance and even in spite of experience. Begin with the body of science, to which there necessarily corresponds the world as defined by physics, and the triangle becomes subjective. Experience moves inside. Psychological life is set opposite the world.

The conclusion that the subjective (psychological) disrupts what is real is inextricably tied to this argument which imposes a metaphysics of opposition on the figure. Experience, however, rejects this argument *and* its conclusions. For experience the reality of the figure is not restricted to the lines and the circles. Experience does not exclude the triangle from what is real. Experience embraces the entire figure as real. Nevertheless experience does notice a difference between the character or quality of the lines and circles and the triangle. Lines and circles make their appearance in a different fashion than the triangle. The lines and the circles appear fixed and stable; the triangle has a more dynamic quality to its appearance. The triangle appears in movement in the sense that it seems to play on the border of appearance and disappearance. It alludes to its presence rather than stating it directly. It is *elusive.* Notice this last term! What the science of psychology calls *illusion,* psychological life experiences as *elusive.* The significance of this distinction will be discussed later. For the moment, however, we are faced with a question: how does the experienced elusiveness of the triangle modify our understanding of the Ponzo figure?

Again we must go back to the figure and unlike the advice which Kanizsa gives for a similar figure — to examine the contours closely, thus making them disappear —,[39] we must allow our eyes a free play with the figure. What then do we notice? We notice that the movement of the triangle is among the *gaps* or the *breaks* in the circular figures. The triangle is in motion and it sets our eyes in motion, as if we the see-ers expected to find or to corner the triangle in one of those gaps. Indeed, at times the triangle seems to radiate from the gaps, while at other times it seems to intrude upon the dark, circular figures and to disrupt them. But in either case it seems that the appearance of the triangle is essentially bound up with the gaps or the breaks in those figures which are experienced as more stable, more fixed, and perhaps, as we would be tempted to say, more real. The triangle seems to appear with the "break-up" or the "break-down" of "the real," that is through the gaps or the fissures of what is fixed in this instance by prescription. The triangle seems to appear with the *disruption* of "the real," with its un-fixing, with setting in motion again what is initially fixed by prescription.

The *Ponzo illusion* is used to demonstrate two facts about psychological life: its *subjective* character and the *effect* which it nevertheless has upon the real. The *Ponzo figure*, on the other hand, demonstrates two surprisingly different points: the *elusive* rather than the subjective, illusory character of psychological experience, and the appearance of psychological experience not as an *effect upon* the real but with a *disruption of* it. This latter point needs to be stated again. *Psychological experience is not what disrupts the real. On the contrary, psychological experience appears as a disruption of the real.* The latter statement is an entirely different conclusion from the former. There is no dualism, no metaphysics of opposition between reality and psychological experience in the latter. There is only the recognition that psychological experience shows itself when matter matters in another way, when the world changes, at the "break-up" or "break-down" of the given. This latter conclusion is, moreover, so obvious and so required by experience that even Kanizsa must finally allude to it. At the end of the article, when he is considering some hypotheses to explain these subjective figures — brightness and texture gradients, the partial activation of contour-detector cells in the visual system —, he says that the "primary factor seems to be the tendency to completion."[40] He recognizes, therefore, that the incompletion of what appears, its interruption, its disruption, is related to the appearance of these "subjective" (psychological) figures. Incompletion, however, belongs neither to physical figures in themselves nor to a physiological system. It is a psychological reality. His last point, then, undoes his argument and his conclusion, and moves the figure closer to how it is experienced.

The discussion here has focused on the triangle, while Kanizsa's example emphasized the two vertical lines. How does his concern about these two lines fit into the discussion? The answer is rather simple. His assertion that the two lines are the same length already presumes the prescribed opposition between psychological (subjective) experience and (objective) reality. But, guided by the figure as it is experienced, the claim cannot be made, precisely because no question about the comparative length of the lines ever arises. For experience, the length of the lines is not an issue. Nevertheless, if we grant this prescription of reality, this definition of what is objectively real in advance of experience, then the *difference* between the measured line and the experienced line shows once again that psychological experience appears as a disruption of the real. The line on the left does stretch and change its length. Psychological experience does *matter*: it makes a difference and it is how the matter of what is real matters in another way.

THE FUNCTION OF PSYCHOLOGICAL LIFE

While the value of the previous example lies in the very visible way it illustrates the function of psychological experience — as a disruption ("break-up" or "break-down") of reality, psychological experience alludes to a world of experience which is elusive —, the limitations of the example are evident. On one hand, the example concerns only perceptual experience. On the other hand, it concerns itself with a conception of reality which is prescribed in advance by the posture of science. Let us broaden the scope of this discussion, therefore, with a few additional remarks.

In the first place we may recall here the Cocteau example. Cocteau is standing on the street in the grip of an intention. He has had a glimpse of his childhood again, but he wishes to recapture it more vividly. Failing at first by touching the wall, he finally succeeds when he interrupts his usual, familiar posture. He stoops down; he closes his eyes; he traces his finger along the wall. At this moment of disruption, the familiar, taken-for-granted wall of brick and stone disappears. That wall which he may have passed many times before, that wall which countless others would leave unnoticed, that wall, like the walls of everyone's childhood home, which is fixed in its meaning by the forgetfulness of daily habit and routine, breaks down and alludes to a memory which remains elusive. Let Cocteau stand up again and the habitual wall will immediately reassemble. The memory will fade. It will disappear in the solid, everyday familiarity of the wall.

In the second place the experience of emotions further illustrates the function of psychological life. Emotional experiences are, if nothing else, disruptions or breakdowns of the routine habits of one's daily life. One never *has* an emotion. On the contrary, one *is* an emotion and the emotion which one is is the altered face of things. The road between my home and my office, for example, *lengthens*, with my impatience to be home, just as it *flattens out, narrows*, and becomes a *dull, colorless* stretch of grey ribbon when I must reluctantly travel to my office to grade a mountain of student examinations. The road changes. I am impatient. These two statements are equivalent, and to say one is to say the other. Human emotions do not change the things of the world in the way that milk added to coffee changes it. Human emotions are these changed appearances, these disruptions of the usual faces of things. Of course these disruptions are not *empirically* sensible. No camera would ever record the change in the length of the road. Nevertheless they are real, and more real in fact than the odometer reading in my car which always measures the constant length of five miles. Moreover, each one of us knows the variety of emotional experiences — anxiety is not anger —

because each one of us lives this variety as so many changes of the world. Indeed, if emotional experience were not such a change, if it were not anchored in the fabric of the world, if the world were a fixed and immutable reality over there on the other side of subjective, emotional experience, would we not be condemned to spend most of our waking life in intellectual puzzlement about what we experience? But such an effort is not our task because each emotion is a transformed world, because each emotion is how the world matters in another way.

Whether we consider perception, memory, or emotions, therefore, the conclusion is the same. Psychological life does appear as a disruption of the real, where the real is understood to mean the fixed, habitual, taken-for-granted character of events and things. That fixing, moreover, need not be limited to the view of science which prescribes in a systematic way this reality of things. It also includes in a much broader fashion that fixing of reality which marks the character of habitual, daily life. We become used to things, to events, to others, and to ourselves in the ways that we use them and are used by them, and in the easy comfortableness of that familiarity we begin to fall asleep psychologically. I live on the street but no longer notice the color of the houses or the number of trees which line the street. Or I chat with my friends but no longer hear what they say, since we always seem to say the same thing. But when things break up, or when events break down or are disrupted, psychological life emerges again. The cracks and the fissures, the gaps and the breaks, the moments of disruption, allude to another perspective on things which remains elusive. That perspective is the psychological one.

THE FUNCTION OF METAPHOR

In one chapter of *The Rule of Metaphor*, Ricoeur considers metaphor in terms of deviation, and initially he points out how this issue of deviation already presumes the prior issue of "deviation from what." There is figurative language because there is language which is non-figurative. There is language which recognizably is a norm. The problem, however, is to identify this *norm-al* language while recognizing that an absolutely non-figurative language does not actually exist. For Aristotle the norm was the standard meaning of words, a position which the nineteenth-century rhetorician Pierre Fontanier also adopted. In his works, according to Ricoeur, "Figurative meaning contrasts with proper meaning within current usage."[41] For Jean Cohen, on the other hand, the deviation of figurative language is best measured in terms of its contrast with that system of language which by intention if not in achievement proposes to be non-figurative in the extreme. This is the language of science. Thus either by *habit* or by *prescription* a "steno-language" appears,[42] a language, however, whose use echoes or reflects a metaphorical deviation.

Deviation occurs in the *using* of language. It occurs in speaking. Deviation belongs not to language but to speech. There are no literal words-in-themselves and no words which by themselves are metaphorical. There is no literal language-in-itself any more than there is language that is only metaphorical. Rather there are words which are spoken, in the broadest sense of this term, and in that speaking words animate, reflect, deepen, and figure each other in such a way that some may take on new meaning, deviant meaning, in relation to others which do not. This view does not deny, of course, that every word brings with it a history. It asserts only that this history is a history of previous reflections which are now more often than not forgotten. This view of deviation insists, therefore, only that this history is not a fixed or permanent norm against which the deviant use of words can be measured. To claim that the word is such a fixed reference is to engage in the *dictionary fantasy*, which is to suppose that we speak the language of the dictionary. Dictionaries, however, presume a speaking community. Language presumes speech. Every utterance is always to some degree deviant. *Speech*, we might say, *always disturbs language.*

Deviation is not a movement *away from* the literal *to* the metaphorical, but the consequence of the *interaction* of words, the outcome of their inter-animation. Thus Max Black in speaking of metaphor says that it is "*a sentence* or another expression in which some words are used metaphorically while the remainder are used non-metaphorically."[43] In a sentence, in living speech, there is a mutual impregnation of words, the consequence of which is at times a living image, a fruitful metaphor. Metaphorical expression is a deviation, but it deviates from a norm only because it appears through a norm. It is a disruption of a norm only because it is a norm disrupted by the mutual reflection of words. As Cleanth Brooks says in speaking of poetic language which is by necessity metaphorical: "The terms are continually modifying each other, and thus violating their dictionary meanings."[44]

As an example of metaphor's deviation, consider these four lines from Richard Wilbur's *Things of This World*. They are quoted by Philip Wheelwright:

> But seeing rose carafes conceive the sun
> My thirst conceives a fierier universe.
> And then I toast the birds in the burning trees
> That chart their holy lucid drunkenness.[45]

The word *toast* is a pivotal term in these lines and around it a semantic tension gathers. Toast is ambiguous. Is the word meant to conjure up an extraordinary breakfast scene of rose carafes and toasted birds? This is rather unusual fare, and yet it is one possibility considered by Wheelwright, a possibility supported by *rose carafes* and *thirst*. These terms can reflect this more customary and usual sense of the word *toast*. Toasting one's breakfast food, even if it is the birds in the trees filled with the hot breath of the sun, is a legitimate expectation which arises from what Dwiggins calls a "contextual pressure"[46] exerted by these other terms. Wheelwright suggests, however, that this meaning seems inappropriate to the poem, and in any case it is not the only meaning. The rose carafes which conceive the sun also suggest another more deadly presence of the sun which now burns the trees and parches one's throat. Indeed one can imagine through the bright, and even blinding sun sparkling through the rose carafes, a vision of the created sun of nuclear holocaust, a grim vision of catastrophe supported by the terms *fierier* and *burning*. These terms reflect another and different meaning of the word toast. In this context "I," humanity, incinerate the world.

But a third meaning is also possible. The toasted birds of the breakfast table and the toasting of birds in a fierier universe can give way to *a toast* offered by a merry reveler. Eyes blurred by the grape of Dionysus, this bacchanalian figure may lift his head and catch sight of the sun's painful light in the rose carafes, and feeling its parching heat he may raise his glass in lip-swollen tribute to his companions, the birds. And here again the other words of the poem support this meaning. *Rose carafes*, *thirst*, and especially that *holy lucid drunkenness* reflect such a joyful, frivolous toast.

Four lines and three different scenes! Four lines and three different figures! *Toast* plays back and forth among these other words, and its meanings appear through them and change them. In this respect *toast* and the meanings which it has and which it engenders within these lines are like that elusive triangle which appears through the fixed lines and circles and which changes them.

But what is the meaning of the term *toast* and of the lines which pivot around this term? Wheelwright says that we cannot decide. He is correct. The meaning cannot be fixed because the poet has arranged things in such a way that the term and the meaning of the lines stay in motion. Let *toast* and other words reflect one meaning, and as soon as it seems fixed it is disrupted by another reflection among the terms. In the way in which the poet constructs his lines, the term *toast* takes on a metaphorical function. And that function is nothing less than to *disrupt* the fixing or the freezing of meaning. Literal meanings are broken down. The word and the lines *allude* to meanings which remain elusive. Metaphorical expression serves a de-literalizing function.

T. S. Eliot has written that the task of the poet, who is a maker of metaphor, is to "*dislocate* language into meaning."[47] We have just seen an instance of this dislocation with the poet Richard Wilbur. But what the poet does with skill and with intention happens psychologically. Psychological life, like metaphor, is a disruption of the real in the sense of what is lived literally in a taken-for-granted and forgetful fashion. But unlike metaphor, psychological life is more often than not the experience of disruption rather than its planned creation. A metaphor, we might say, is an explicit psychological act, while psychological experience is a living metaphor. Regardless of this distinction, however, metaphor and psychological life do share the same function. Wheelwright speaks of this function in the following way: "What really matters in a metaphor is the psychic depth at which the things of the world, whether actual or fancies, are *transmuted* by the cool heat of the imagination."[48] And Dwiggins in his work on metaphor makes the same point. "Each metaphor," he says, "is a call to transcend the habitual limits of the 'real,'" by which he means the everyday world of mere fact. Moreover, if we hear this call of metaphor, then "we regain (or retain) our playful freedom in the face of the congealments, however much needed, of the everyday."[49] Disruption, then, characterizes the life of metaphor as much as it characterizes psychological life. Disruption characterizes psychological life as a metaphorical reality.

Psychological Life as a Metaphorical Reality: Implications

Mirrors, shadows, and reflections; a bottle of wine and a cup of tea; purple finches and Newton's spectrum; an infant before a mirror and a story about Sunday morning; the pumping heart and the Baroque world; Cocteau's diary entry and Hölderlin's joyous waves; a modern psychological experiment performed by Stanley Schachter and Jerome Singer and a poem by Wallace Stevens: each of these examples has illustrated the metaphorical character of psychological life. Three implications of this recovery of psychological life as a metaphorical reality are presented below.

Psychological experience as a metaphorical reality is neither a thing nor a thought. It is not an empirical fact nor a mental reality. As such, therefore, it is neither the empirical truth nor the logical consistency of experience which matters psychologically. On the contrary, as a metaphorical reality it is the way of seeing which opens up a world which matters and which must be understood. A metaphor establishes a world, and one understands a metaphor by participating in its vision. To check the empirical validity or logical consistency of a metaphor in advance of this participation is to refuse the metaphorical dimension of the metaphor. To check for the empirical or logical truth of a psychological experience in advance of experience, or even in spite of it, is to transform the domain of psychological life into science or philosophy. Psychological experience may show itself through science or philosophy. But that is an entirely different matter from saying that psychological experience is either scientific or philosophical. Experience is a world and the metaphorical character of experience deepens and reflects the world as story even as it re-figures the person as a character in a tale. Psychological experience inclines one toward a view of the world. Taking up that inclination, one is then able to explore the boundaries and the limits of that world.

The metaphorical character of psychological life also has implications for the *craft* of psychological studies. Because psychological experience is indirect, because it reveals itself only by concealing itself, psychological life is always in need of being *recovered*. More specifically psychological life tends to cover itself in the habitual tasks of daily life, in those taken-for-granted, literalizing attitudes and perceptions of everyday living. As such, therefore, we may say that psychological craft consists in bearing witness for what lies forgotten beneath the literalizing attitudes of daily and scientific life. In this regard the psychologist is not so much a discoverer in search of new truths or stories, or a creator of fresh ideas or tales, but, on the contrary, a witness whose work embodies the unheard (of) stories of an age in the sense of that which an age most desires to forget.

Finally the metaphorical character of psychological life also has implications for the *psychological attitude*. What, we may ask, is the attitude or the demeanor of the psychologist-witness? Does the psychologist bear witness like the prophets of old, threatening destruction? Is the psychologist a messenger of the gods like the figure of Hermes?[50] I think that the psychologist's demeanor is not so serious. On the contrary, the psychologist as witness is, by virtue of being psychological, never so certain in the task as these figures can be. The indirection of metaphor means that psychological life is *elusive*. We saw this feature most clearly in the discussion of the metaphorical function of psychological life. Consequently the psychologist who bears witness can "only" *allude* to what is elusive. No direct statements with the seal of certainty can be made. No prophecies can be given. *The psychologist alludes to what is elusive!* The psychologist speaks through the mode of story and hence points to but does not define what appears indirectly and what remains indirect.

As such, therefore, it is the attitude of *play* which best characterizes the psychologist-witness, since *allusion* and *elusive* are both rooted in the Latin word *ludere*, which means to play.[51] The psychologist, who moves playfully toward that which moves playfully away, touches the elusive but does not control it. With this reference to play I do not mean to suggest, however the frivolity of games, the sense of play as escape which marks our modern age.[52] I mean, on the contrary, the insightful play of metaphor. A metaphor is a play upon words, and psychological life as a metaphorical reality is a play upon the world. It is a dramatic tale.

Conclusion

When Thomas Sprat published his *History of the Royal Society*, he wrote these words in praise of its scientific members:

> They have therefore been most rigorous in putting in execution, the only Remedy, that can be found for this extravagance: and that has been, a constant Resolution, to reject all the amplifications, digressions, and swellings of style: to return back to the primitive purity, and shortness, when men delivered so many things, almost in an equal number of words. They have exacted from all of their members, a close, naked, natural way of speaking: positive expressions; clear senses; a natural easiness: bringing all things as near the Mathematical plainness, as they can.[53]

The extravagance of which Sprat speaks is metaphor, and the date of these words is 1667. In the same age that the human heart and the space of the world in which it beats become empty of psychological life, there is a campaign to empty language of metaphor. Campaign, moreover, is not too strong a word, since in 1670 we find Samuel Parker going "so far as to advocate an Act of Parliament forbidding the use of 'fulsome and luscious' metaphors."[54] In an age when the science of psychology seeks to purify itself of the psychological, language seeks to purify itself of the metaphorical. Certainly this "coincidence" is no surprise. This work has traced and has attempted to recover the common grounds between metaphor and psychological life. The fate of meta-

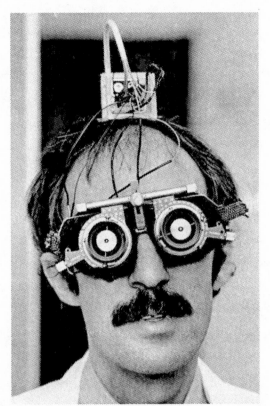

Figure 8. The face of modern psychology. Photo by Mark Perlstein/ *Dallas Times Herald,* October 9, 1979, p.1.

phor seems to be historically linked in modern times with the fate of the psychological. At the moment this may be cause for celebration. Cleanth Brooks has said: "The most fruitful modern criticism [is] a rediscovery and recovery of the importance of metaphor."[55] The time may be propitious, then, for a recovery of psychological life as a metaphorical reality.

Closing Lines: A Final Remembrance

If the psychologist bears witness for what would otherwise be forgotten in being taken for granted, it is fitting that this book should close with something to remember. Consider the face which is presented in Figure 8. It is the face of modern psychology. Look at that face and study it! A faint smile appears on the lips. Or is it an expression of bewilderment? Mona Lisa smiles, and her face may be the earliest face of modern psychology. Has our psychological life come from the Mona Lisa to this face? From that earliest face to this latest one there is this difference: what is only suggested in the former is now explicit in the latter. The *interiorization* and *literalization* of psychological life is the theme of that face, the face of a psychologist who is investigating dreams. He "looks" inside, away from the world. His "eyes" look at his dreaming brain. We should not forget what he is doing. At the close of this work, we should remember that face. At this final exit we should no longer take that face for granted. As we close we should allow that face to disturb our dreams, particularly that cultural dream which we share and which is called the science of psychology.

AFTERWORD

Psychological Life: From Science to Metaphor was a first step on a journey, which began with curiosity. Trained as a phenomenologist, I was also by temperament always something of a daydreamer, content to let explanations of things given to me dissolve in reverie. Today, I understand that the daydreamer is a born phenomenologist, and that a phenomenologist is a "grown-up" daydreamer. Both are witnesses for experience rather than critics in search of explanations, witnesses in service to presence before becoming critics in pursuit of meaning. As such, each one practices a kind of fidelity to experience as it takes place. After all these years, I still recall the place and the occasion where, in a mood of reverie, the work of this book began with a wondering about the character or nature of psychological life on its own terms. And I recall the feeling of that moment. I was gripped by something larger than myself, possessed by a question, which, even then in some dim way, I felt as a terrible gift, a vocation, which was calling me into a life and a work not of my conscious choosing.

A phenomenology of the mirror experience was the response to this question. Through the mirror a material reality is transformed into an image, and the image is as far on the other side of the mirror as the material reality is on this side of it. The mirror image is a deepening of material reality. It is the depth of what we ordinarily define as real, when we identify reality with matter that is visibly situated in local time and space.

When we distance ourselves, however, from this experience, and, via the science of optics, explain the image as a virtual reality, we dismiss it as a presence that does not matter. Alongside the density of facts, its virtual presence has no weight. Content with the explanation, the haunting reality of the image is lost.

For phenomenology, however, experience is the starting point of reflection. In spite of the explanation, therefore, the image in the depths of the mirror's world is real. Its ghostly presence as a hauntingly familiar and yet strange one, a figure who is and is not you, matters. As reasonable as you are, let the mirror crack and the image shatter as you are looking at it, and you will, for a moment, wonder and, perhaps, worry. In this moment, factual explanations and/or rational ideas are dissolved in the broken image.

On its own terms, psychological life matters as image. From the side of depth psychology, Jung made the same claim, and within phenomenology, the image character of psychological life is found, for example, in the work of Bachelard and, to some degree, in that of Merleau-Ponty. But this claim was not the core insight of this book. Rather, the primary contribution of *Psychological Life* was, and still is, the development of the metaphoric quality of the image as the ontological ground of psychological existence. The dynamic tension of this book was the move from mirror to metaphor.

This move from mirror to metaphor occurs because both image and metaphor belong to a domain of reality that is neither empirically factual nor conceptually rational. Each presents a subtle world, which is neither the interior, private space of mind nor the exterior, public space of matter. Both describe a no-where world, if you wish, that is nevertheless now-here, a world that alludes to a reality, which remains elusive.

The mirror image, for example, is over there in the world. It is not a thought, and yet its presence in the world is not like that of a thing. The image is visible in the world, but not in the same way that the mirror itself is a visible presence. I can touch the glass on the mirror, but I cannot touch the image in its depths. But it can touch me, move me, solicit me in a way that is often surprising and even disturbing. Its reality and presence arises, like smoke, somewhere between thoughts and things.

A metaphor, too, is neither a thing nor a thought. It is the witnessing of a vision that arises in that no-where place between mind and matter, as if a secret dialogue has already taken place between one's heart and the mystery of things. Recall the example in the book, taken from the literary critic Howard Nemerov. Looking at some birds in his garden, Nemerov believes he is seeing a purple finch. Unsure, however, he compares his vision with a factual account of this bird from a field guide. It is not the facts, however, that persuade him of the reality of the purple finch. Rather, it is the surprise of the metaphor: a purple finch is a sparrow dipped in raspberry juice!

A metaphor is an invitation into a way of experiencing the world, a prescription for vision, and in its birth it does erupt as a surprise and delight. It is not a reasonable act, nor is it based upon careful empirical comparisons, which measure and weigh the likenesses and differences between the two terms of a metaphor. Reasons come later, after the metaphor has erupted. A metaphor makes sense after the fact so to speak. In this regard, a metaphor works in the same way as a dream. It has us before we get it.

Indeed, I would now suggest that a metaphor is a kind of waking dream. Dream and metaphor are both ways of living with soul in mind, and each dissolves our conventional wisdom about things and thoughts. Metaphor and dream invite us to see through the fact minded literalisms of our individual and collective minds. Each is a kind of psychological alchemy, a work of dissolving and de-literalizing old habits, customs, and routines. In this respect, psychological life as a metaphoric reality is not about solutions. It is about dis-solutions. In the final chapter of this book, I spoke to this point in terms of disruption as the metaphoric function of psychological life. Those moments when our facts and ideas breakdown are the occasions when the image breaks through.

As the discussion of the purple finch already indicates, the metaphoric reality of the image has its counterpart in the image sense of metaphor. The sparrow dipped in raspberry juice is an image of a world that is real. The bird is there in the garden for Nemerov and for us to see. The image in the metaphor is not a conceptual idea in his mind. But neither is it a fact in the world. If, for example, in a fit of empirical frenzy, Nemerov rushed into his garden and managed to grab hold of the bird, his hands would not drip with juice.

A good example of the metaphoric quality of image and the image quality of metaphor is Magritte's famous painting of a pipe, which he titled, "Ceci n'est pas une pipe." The title grabs our attention, because it alerts us to what we already know and live in the presence of a painting. We know a painting is a different kind of reality. A painting does not just re-present a world, it is a world. A painting is a portal into a world of experience, and in its presence we step through the canvas into the depths of its world, like we do in the presence of a mirror. We know Magritte's pipe is not a pipe in the factual sense, and we know it is not just an idea in his mind, because the pipe is there in the painting for us to see. It is an image-pipe, and his title reminds us that we do not mistake the image for the thing. The title reminds us that before we think about things, we live in the world through the metaphoric reality of the image. And, when we are surprised in this fashion, disrupted and jolted out of our usual ways of thinking and being, even the pipe in one's hand might reveal itself in new ways. The story of the wine bottle in *Psychological Life* is a good example of how the ordinary world of things are haunted by images.

Metaphor, as the gnosis of the image, and not fact or idea, is the ontological ground of psychological life. This was the primary theme and the contribution of *Psychological Life*, and it is this foundation that has guided all my work since the publication of this book in 1982. In one way or another, the books and the essays, which followed this one, have been concerned with articulating the art of psychological life as the cultivation of a metaphoric sensibility. I want to make some remarks here as a way of bridging this book and those essays.

To live psychologically, to live in the world with soul in mind, requires a radical shift from an empirical and/or intellectual sensibility to a metaphoric sensibility. Psychological life is not in the facts of one's history or biology, any more than it is in the theoretical ideas we create about those facts. It is given through the images and the stories that those images unfold. A metaphoric sensibility attunes us to the image quality of those facts and ideas, the subtle ways in which this "prima materia" is re-figured as a story, like the image of the person through the mirror is re-figured as a character in a tale. Metaphoric consciousness is a leavening of fact with fantasy, a seasoning of an idea with a fiction, the transformation of an event into an experience. It is the kind of work, which the poet John Keats alluded to when he called the world "the vale of soul making."[1]

A metaphoric sensibility understands psychological life to be a deepening of nature and mind as image. Dreams do this work of deepening every night for the individual, and art does it for the collective. Van Gogh's "Starry Night" is a good example. This painting reveals the stars in a way that imagines their hitherto concealed depths. Through this image we step into a new starry night, and once one has seen that painting the starry night can never be what it was before. His painting changes the world. In this respect, I would say today that living with soul in mind continues the on-going act of creation. Living psychologically is a creative art, the way in which we participate in the divine, including its shadows and destructions.

Metaphoric sensibility is the capacity of seeing and stepping through the giveness of the material world into the depths of an image. Because this action changes the world, the cultivation of a psychological consciousness is a subversive art, which is always counter to institutionalized ways of knowing and being. Soul is not a republican virtue. It is, as Jung said, "an opus contra naturam,"[2] a piece of creative subversion, which phenomenology would describe as the bracketing of the natural attitude.

One of the gifts of phenomenology is that it constantly returns us to those very same collective conditions, which the work of soul undoes. And it does this, because it begins its reflections with the living body situated in the collective matrices of culture and history. When Van Gogh paints the starry night, it is not a disincarnate mind that paints. "The painter takes his body with him," Merleau-Ponty says.[3] The starry night sky penetrates the painter's body, and through his flesh reveals heretofore undreamed possibilities.

There is as much mystery in this penetration as there is ordinariness, for the same process takes place with the mirror. In the mirror experience, the image is not seen in the mirror. Indeed, if you attempt to look at the image with this idea in mind, you will focus your eyes on the glass and the image will fade. You will also probably get eye strain. The engaged body, living through this situation, knows and lives the psychological truth of the image. Its eyes penetrate the surface and fall into the depths. The eyes see the image over there on the far side of the glass, because the image has already penetrated the engaged body from that place. The engaged body, solicited by the image, follows the track of this solicitation. It steps through the looking glass, as it were, into the depths of the image.

Because phenomenology is an embodied style of thinking, it is the indispensable and necessary attitude for psychological life. The engaged body is the pivot where fact and image intersect, the locus of a transformation where the facticity of the human flesh becomes a living metaphor through gesture and language. Van Gogh's eyes, for example, are not cameras, which simply record the starry night sky. They are not bits and pieces of anatomy, and there is more to his seeing than meets his eyeballs. Van Gogh's eyes are inquisitions of the starry night, whose style might be described as a glance that lingers in the moment, or as a gaze, which loves what it seeks to know. The glance or the gaze, like the glare or the stare, are metaphoric gestures of psychological life, transformations of anatomical facts into imagined and imaginable worlds.

To be psychological is to understand that nature and mind as mirrors of soul are deepened and re-figured as image when the engaged body lingers in the moment. It is only through the quotidian time bound condition of our flesh that the other timeless realm of the image comes through, only through the time bound flesh that the timeless possibilities of the world show themselves. The living body, engaged in its situations, is the portal through which this no-where world of the image falls into time and becomes now-here. It is the pivot where the factual historical world becomes a metaphoric psychological world.

This pivotal moment is a matter of desire, a matter of erotic ties between the sensitive flesh that hungers for the sensible world, and the sensible world that seduces the sensitive flesh. Van Gogh's eyes fulfill themselves through his paintings, and his paintings are the destiny of a vocation between vision and the visible. Image is the offspring of desire. Psychological life is awakened by Eros, as the ancient story of Eros and Psyche indicates.[4] But not only Eros; Thanatos too; not only love, but also loss. If psychological life is the flower of a love affair between flesh and world, then loss and grief are the dark roots of its soil.[5]

These few remarks amplify what is already present in *Psychological Life*. The seductive bond between body and world, for example, is there in the chapter on things and the other, weaving itself as a leitmotif through the various descriptions. In addition, the theme of loss is present in these chapters and descriptions. Indeed, it could not be otherwise, because the phenomenologist who wrote this book was practicing phenomenology as the art of lingering. When one is present to the world in this way, nature and mind reveal themselves as presences haunted by absences, as the time bound shadowed by the eternal. If one lingers in this fashion, if one is patient enough to be a witness for things as they appear, and is capable of suspending for a moment one's ideas, assumptions, and explanations, then the image of the occasion, the image in the moment, comes forth, holding within itself the presence in the moment and the absence, the beauty of the time bound moment and the awe-ful sense of its eclipse. The story of the wine bottle, or the description of the shadows of things, are prime examples of presence haunted by absence, of this chiasm of time and eternity.

As I write these words now, in the posture of a backward glance, I feel a strong sense of gratitude for the spirit of the work that was birthed in this book. There is and has been a vocation in this twenty year journey, a journey in service to the character of psychological life on its own terms. That this vocation was seeded in phenomenology is crucial, because without this foundation what I have offered over the years would have been made from my ideas about the character of psychological life, rather than drawn out of experience. In this respect, phenomenology is fidelity to experience, and in this fidelity what it makes of an experience has the feeling tone of a remembrance. A true phenomenologist is not clever or dazzling. He or she is a witness who awakens one to what one already knows but has forgotten. Phenomenology is truly an-amnesis, a recovery of what has been lost, forgotten, marginalized, or otherwise repressed. At its best phenomenology, as this work of an-amnesis, is a homecoming.

Phenomenolgy as homecoming is what Edmund Husserl intended

when he described the task of phenomenology as back to the things themselves. It is also what Heidegger meant in his description of truth as "a-lethia," the work of un-forgetting. The homecoming is also found in the pithy statement of Erwin Straus, who, in saying that phenomenology is the work of unraveling the un-written constitution of everyday life, suggested that it is the work of giving words to what has already been lived and known. In this context, phenomenology as homecoming finds its traveling companions in the poets. Rilke's *Duino Elegies*, for example, are devoted to the work of lingering close enough to the world that one is able to hear the appeal of things to become invisible through us via language. Phenomenologists and poets engage in the work of saying the words of the world that have been whispered to them.

Reading Husserl, Heidegger, Straus, and others like Merleau-Ponty, is a remembering, as difficult as their work can be to the mind that seeks understanding. But phenomenology as homecoming does not work itself initially or primarily through the mind. The homecoming is heart-work. The an-amnesis begins with the awakened heart, through a heart that is touched and moved to remember. Gaston Bachelard works in this fashion at the level of the heart. So too does J. H. van den Berg. His work in fact is a cultural-historical homecoming. In his metabletic studies, the crusts of history are removed from our eyes. Through his work, one realizes that the worlds we take for granted are perspectives in a drama of changing landscapes. In his hands, phenomenology as homecoming is a cultural therapy, which changes the heart. More than anyone else, and there are many to whom I owe a debt, he inspired and informed this book and the work that has followed.

In writing this Afterword, I am aware of how this book and the work that has followed has been a continuing dialogue among these phenomenologists, depth psychologists, especially Freud and Jung, and the poets. To describe the key moments of this dialogue is not possible here, and I even doubt that I could do so. I know only the rough outline of this conversation in which I have been first an eavesdropper and then a bricoleur, a rag picker, who has gathered up bits and pieces of that conversation and made of them a tattered cloth. Imperfect, frayed, loosely woven, but a tissue of themes nevertheless. Take two ends of this cloth, billow it so that it becomes an enveloping canopy. At one end is the theme of image and the metaphoric nature of psychological life. At the other, it is the imaginal and its metaphoric structure as the autonomous domain of soul.

Image belongs to the imaginal world, like fact belongs to the empirical world and idea to the conceptual world. Image, fact, and idea are the ways through which each of these different ontological domains show themselves. Each is also the specific way in which we know these domains: image as a metaphoric gnosis, fact as an empirical one, and idea as a rational way of knowing and being. In moving from image to imaginal, I have only been re-turning to and turning over the core theme of *Psychological Life*. Image and its metaphoric reality already argued for the ontological autonomy of psychological life. The imaginal is and has been a way of furthering that claim.

The imaginal is the term that Henry Corbin gives to those regions of reality and experience explored by the Sufi mystics nearly a thousand years ago. A careful phenomenologist, Corbin[6] differentiated the imaginal from the imaginary, and in so doing affirmed the ontological validity and primacy of this world as an intermediate and intermediary world. Like the image, the imaginal world is neither the sensible, empirical, nor the intellectual, conceptual world. This other world is not the time bound world of our empirical-rational sensibility. It is not the cultural-historical world. But, again like the image, it shows itself through the material world, as breakdowns of the cultural-historical time bound world that are breakthroughs of the timeless world. The imaginal is the chiasm of the historical and the eternal, a pivotal world, like image is the visionary pivot of things and thoughts. In the language of Jung, it is the world of the archetypes playing themselves out through history, preserving and transforming fundamental human experiences. In the language of quantum physics, the imaginal is the quantum field of possibilities before its collapse into local space-time.

Near the end of the 19th century, and in the early years of the 20th, phenomenology was making a place for the eruption or breakthrough of psychological life on its own terms. At the same time, depth psychology and quantum physics were witnessing the breakdown of the Cartesian metaphysics of matter and mind. In the consulting rooms of Freud and Jung, this breakdown of the matter-mind dualism was the breakthrough of soul. In the hands of the early quantum physicists, it was the breakthrough of the quantum field. It is, perhaps, one of the most curious facts of the late 19th and early 20th centuries that the eruption of soul in the consulting rooms of Freud and Jung coincided with the eruption of the quantum in physics.

Jung would call this mutual mirroring of psychological experience and material event an expression of synchronicity. Van den Berg would call it a metabletic moment. However one might describe it, the astonishing point is that simultaneously the imaginal world of soul was breaking through mind and nature. This breakhrough was already occasioned by the void created when, in his *Meditations*,[7] Descartes proclaimed that he found no difference between soul and mind, and then proceeded, in both the Latin and French editions of that text, to use the word for mind rather than soul.[8] In that moment, soul fell into an abyss. It was toward this abyss, that phenomenologists, depth psychologists, and quantum physicists were drawn in the waning years of the 19th century.

The simultaneity of this breakthrough suggests to me today that the imaginal is the quantum field of soul, and the quantum field the imaginal domain of nature. Much significant work about this convergence of psychology and physics, about soul and nature, has been done, but much also remains to be done. In this Afterword, I have taken a backward glance, which has moved me forward. A key aspect of this forward movement since the publication of *Psychological Life*, has been the deepening of the metaphoric nature of psychological life in terms of its aesthetic and poetic dimensions. I hope that these further remarks will tempt the reader into his/her own backward glance to re-collect the reading of this book, a gesture that might deepen and enrich that reading.

Earlier I cited my indebtedness to Henry Corbin for his use of the term imaginal in his discussions of the mystical worlds of the Sufi mystics. In his preface to one of Corbin's books, the literary critic, Harold Bloom, rightly acknowledges the difficult gap we would need to bridge between the Sufi mystics' exploration of the imaginal world and our contemporary techno-consumer world. Admitting this point, he goes on to say poetry as well as mysticism is a threshold to the imaginal realm. Indeed, he says that the imaginal world sometimes has "no name except poetry itself."[9] The soul that struggles from the abyss confirms, I believe, Bloom's point. The soul that arises from the abyss speaks in a poetic voice, and the imaginal world of soul is an aesthetic landscape.

A major consequence of these claims is that the discipline of psychology is closer to the arts than it is to the sciences. Over the years, I have elaborated these claims in other books and in essays, some of which are now in press in a collected volume.[10] While this Afterword is neither the time nor the place to spell out even a few of these elaborations, I do want to note one thing. The soul's poetic voice and its imaginal landscapes require an aesthetic sensibility, which is a way of knowing with and through the heart, a way of knowing that is neither benumbed by un-examined facts nor bewitched by clever ideas. It is a feeling sense, which is passionate, a way of knowing and being that is in sym-pathy with what it seeks to know, a way of knowing and being that is compassionate and attuned to its object. In the late 17th century, Blaise Pascal, counterpart to Descartes, recognized this special gnosis of the heart, when he said that "the heart has its reasons that Reason does not know."[11] Moreover, for the Sufi mystics the heart was the organ of perception for the imaginal world.

The heart already had a central place in *Psychological Life*, although when I wrote this book I knew nothing of Corbin's work. The recovery of the heart as a metaphoric reality prepared the way, however, for the imaginal heart. Working with William Harvey's 17th century description of the heart as a pump, I showed how his empirical studies and factual account was and is also an image of the heart, no more valid than the images of the heart preserved in its etymology, where it is the seat of memory and courage. Each is real but real in a different way. The broken heart is a metaphor, whose reality speaks of one's loss, like the pumping heart is a metaphor, whose reality speaks of our cardiac condition. If I tell you my heart is broken, I do not want you to call a cardiologist. On the other hand, I do want the cardiologist to attend to an arrhythmia.

The broken heart is a subtle heart, related but not reducible to the pump. The pumping heart too is a subtle heart. Both are metaphoric

possibilities, and each of these images are metaphoric possibilities because at the heart of the matter, the heart, the body, nature is an imaginal domain, which collapses into cultural-historical expressions.

To dismiss this difference, as we have done while standing at the
abyss; to reduce the broken heart as an imaginal reality to the factual
heart as a pump; to take Harvey's factual claim that the heart is a pump
literally and forget that this claim rests upon a metaphoric vision, is to
lose the soul of the heart. The power of the fact, which explains the
primary function of the heart as one of changing venous into arterial
blood by circulating it through the lungs, and the wonders of modern
medicine that flow from this fact, have seduced us into sleep. And in this
sleep we have forgotten that even within the explanation there remains a
hint of the heart's soul and its alchemical powers to transform the gross
matter of the world into its subtle forms. Asleep to the metaphoric
character of the pumping heart, to its image sense, the breath of soul has
become the oxygen of the lungs. When this happens, we lose not only
our awareness that the imaginal is real. We also lose the related insight
that the real is fundamentally imaginal, that the world that we measure
and explain through our facts, and systematize through our ideas, is a
tissue of metaphors.

The passage from image to the imaginal needed this recovery of the
heart and its own ways of knowing and being these subtle realms. As I
said above, I truly did not know this when I wrote this book in 1982.
But the heart of the work did. Somehow it was all there, a vocation, a
destiny, a work to be done. In this span of time, my companions have led
me to the edge of the abyss, and at this place I have been stretched
beyond myself, held in a tension between phenomenology on one side
and depth psychology on the other. Suspended above the void, it has
been the poets who have stood under me, and under-stood the work that
has been a vocation. It has been the poets, because, as John Keats observed, they practice a kind of patient fidelity in the face of the wonders
of experience. Keats called this attitude "negative capability," which he
described as the ability "of being in uncertainties, Mysteries, doubts,
without any irritable reaching after fact and reason."[12]

There are times now when I wonder if it is better to be a failed poet than the good scientist in the heartwork of soul making. In "A Midsummer Night's Dream," Shakespeare says, "And as imagination bodies forth/ The forms of things unknown, the poet's pen/Turns them to shapes, and gives to airy nothing/A local habitation and a name."[13] Is it better to give for a moment some form to the subtle vapors of soul than to freeze or condense these vapors into the icy dungeon of our facts or ideas?[14] Is it wiser to be in service for a moment to a saying that is a showing of a truth that moves and touches the depths of the heart before it stirs the surface of the mind? In the realm of soul, is the moment's epiphany and our witnessing of it enough? Is it enough to give the no-thingness of soul a locality that is momentary?

Phenomenology at its best does this. Its descriptions need no further explanations, when they are born of a lingering in the presence of what is given. As a mode of presence, the descriptions of phenomenology are enough for the ways of the soul, especially when they adhere to that notion of negative capability, which allows us to be witnesses before we become critics.[15]

So, is it better and wiser to practice the art of soul making in the company of the poets? To this question I would say, "Yes!" And in this backward glance, I would add that while I found my way into psychology through philosophy, I have found my way out through poetry.

Am I done, then, with psychology? To this question, I must say, "No!" In finding my way out, I have found that psychology in its best moments is a transitional space, a half-way house between truth and beauty, wherever they may be found for a person. In this regard, I believe that psychology is less a habitat than it is a journey, and what matters is who takes the journey and how one goes. Psychological work demands character, fidelity to that destiny that draws you out of your heritage, to that vocation which chooses you for a work and makes use of you. It demands too that you be a character, someone outside the norm, willing to take on this risky business of soul making, someone who is vital, instinctual, perhaps even at times crude in service to upsetting the conventional wisdom of things, someone outrageous, funny, ambiguous, someone, finally, who is a fool in love with paradox and irony, a lover of the soul.

However one does that, it seems to me now that what matters is the joy of recognizing that being in service to soul is not the province of psychology or psychologists. Rather, it is the province of anyone and everyone whose life, when touched by soul, is transformed and becomes psychological. In this moment of becoming psychological, one steps through the mirror, an action that deepens, re-figures and reflects the ordinary events of one's life as an image, as a story, and one steps into the imaginal and subtle worlds of the soul. In this moment of soul making, one has a change of heart about everything, and whether it lasts for a lifetime or a second does not matter. It happened, and that's what matters, because in that moment one has a glimpse of that other realm from which each of us has come, that other place, which being nowhere is now-here, that subtle realm of the imaginal world, a moment when the timeless collapses into and intersects with the time bound, a moment in time of the eternal when one glimpses the soul image of his or her embodied form, the face, if you wish, that you have and have always had, the image of the soul twin in the mirror of eternity. In such moments, the appeal of psychology is to the pilgrim and the orphan that each of us is,[16] an appeal that turns one around, a moment of re-turning, when soul work becomes homework, when soul work becomes the journey of the heart to remember its home in those subtle realms of the imaginal world before it fell into time.

In search of the autonomous character of psychological life, I have wandered across disciplines, the wanderings of a gypsy soul in search of home. Curiously, my name, Romanyshyn, means "son of a gypsy." Is one's work seeded in a name? Is what is in a name a heritage that is a destiny? I do not know. What I do know, however, is that in these wanderings, I have found temporary shelters along the way, sanctuaries in the soul and in the world. My favorite one is at the intersection of the time bound world and the timeless soul. It is a bar where the custom of closing time still reigns. "It is time, gentlemen," the barman of this imaginal landscape says. Would that closing time was such a clear and simple declaration for all the moments of transition in our lives! Would that we all had such a barman of the soul! But let the wish be as it is. Let it rest in its subjunctive mood, a mood that is friendly to the imaginal domains. And let it be closing time for us—for now!

NOTES

Forward

1. William Harvey, *Exercitatio anatomica de motu cordis et sanguinis*, as quoted in J. H. van den Berg, *Het menselijk lichaam*, 2:32.
2. Emilio Parisano, *Recentiorum disceptationes de motu cordis, sanguinis et chyli*, as quoted in ibid, p. 33.
3. Emile Guyénot, *Les Sciences de la vie aux XVII⁴ et XVIII⁴ siècles*, as quoted in ibid.
4. See G. Joseph, "Geschichte der Herztone vor und nach Laennec bis 1852," as cited in ibid, p. 34.
5. Ibid., p. 35.
6. Ibid., pp. 37-42.
7. Thomas S. Kuhn, *The Structure of Scientific Revolutions*, p. 10.
8. See H. Wolfflin, *Renaissance und Barock*.

Introduction

1. A detailed presentation of the significance of introductory texts to a discipline can be found in Robert Romanyshyn, "Psychology and the Attitude of Science," in *Existential-Phenomenological Alternatives for Psychology*, ed. Ronald S. Valle and Mark King.
2. Clifford T. Morgan, Richard A. King, and Nancy M. Robinson, *Introduction to Psychology*, pp. 146-175.
3. Ibid., p. 158.
4. I am not saying here that science is a myth. But I am saying that our uncritical regard for it gives it a mythical power in our lives. My attitude to science and specifically to psychology's claim to be a science will become clear as the book develops.

5. But is not psychology's explanation of this experience correct? Is not the example which I cannot remember inside me? Despite psychology's explanation, which is visualized so dramatically in Figure 1, the way in which our everyday language describes this experience preserves another and a different story. The example I wish to use but cannot remember lies on the tip of my *tongue*, and in locating the experience in this way I am describing what seems most essential about it. Until I remember, *we* cannot begin. Until I remember the example, our relation, which is this book, is suspended. We wait together for the word which is crafted by the tongue. We wait together for the tongue, this organ of the body which ties us together in speech, to shape this experience. Placing the example which I cannot quite remember on the tip of the tongue, our everyday language informs us that this experience is a *relational* phenomenon. It tells us that this experience is a matter which lies between us, a matter which matters as much to you as it does to me.

Moreover, insofar as one would never appeal to another to inspect the tip of one's tongue in order to help one to remember, our everyday way of describing this experience suggests that our way of speaking about experience is not literal, perhaps because experience itself is not something literal.

The intention of this work is to recover the relational and non-literal character of psychological experience. This aim requires a critical and historical inquiry into the tendency on the part of modern scientific psychology to interiorize psychological experience and to treat this interiorization in a literal fashion. Moreover, the current definition of psychology as a science of behavior does not achieve this aim. On one hand psychology's concern with behavior is motivated by a rejection of interiorization primarily on methodological grounds. Interiorization is rejected in fact, which means it continues to exist in principle. Indeed this ghost of interiorization haunts the science of behavior every time psychology turns to physiology, a literalization of this interiorization. Of course, Skinner's radical behaviorism seems more critical on this score, but even with Skinner the rejection of the inside space is equivocal. Correctly criticizing "the damaging effect of the inner-directedness of physiological, as well as mentalistic, inquiry," he nevertheless goes on to say that the account of the behaving organism given by the future physiologist "will be an important advance over a behavioral analysis" (B. F. Skinner, *About Behaviorism*, pp. 214-215). This account, according to Skinner, will not "invalidate the laws of a science of behavior" (ibid, p. 215), but will complete it. With respect to its own future, then, Skinner's radical behaviorism seems to be not sufficiently radical on this issue of the interiorization of psychological life.

On the other hand, insofar as the ghost of interiorization haunts the science of behavior, Skinnerian or otherwise, psychology's turn to behavior already established the nature of the behavior toward which it turns. Behavior becomes the other side of the inside. It is the outside of the inside, its complement or mirror image. It is pre-established as a visible, observable thing. Indeed, it is visible and observable precisely because it is a thing, like the things and/or objects in the world. But behavior is not a thing, and its observability is not a given but an achievement. Chapter 3 addresses this issue. Here I wish to say only that a critical examination of this theme of interiorization leads to and requires a thorough re-visioning of the notion of behavior.

6. Wallace Stevens, *Poems*, sel. Samuel French Morse, p. 109.

I. Psychology and the Metaphor of Science

1. All three statements — by Herman Ebbinghaus, Richard Mueller-Freienfels, and Robert S. Woodworth, respectively — are quoted by François H. Lapointe, "Who Originated the Term 'Psychology'?" *Journal of the History of the Behavioral Sciences* 8, no. 3 (July 1972): 328.

2. Ibid., p. 329.

3. James Hillman, *Re-Visioning Psychology*, p. 90.

4. Ibid., p. 51.

5. The scientific laboratory and the medical clinic have been the only two *places* in modern times where psychological life has appeared. In the former it has appeared as illusion, in the latter as symptom or dream. The purpose of this book is to present something of the history of that former appearance. A consideration of the latter theme is post-

poned for another work. In conjunction with the latter theme, however, I recommend Michel Foucault's *The Birth of the Clinic.*

6. Ernest Klein, *A Comprehensive Etymological Dictionary of the English Language,* p. 157.

7. Van den Berg has worked out a unique and important historical approach to the study of psychological life. He terms his approach metabletics, a theory of changes, and a theoretical account of it can be found in J. H. van den Berg, *The Changing Nature of Man,* and in *Humanitas* 7, no. 3 (winter 1971). Applications of this approach to psychology can also be found in these two works. The interested reader should also see van den Berg's *Divided Existence and Complex Society,* a metabletic study of depth psychology. In addition to these three works, there are English translations of some of his phenomenological studies. Most notable among them are *The Psychology of the Sickbed, A Different Existence, Dubious Maternal Affection,* and *Medical Power and Medical Ethics.* I make mention of him in some detail because his influence bears heavily on this work.

8. Maurice Merleau-Ponty, "Eye and Mind," trans. Carleton Dallery, in *The Primacy of Perception,* p. 168.

9. John Archibald Wheeler, "The Universe as Home for Man," *American Scientist* 62, no. 6 (November-December 1974): 689.

10. The relationship of this work to depth psychology is ambiguous. On one hand Freud's psychoanalysis is a continuation of that cultural dream called scientific psychology. After all, Freud began with his *Project for a Scientific Psychology.* But this work was abandoned and on that occasion in his life when he was presented with a handsomely bound copy of it, after believing that he had destroyed all existing copies, he fainted. Freud's own relation to science as a psychologist was ambiguous, or perhaps we should say here ambivalent. In either case the *Project* was a *failed success.* It was a failure in the sense of continuing the dream of psychology as a science which was its intention. It was a success in the sense that this failure led to psychoanalytic psychology, to a psychology which moves in the realm of symbol rather than fact. There is a work of de-literalization in depth psychology and in this regard a convergence between this psychology and the one presented here. But

there remains the interiorization of psychological life in Freud's psychology as well as a tendency to re-convert the symbol into the fact insofar as Freud replaces the individual patient's wish with a cultural deed at the dawn of human history. In this regard there is a divergence between this work and his psychology. With respect to these issues and specifically with respect to the notion of the unconscious see Robert Romanyshyn, "Unconsciousness, Reflection and the Primacy of Perception." See also the discussion of the unconscious in Chapter 3 of this work.

11. This notion of the natural attitude is a theme which characterizes phenomenology, the approach which is taken in this work. In daily life we live on the empirical level where we assume the factual character of things. But this assumption, which makes us "merely fact-minded people" (Edmund Husserl, *The Crisis of European Sciences and Transcendental Phenomenology*, trans. David Carr, p. 6), hides a forgetfulness for the intentionality of human life. We rest in things, forgetful of how the appearance of things is the necessary (noematic) correlate of embodied conscious action in the world (noetic acts). Phenomenology seeks to recover, then, that intentional structure of human life, that noematic-noetic correlate, that relation of reflection, as it is called in this work, by temporarily bracketing the assumptions of naïve life. A phenomenologically based psychology shares this procedure. But a noticeable difference between the aims of phenomenological philosophy and a phenomenologically based psychology, a psychological psychology, lies in the *specificity* of what the latter recovers. In the psychological domain, the recovery of intentional life reveals itself as figure and story. In other words, to practice phenomenology in psychology is to recover beneath the natural attitude of daily life in which we dwell as empirical persons in a factual world the world as story inhabited by phenomenal figures. This book is an extended illustration of this theme. Readers who are interested in the philosophical side of phenomenology are advised to consult the readable introduction provided by Richard M. Zaner's text, *The Way of Phenomenology*. Parts 1 and 2 of Husserl's *Crisis of European Sciences* are also recommended, even though they are more

difficult for the beginning reader in phenomenology.

12. The significance of *disruption* in recovering psychological reality is not unlike the role which disruption plays in the recovery of truth
in the works of Heidegger. Of course, I do not mean to suggest here a
direct parallel. But the coincidence does acknowledge again the indebtedness of this work to a phenomenological style of thinking, even as it
suggests that a genuine psychology is phenomenological in attitude. For
a discussion of this role of disruption in Heidegger's thought, the reader
is referred to William B. Macomber's book, *Anatomy of Disillusion*.
While he does not explicitly use the term *disruption*, the notion is clearly
demonstrated in his book. In Heidegger's own work the reader will find
an illustration of this theme in his essay "The Origin of the Work of
Art," which appears in *Poetry, Language, Thought*, trans. Albert
Hofstadter.

13. Hillman, *Re-Visioning Psychology*, p. 91.

14. Compare the work of Hillman, especially *Suicide and the Soul*.

15. Husserl, *The Crisis of European Sciences*, p. 203.

16. Nicolaus Copernicus, *De revolutionibus orbium caelestium libri
VI.*

17. Andreas Vesalius, *De humani corporis fabrica libri septem.*

18. Robert Romanyshyn, "Copernicus and the Beginnings of Modern Science," *Journal of Phenomenological Psychology* 3, no. 2 (Spring
1973): 187-199.

19. Quoted by Edwin Arthur Burtt, *The Metaphysical Foundations of Modern Physical Science*, p. 79.

20. This notion of the abandoned body is to be found in the Epi-
logue to van den Berg's *Medical Power and Medical Ethics*.

21. Burtt, Metaphysical Foundations, pp. 84-86.

22. Norwood Russell Hanson, *Patterns of Discovery*, p. 177, n. 6.

23. René Descartes, "The Dioptrics," in *Descartes: Philosophical
Writings*, ed. and trans. Elizabeth Anscombe and Peter Thomas Geach,
p. 245.

24. René Descartes, *Treatise of Man*, trans. Thomas Steele Hall, p.
xxxv.

25. Ibid., p. xxiii.

26. B. F. Skinner, "The Machine That Is Man," *Psychology Today* 2, no. 11 (April 1969): 20-25, 60-63.

27. Frank Geldard, *Fundamentals of Psychology*, p. 1.

28. Gaetano Kanizsa, "Subjective Contours," *Scientific American* 234, no. 4 (April 1976): 48-52.

29. Van den Berg, *The Changing Nature of Man*, pp. 230-231.

30. "When Silence Reigns," in *Selected Prose of Rainer Maria Rilke*, trans. G. Craig Houston, p. 4.

31. Van den Berg, *The Changing Nature of Man*, pp. 230-231.

32. Freud's study of the Mona Lisa does not emphasize this estrangement of the landscape, this *interiorization* of psychological life. On the contrary, *it presumes it.* But is one able to read the Mona Lisa in Freud's way, as the presence of an absent, forgotten memory, because one has already located psychological life on this side of the world? My argument here does not concern the validity of Freud's interpretation. Rather it concerns the ground upon which his interpretation rests. The condition for the possibility of a *psychoanalysis* of the Mona Lisa arises precisely because psychological life has been displaced from the world. See Sigmund Freud, *Leonardo da Vinci and a Memory of His Childhood*; also see note 10 of this chapter.

33. Walter Pater, *The Renaissance*, p. 130 (emphasis added).

34. Ibid.

35. George Schwartz and Philip W. Bishop, eds., *Moments of Discovery* 1: 396.

36. Ibid., p. 399.

37. Alexander Pope, "Epitaph on Sir Isaac Newton," quoted by Marjorie Hope Nicolson, *The Breaking of the Circle*, p. 154.

38. John Keats, "Lamia," quoted by Marjorie Hope Nicolson, *Newton Demands the Muse*, p. 2.

39. Schwartz and Bishop, eds., *Moments of Discovery*, p. 395.

40. *A New English Dictionary on Historical Principles*, ed. Sir James A. H. Murray et al., 5:43.

41. Ibid., p. 44.

42. See Paul Hazard, *The European Mind (1680-1715)*.

43. The everyday world in which we live is a world which solicits

our belief, and our actions in the world are grounded in what Merleau-Ponty calls a "perceptual faith" *(The Visible and the Invisible*, p. 3). A patient's hallucinations are evidence of a description of that belief. The believable world is in question. The hallucinations are not a matter of wrong or insufficient knowledge. They are not bad judgments. In this light it is not surprising that the term hallucination appears when our relation to nature shifts from the mode of belief to that of reason. The historian Marc Bloch describes this shift in terms of interpretation versus observation, and Lucien Febvre speaks of it in terms of the increasing reliance on vision in the seventeenth century. But it is not just a new emphasis on the eye which matters here. Rather it is also the changed meaning of the eye which counts. A Newtonian eye, the eye of science, is a reasoning eye, a calculating eye, a measuring eye. It is these features, which now characterize vision, which account for the significance of this shift and prepare the way for a mistaken vision, for hallucination. See Marc Bloch, *Feudal Society*, trans. L. A. Manyon, vol. I, and Lucien Febvre, *Le problème de l'incroyance au XVI siècle*. With respect to the miracle and the notion of belief, see van den Berg, *The Changing Nature of Man*, Ch. 4.

44. Husserl speaks of the world of science as a "garb of ideas" thrown over the everyday world of life (*The Crisis of European Sciences*, p. 51). He is clear, however, that this way of speaking does not challenge the validity of scientific constructs. It "only" brings into question the forgotten ground of science. The purposes of this work are to show the mode of psychological existence which appears through the world of science and to indicate what this style conceals of psychological life.

45. The fate of the dream in scientific psychology is different from its fate in depth psychology. In the latter, especially with respect to Freud's work, the dream becomes another path toward psychological life, and through it another understanding of psychological life emerges. Indeed we might even say that with the dream and with the symptom, the "dream" of scientific psychology is disrupted. But to follow this path would take us beyond the boundaries of this work. We would have to show how Freud's work both disrupts the "dream" of scientific psy-

chology, even while it continues it. In the present work the intention is to show how the dream is incorporated into the "dream" of scientific psychology, how the laboratory enters the clinic. Compare notes 5 and 10 to this chapter.

46. Descartes' account of the experience was originally contained in his youthful journal *Olympica*, now lost. Parts of it, however, were preserved by Descartes' biographer Baillet and the philosopher Leibnitz. My presentation draws on the material in Jacques Maritain, *The Dream of Descartes*, trans. Mabelle L. Andison, pp. 13-29, and Bernd Jager, "The Three Dreams of Descartes: A Phenomenological Exploration," *Review of Existential Psychology and Psychiatry* 8, no. 3 (Fall 1968): 195-213.

47. Maritain, *The Dream of Descartes*.

48. Jager, "The Three Dreams of Descartes."

49. Maritain, *The Dream of Descartes*, p. 21.

50. Audrey Haber and Richard P. Runyun, *Fundamentals of Psychology*, p. 64.

51. I purposely avoid here a consideration of whether these events are understood as the *causes* of the experience, as the *conditions* of it, or as its *parallel* accompaniment, because all three positions are variations of the same point: *the events are the facts of experience*. This point commits psychology to none of these positions while allowing any one of them. Starting with it, psychology can adopt the strong position of causality, the middle one of conditionality, or the weak one of parallelism.

52. This is Colin Murray Turbayne's notion of metaphor. See his *The Myth of Metaphor*, Ch. I.

53. These remarks on metaphor and psychological life as metaphorical anticipate the theme of this work, the explicit subject of the final chapter. They arise here because the feature of literalization in psychology conceals psychological life as a metaphorical reality. When this feature is the focus of discussion, what is hidden begins to be recovered.

54. In one respect it is questionable whether even a scientific physiology *ever* deals only with facts. Insofar as it deals with the human body, its findings are *initially* understandable only through the body as an ex-

perience of the world. In other words, physiology must always, at least initially, establish itself through the vehicle of the experienced world. It is, therefore, always a *reflection*. It is foundationally *psychological*. Now, of course, this acknowledgment does not reduce physiology to psychology, the reverse error of scientific psychology as evidenced in the example. It means only a recognition of how psychological life is always in the middle of things, and hence how a psychological point of view can always legitimately be taken in any human endeavor. A genuine psychological point of view is not imported from the outside. On the contrary it is recovered at the heart of any specific endeavor. It is a way of *deepening* that endeavor, recovering how it *matters* in another way.

55. This notion of a metaphorical understanding of the body in a psychological psychology is developed in detail in Chapter 4.

2. Reflections of the Psychological World: Things

1. Martin Heidegger, "The Thing," in his *Poetry, Language, Thought*, trans. Albert Hofstadter.

2. Quoted by Christian Norberg-Schulz, *Existence, Space and Architecture*, p. 36.

3. Maurice Merleau-Ponty, *Phenomenology of Perception*, trans. Colin Smith, p. 383.

4. J. H. van den Berg, *The Phenomenological Approach to Psychiatry*, p. 28. This work has been re-issued in changed form under a new title, *A Different Existence*.

5. Van den Berg, *The Phenomenological Approach to Psychiatry*, p. 29.

6. Ibid.

7. Kakuzo Okakura, *The Book of Tea*, ed. Everett F. Bleiler, pp. 30-31 (emphasis added).

8. Ibid., p. 35.

9. See M. Jacobs, "Geometry, Spirituality, and Architecture in Their Common Historical Development as Related to the Origin of Neuroses: A Summary," *Humanitas* 7, no. 3 (Winter 1971): 291-320.

10. Norberg-Schulz, *Existence, Space and Architecture*, p. 32.

11. See Robert Romanyshyn, "Experience Takes Place," in *Dimensions of Thought*, vol. 2, ed. Ralph H. Moon and Stephen Randall, pp. 153-178.

12. Behaviorism, of course, rejects this interiorization of psychological life, and Skinner's work is witness to its battle against mentalism. But its rejection is on methodological grounds, and this means that in principle that spectre of mentalism, the ghost of interiorization, still haunts this psychology. The ghost remains because behaviorism begins with the world as it is already defined by science, with the so-called objective world of empirical events. As we saw in Chapter I, this way of beginning modern psychology necessarily moves psychological life inside. Behaviorism is a countermove without however the necessary re-visioning of the "outside" world which makes this move "inside" initially necessary.

13. Paul Ricoeur, *Freud and Philosophy*, trans. Denis Savage, p. 7.

14. Quoted by Hazard, *The European Mind*, p. 401.

15. *The American Heritage Dictionary of the English Language*, ed. William Morris, p. 1544.

16. Plato, *Timaeus*, 47a. I am citing the translation by Benjamin Jowett published in *The Collected Dialogues of Plato*, ed. Edith Hamilton and Huntingon Cairns, p. 1174.

17. *American Heritage Dictionary*, p. 1524.

18. The opposition of culture and desire is the theme of Freudian psychology. In the nineteenth century culture becomes the enemy of desire, and desire retreats underground. Is it because in the nineteenth century psychological life has become so *interiorized* that the earth can no longer be remembered as home? After three hundred years or more of successful scientific-technological achievements, does Freud begin to hear the voice of a homeless wanderer who has no place in the world?

19. It is interesting that the word *nostalgia* first appeared in the English language in 1780 in relation to a condition suffered by soldiers away from home. Is it possible that by the nineteenth century people had become so psychologically homeless that desire, which originally concerns our place upon the earth, began to speak forcefully and noticeably through the *disruptions* of pathology?

20. Van den Berg, *The Phenomenological Approach to Psychiatry*, p. 32.

21. Merleau-Ponty, *Phenomenology of Perception*, p. 383.

22. The way in which we understand psychological life finds its complement in the way in which we understand the world. In a psychological psychology, psychological life is a reality of reflection and hence an understanding of the world is also as a reflection, that is as neither fact nor idea. On the other hand, scientific psychology's interiorization and literalization of psychological life find their necessary complement in the physicalizing of the world. The world is only an empirical, neutral realm of factual materiality (see Chapter I). To re-vision psychological life is to re-vision the world (and the human body). Things, body, and psyche are a system of mutual reflections.

23. Robert Romanyshyn, "Psychological Language and the Voice of Things," *Dragonflies: Studies in Imaginal Psychology* I, no. I (Fall 1978): 83-84.

24. There are times when we are psychological and there are times when we are not. Just as one's psychological life hides itself, and/or tends to be forgotten, we may say that the world also forgets its psychological life. At noon and at night the world forgets itself psychologically. In these moments it gives rise to a psychology which forgets the psychological. In this respect we may say that the scientific conception of the world belongs to these times of high noon and night. These are its moments. Newton goes into the *dark* to study the *light*. Descartes *dreams at night* a new dream of reason founded on *clear* and distinct ideas. Freud builds a *scientific psychology* from the fragments of the *night*.

25. Schwartz and Bishop, *Moments of Discovery* 1:399.

26. Merleau-Ponty, *Phenomenology of Perception*, pp. 306-307.

27. Merleau-Ponty, "Eye and Mind," in *The Primacy of Perception*, pp. 182, 186 (emphasis added), 164, 168.

28. Liliane Brion-Guerry, "The Elusive Goal," trans. John Shepley, in *Cézanne: The Late Work*, ed. William Rubin, p. 80.

29. Merleau-Ponty, "Eye and Mind," pp. 166-168.

30. Ibid., p. 182.

31. The reason for the quotation marks should be clear from the

previous discussion. The relation of a thing to a shadow or a reflection is not one of possession but of a deepening of one thing through another. A thing does not "have" a reflection if one is seeing and speaking psychologically. Rather the reflection is the depth of one thing through another. It is the means by which things *re-figure* each other. It is the imaginal connection between things.

32. José Ortega y Gasset, *Meditations on Quixote*, trans. Evelyn Rugg and Diego Marín. All quotations are taken from pp. 88-89.

33. Romanyshyn, "Psychological Language and the Voice of Things," p. 74. The example is taken from Hanson, *Patterns of Discovery*.

34. I put "stands" in quotation marks to draw attention to the metaphorical style of embodiment which marks Kepler's vision. It is the style of embodiment which belongs to the corpse. It is the stance of the corpse. See Chapter I.

35. See Allen Tate, "The New Provincialism," in *On the Limits of Poetry: Selected Essays (1928-1948)*, p. 293. Tate's quote is a liberal borrowing from Blake. Tate writes: "From now on we are committed to seeing *with*, not *through* the eye: we, as provincials who do not live anywhere." That is the point! To see with the eye, to adopt the body of science, is to lose one's place in the world, one's home. Blake's own words are: "What it will be Questioned When the Sun rises do you not see a round Disk of fire somewhat like a Guinea O no no I see an Innumerable company of the Heavenly host crying Holy Holy Holy is the Lord God Almighty I question not my Corporeal or Vegetative Eye any more than I would Question a Window concerning a Sight I look thro it & not with it." See *The Poetry and Prose of William Blake*, ed. David V. Erdman, p. 555.

36. Hanson, *Patterns of Discovery*, p. 182, n. 6.

37. I should not say "gazes" here because that word connotes a style of seeing. It indicates a way of seeing which differs, for example, from staring or peeking. To see is to take up the eye of anatomy and physiology for the task of expression. Scientific psychology, however, restricts the vision of the eye. It deals with the "minimal" eye in order to literalize its account of vision. Thus I should speak in terms of light stimuli and retinal sensations. I should do this for consistency. But then we

would miss the ironic paradox in modern psychology: the way in which it sees the life of vision is not accounted for by that vision.

38. In the context in which it is written, this statement is more or less correct. Freud's depth psychology continues the cultural dream of modern psychology as a science insofar as it interiorizes psychological life. But Freud's depth psychology is, in another sense, the breakdown of this dream insofar as Freud's psychology recovers the non-literal character of psychological life. In *Studies on Hysteria*, for example, Breuer, in conjunction with Freud, says: "It is only too easy to fall into a habit of thought which assumes that every substantive has a substance behind it — which gradually comes to regard 'consciousness' as standing for some actual thing; and when we have become accustomed to make use metaphorically of spatial relations, as in the term 'sub-consciousness,' we find as time goes on that we have actually formed an idea which has lost its metaphorical nature and which we can manipulate easily as though it were real. Our mythology is then complete" (Sigmund Freud and Josef Breuer, *Studies on Hysteria*, trans. James Strachey, p. 271). See also note 10 to Chapter 1.

3. Reflections of the Psychological World: Others

1. Maurice Merleau-Ponty, "The Philosopher and His Shadow," in *Signs*, trans. Richard C. McCleary, p. 159; Merleau-Ponty, "Eye and Mind," in *The Primacy of Perception*, p. 168.

2. George Herbert Mead, *The Philosophy of the Present*, ed. Arthur E. Murphy, p. 169 (emphasis added).

3. The position I am adopting here is that of Merleau-Ponty. It is not a dualism of cognition and perception, of mind and body, but a recovery of the mindful body, or the incarnated mind. Essential to this view is a recovery of the lived body which in turn allows a recovery of self and other in a psychological way. A psychological psychology builds on the foundation of phenomenology, and indeed it is Mead's failure to rethink critically the meaning of human embodiment which makes his social psychology fall somewhat short of a genuine psychological account. But in this chapter I am not specifically concerned with refuting

Mead's views or with presenting those of Merleau-Ponty. On the contrary, acknowledging my indebtedness to Merleau-Ponty and to phenomenological thought in general, my intention is to sketch a (social) psychological psychology which arises on this foundation. Readers who are interested in either Merleau-Ponty or Mead are referred to the following introductions: for Merleau-Ponty, see John Sallis, *Phenomenology and the Return to Beginnings*; for Mead, see David L. Miller, *George Herbert Mead: Self, Language, and the World.*

4. Merleau-Ponty, "The Child's Relations with Others," trans. William Cobb, in *The Primacy of Perception*, p. 128.

5. I am using the word "casts" here for convenience. Any notion of projection and/or of the reflection as a possession of the self is not intended. Compare Chapter 2 and the discussion of shadows and reflections.

6. These initial remarks already indicate a double *confusion* between self through other and other through self. The specular image is initially and originally *not me* but an-other. And the other is initially and originally coincidental with this appearance of this reflection which *is me*. Compare Chapter 1 and the discussion of the mirror reflection.

7. Merleau-Ponty, "The Child's Relations with Others," p. 128.

8. Ibid., p. 129.

9. Ibid., p. 130.

10. Ibid., p. 132.

11. Ibid. (emphasis in original).

12. Belief matters! This phrase has to be heard in two ways. On the one hand it indicates that psychological reality is not what is real in an empirical sense. Hence *belief* matters. This is, what one *believes* about reality matters. On the other hand, it indicates that psychological life, as belief, matters in the sense that the matter of reality matters in another way. Hence belief *matters*. Psychological life makes a difference with respect to what is real.

13. Merleau-Ponty, "The Child's Relations with Others," p. 137.

14. I am not suggesting here that psychological life is child's play. But I am certainly suggesting that a playful attitude defines a psychological approach to the world. Nothing seems to distance one from a psy-

chological presence to reality as much as a morbidly serious attitude.

15. Merleau-Ponty, "The Child's Relations with Others," p. 137.

16. Ibid., p. 136.

17. Ibid., p. 141.

18. Ibid., p. 148 (emphasis added).

19. Ibid., pp. 154-155 (emphasis added).

20. Ibid., pp. 153-154.

21. Ibid., p. 154.

22. Quoted in ibid., p. 148.

23. Jean-Paul Sartre, *No Exit and Three Other Plays*, trans. Stuart Gilbert et al., pp. 46-47.

24. Hanson, *Patterns of Discovery*, pp. 6-7.

25. William Harvey, *Exercitatio anatomica de motu cordis et sanguinis in animalibus.*

26. These few remarks are like those in Chapter 2 regarding Johannes Kepler and Tycho Brahe. In both places it is a question of reconceptualizing psychological reality. This reconceptualization is the explicit theme of the final chapter, although the earlier chapters already indicate the need for this reconceptualization. But enough has already been said to suggest what that final chapter will say. Psychological life as a reality of reflection, this reality which is characterized by identity and difference, is a metaphor. The issue of validation, then, concerns how a metaphor is valid and how it is validated.

27. I am limiting myself here to the five observations given in the example. One could imagine, however, an observation which interprets Harvey's reluctant behavior in terms of the annual rainfall in London between 1616 and 1628. Obviously this observation would not merit the same consideration shown to the other five. *Why*, however, is another issue, the issue of validation (see previous note), which would take us beyond the boundaries of the present discussion.

28. Stanley Schachter and Jerome E. Singer, "Cognitive, Social, and Physiological Determinants of Emotional State," *Psychological Review* 69, no 5 (September 1962):379-399. Quote is from p 394.

29. Note that for the latter situation the Epi Mis group is not included. The reason for this absence in the author's design of the ex-

periment does not, however, concern this discussion. See ibid., p. 386.

30. Schachter and Singer, "Emotional State," p. 397.

31. Ibid., p. 393.

32. Ibid., p. 388.

33. Ibid., p. 395.

34. Ibid., p. 397 (emphasis in original).

35. James Hillman, "The Fiction of Case History: A Round," in *Religion as Story*, ed. James B. Wiggins, pp. 123-173.

36. *American Heritage Dictionary*, p. 1548.

37. James Agee, *A Death in the Family*, p. 94.

38. For a more detailed treatment of the imaginal and its place in psychological life see Mary M. Watkins, *Waking Dreams*. She elaborates this theme far beyond what I can do here. My intention is merely to introduce this mode of understanding as the one which properly belongs to psychological life insofar as psychological life as neither fact nor idea does not belong to empirical or rational modes of understanding.

39. Merleau-Ponty, "Indirect Language and the Voices of Silence," in *Signs*, p. 75.

40. In *The Changing Nature of Man*, van den Berg describes how Freudian depth psychology fails to appreciate this difference. When Freud discovered that the accounts of his patients were not factually true reports of actual past events, he and the new science of psychoanalysis were in grave circumstances. Freud himself says of this period: "When I realized that these sexual approaches had never actually occurred, that they were just fantasies made up by my patients, or perhaps even suggested by myself, I was at my wit's end for some time" (cited in *The Changing Nature of Man*, p. 134). Freud, however, found a solution which extended the scope of his theory from neurotic patients to humanity in general. The *individual deed* was replaced by the *universal wish*. Van den Berg rightly points out, however, that what Freud saw as universal wishes buried in a primeval past — the murder of the father, the ritual totem meal, the Oedipus drama — were the patients' *fictions* created to explain to the therapist their present miseries. The patients created this past because in the present the sexual aspect of their lives could find no reflection in the world with others, including the thera-

pist. He, too, was busily concerned with removing sexuality to the safe distance of the remote past. Van den Berg provides the historical details for this retreat to the past in the nineteenth century, and it is not necessary to repeat them here. What is to be noted, however, is that when human experiences find no reflections, when those experiences of human life which are present must be lived as an absence, psychological life as story becomes fiction.

41. Ernest Becker, *The Structure of Evil.* Although Becker's intentions seem obscured by his terminology — he adopts a phenomenological perspective but writes of history in an empirical fashion — the main purpose of his historical-cultural studies seems clear. Since the collapse of the medieval world, the West has attempted to found what Becker calls "a science of man as anthropodicy." Becker details the history of this effort, and it is clear that its intention is neither empirical, real, and factual, nor intellectual, ideal, and fictional. These dichotomies have failed to grasp this domain, the domain which I call in this work the psychological. Becker's works provide, I think, a cultural-historical background for the concerns of phenomenology.

42. My remarks here follow the work of Isaiah Berlin, *Vico and Herder.*

43. R. G. Collingwood, *The Idea of History*, p. 64.

44. Merleau-Ponty, "Eye and Mind," p. 168.

45. Van den Berg offers a different illustration which, however, leads to the same point. Discussing Breuer's and Freud's joint work, van den Berg emphasizes how indispensable Breuer's presence was to one of his hysterical patients. A patient who was hysterically blind would begin to speak only after she convinced herself that she was in the presence of Breuer. Van den Berg asks, why did she need another person, and not just anyone, but particularly Breuer? He says that neither Breuer nor Freud knew what to do with this observation. For van den Berg, however, it indicates unconsciousness as a social phenomenon (*The Changing Nature of Man*, p. 118).

46. Freud's self-analysis, which in many respects inaugurated psychoanalysis, began in the same year that Bram Stoker's *Dracula* appeared: 1897. Is there cause for wonder here? Neurotics and vampires appear in

European consciousness at the same time.

47. See, for example, some of the descriptions of Viennese life at the time of Freud in the excellent book by Allan Janik and Stephen Toulmin, *Wittgenstein's Vienna*.

48. Merleau-Ponty, *Phenomenology of Perception*, p. 369 (emphasis added).

49. I paraphrase here a remark by T. S. Eliot. See "The Metaphysical Poets," in *Selected Essays: 1917-1932*, p. 247.

50. Merleau-Ponty, *Phenomenology of Perception*, p. xi (emphasis added).

4. Reflections of the Psychological World: Body

1. Klein, *Comprehensive Etymological Dictionary*, p. 245.

2. This connection between emotions and the human heart which is recognized in daily life is treated in a recent work by Stephen Strasser entitled *Phenomenology of Feeling: An Essay on the Phenomena of the Heart*, trans. Robert E. Wood. The phenomenology of the heart which he offers is an essay on human feelings, a phenomenology of emotions. See also the recent work of James Lynch, *The Broken Heart: The Medical Consequences of Loneliness*. The title itself bears witness to how the old idea of the heart as the seat of emotions persists in modern medicine.

3. Henri Clouard and Robert Leggewie, *Anthologie de la Littérature française*, 1:242.

4. See Ricoeur, *Freud and Philosophy*. Ricoeur's work fully elaborates this tension in Freud's depth psychology, and he sees both the value and the limits of this tension. The limits here are important. They involve a too narrow conception of symbol in Freud's work which arises, I think, because of a too narrow conception of the body. Freud's psychology tries to be psychological in the shadow of the corpse, that is on the ground of the biological body.

5. *American Heritage Dictionary*, p. 1522.

6. These remarks on memory amplify those made in the introduction. They suggest that *psychology's* search for memory in the brain

misses the *psychological* significance of human memory. First, in *misplacing* memory in the brain, it makes it a matter of mind, of thought, an intellectual matter. Our life tells us, however, that this "memory" is at most a matter of information and that it does not touch what is particularly human about remembering. That which really matters, that which is more than the retention of information, touches the heart. Second, in *placing* memory in the brain, psychology means the issue of place *literally*. Place means location. The place of memory in a life becomes a literal space. But memories are not lodged *in* our hearts. We remember *with* and *through* our hearts.

7. The two works of Hannah Arendt referred to in this story are *Eichmann in Jerusalem* and "Reflections," a three-part serialization which appeared in *The New Yorker* (November 21, November 28, and December 5, 1977) of her book *Thinking*, the first volume of her trilogy *The Life of the Mind.*

8. Norbert Elias, *The Civilizing Process*, trans. Edmund Jephcott, p. 102.

9. Harvey, *Exercitatio anatomica de motu cordis et sanguinis in animalibus.* This is the original publication. The translation used here is entitled *An Anatomical Disquisition on the Motion of the Heart and the Blood in Animals*, in *The Works of William Harvey, M.D.*, trans. Robert Willis, pp. 3-86.

10. Harvey, *Anatomical Disquisition*, p. 5.

11. Ibid.

12. As oversimplified as this instance may seem, the reader should recall the examples given in Chapter 1. The science of psychology literalizes psychological experience by seeing it as its material condition. Physiology becomes the foundation of behavior. Brain is behavior. This is a metaphor, but it is taken literally.

13. Harvey, *Anatomical Disquisition*, p. 31 (emphasis added).

14. Pedro Laín Entralgo, "Harvey in the History of Scientific Thought," *Journal of the History of Medicine and Allied Sciences* 12 (April 1957): 222 (emphasis added).

15. Harvey, Anatomical Disquistion, p. 32.

16. Laín Entralgo, "Harvey," p. 221.

17. J. H. van den Berg, *Zien: Verstaan en verklaren van de visuele waarneming*, p. 39. The English text is taken from a private, unpublished translation.

18. See, for example, the work of Sir John Eccles, *The Understanding of the Brain*.

19. The notion of a divided heart, of the "cor duplex," is older than Harvey, but the point is that in Harvey's work this notion becomes literal. The issue here is the same one which appeared with the courageous heart. A reality of human life becomes literalized in the attitude of science. The consequence is that the "cor duplex," like the courageous heart, becomes unreal, only a metaphor, while "Harvey's" divided heart, like the pumping heart, is forgotten as a world.

20. Walter Pagel, *William Harvey's Biological Ideas*.

21. Laín Entralgo, "Harvey," p. 220.

22. Harvey, *Anatomical Disquisition*, p. 17.

23. It is a question whether van den Berg would agree with the way the changing character of the body is presented here. Certainly our historical perceptions of the body change, but does the body *matter* in another way? But even if there is not agreement on this point, I would claim that the position which is adopted in this work has its foundation in van den Berg's approach. With regard to the *materiality* of nature, for example, he asks about the meaning of scientific discoveries. Are they "discoveries of that which is there? Or do the physicist and chemist discover *the matter of his time*, or rather, *his time and himself*" (*Divided Existence and Complex Society*, p. 132; emphasis in original). This passage seems to suggest that matter does matter in another way. And if that is true of the materiality of nature, then why not of the materiality of the body? Can we not wonder if the anatomist and physiologist discover the body of their time and themselves?

24. For support of this view the reader should look at Owen Barfield, *Saving the Appearances*, Ch. 5.

25. Harvey, *Anatomical Disquisition*, p. 3.

26. C. V. Wedgwood, *Oliver Cromwell*, p. 28.

27. Ibid., p. 32.

28. Quoted in Christopher Hill, "William Harvey and the Idea of

Monarchy," *Past and Present* 27 (1964): 55.

29. Ibid., p. 56.

30. Harvey, *Anatomical Disquisition*, pp. 9, 19, 21.

31. Quoted in John Thorn, Roger Lockyer, and David Smith, *A History of England*, p. 339.

32. Jacobs, "Geometry, Spirituality, and Architecture," p. 291.

33. Van den Berg, "Living in Plurality," *Humanitas* 7, no. 3 (Winter 1971): 407.

34. Harvey, *Anatomical Disquisition*, p. 29.

35. M. Jacobs, "Depth Psychology: A Passing Cultural Phenomenon," *Humanitas* 7, no. 3 (Winter 1971): 371.

36. Harvey, *Anatomical Disquisition*, p. 22.

37. Ibid.

38. Hazard, *The European Mind*, p. xvi.

39. Christian Norberg-Schulz, *Meaning in Western Architecture*, p. 287.

40. Ibid., p. 292.

41. Helen Gardner, *Art through the Ages*, p. 590.

42. Quoted by Norberg-Schulz, *Meaning in Western Architecture*, p. 287.

43. Miroslav Hanak, "The Emergence of Baroque Mentality and Its Cultural Impact on Western Europe after 1550," *Journal of Aesthetics and Art Criticism* 28, no. 3 (Spring 1970): 320, 318, 323, 324.

44. A. C. Harwood, *Shakespeare's Prophetic Mind*, pp. 35, 33. Harwood's study lends support from a literary point of view to the thesis about psychological life offered in this work. Hamlet, according to Harwood, is a figure with a new style of consciousness. Consciousness is now "localized in the brain and nerves" (p. 34); it is separated from the world. The themes of interiorization and literalization are apparent.

45. Nicolson, *The Breaking of the Circle*, p. 92.

46. Ibid., p. 101.

47. Quoted in ibid., p. 101.

48. Hanak, "Emergence of Baroque Mentality," p. 325.

49. Richard S. Dunn, *The Age of Religious Wars (1559-1689)*, p. 179.

50. R. L. Colie, "Some Paradoxes in the Language of Things," in *Reason and the Imagination: Studies in the History of Ideas (1600-1800)*, ed. J. A. Mazzeo, p. 113.

51. Quoted in Hazard, *The European Mind*, p. 401. Recall the discussion of desire in Chapter 2 and compare it with Locke's understanding. In a scientifically based psychology, desire is uneasiness, a sense of restlessness, a doubt regarding one's place. In the psychological recovery of desire, it concerns the place of humanity: desire is the making of place, the finding of place. In addition, for Locke and the psychology which follows him, desire is an *interior* uneasiness. For a psychological psychology desire places us in the world. Do we become restless and uneasy inside when we turn away from the world, when we have lost our place in the world?

52. I will not give the history of the Sacred Heart in the following remarks, since my intention is to illustrate the *psychological* significance of the change of heart in the seventeenth century. It is important to mention here, however, a few historical notes. The most dramatic and historically significant appearance of the Sacred Heart was to Margaret Mary Alacoque beginning in 1673, and it is this appearance which I will discuss. Earlier appearances are, however, recorded. In the thirteenth century, for example, St. Gertrude (d. 1302) prophesied that a devotion to the Sacred Heart would appear when worship of God and belief in Him had grown *weak* and *cold*. In the seventeenth century Jean Eudes conceived the idea of a public *cultus* in honor of the sacred hearts of Mary and Jesus. According to van den Berg, Eudes first proposed such a devotion in 1629, only one year after the publication of Harvey's text (see J. H. van den Berg, *Het Menselijk Lichaam*, pp. 64-134). Moreover, in 1670, some three years before Margaret Mary's experience, Eudes received permission for a special Mass and office devoted solely to the Sacred Heart of Jesus. Finally, Bainvel adds that the first Feast of the Sacred Heart of Jesus was celebrated around October 20, 1672 (see Jean Bainvel, *Devotion to the Sacred Heart*, trans. E. Leahy).

53. Arthur R. McGratty, *The Sacred Heart*, p. 83.

54. Ibid.

55. Ibid., p. 86 (emphasis added).

56. Ibid., p. 87.

57. See, for example, Meyer Friedman and Ray H. Rosenman, *Type A Behavior and Your Heart.*

58. Blaise Pascal, *Pensées*, trans W. F. Trotter, p. 109.

59. The divided heart appeared in the seventeenth century. The term *neurosis* made its first appearance in 1733 in a work published by George Cheyne entitled *English Malady.* Jacobs offers an intriguing discussion of this point in his *Humanitas* article, "Geometry, Spirituality, and Architecture." See also van den Berg's *Divided Existence and Complex Society.*

60. Lynch, *The Broken Heart*, p. 17.

61. Ibid., p. 3 (emphasis in original).

62. Lynch's book, though excellent, is marked by that kind of non-psychological thinking about the body which is critically examined in this chapter. While he clearly demonstrates the relation between psychological life and the physical body, he still envisions this relation in terms of an interacting dualism. Thus, for example, in speaking of the book's title he says that the broken heart is not only a poetic image. It is also a medical reality. But I think the point should be made the other way around. The broken heart is a medical reality because the heart always *matters* in a psychological way. If one begins with an understanding of psychological life as embodied, and of the body as a psychological reality, then a dualism between the psychological and the physical is avoided. We are embodied, and our sciences of the body today are reflections of a psychological style of life. This viewpoint does not diminish the validity of these sciences. It simply places them in another perspective. It allows us to see science and its achievements in another way.

63. Because the purpose of this work is to write a *psychological psychology*, I do not intend either to answer this question beyond the limits posed by this purpose or to show explicitly the lines of influence which have shaped this work. The reader who is familiar with phenomenology will recognize the obvious debt which I owe to this tradition for a style of thinking.

64. While a psychological psychology is obviously indebted to phe-

nomenology, it is not equivalent to phenomenology. In addition to the recovery of experience in its own terms as it is lived, a psychological psychology must also include the *figuring* of experience. This requirement means the abandonment of the ego as the center of experience, and in this regard a psychological psychology moves closer to depth psychology with its appreciation of the multiplicity of figures and their many stories beyond the ego. The psychology offered in this work is, therefore, indebted to both of these traditions while not being identified with either one of them.

65. Friedrich Nietzsche, *Beyond Good and Evil,* trans. Walter Kaufmann, p. 2. The full quote reads: "Suppose truth is a woman — what then?"

66. Quoted in Julián Marías, *José Ortega y Gasset: Circumstance and Vocation,* trans. Frances López-Morillas, p. 283.

5. The Metaphorical Character of Psychological Life

1. Quoted in van den Berg, *The Changing Nature of Man,* p. 212.

2. We can say, however, that his memory is those neurological events, provided that we hear this statement as a way of speaking rather than as a literal account of what is spoken about. (Recall the discussion of the nightmare in Chapter 1.) *The point is that scientific psychology is psychological when it is recovered as a metaphor.* And yet in this particular case the results obtained may not be worth the effort of recovery. Indeed the first step of recovering the reflections of these neurological events as an experienced world seems unimaginable. This difficulty implies, moreover, that physiology, while a legitimate reflection of psychological life, is not the most fruitful one.

3. Van den Berg, *The Changing Nature of Man,* pp. 215, 213, 214, 216.

4. This is a notion used by Merleau-Ponty. See, for example, the comments made by the translators to a work of his entitled *Sense and Nonsense,* trans. Herbert L. Dreyfus and Patricia Allen Dreyfus, p. xiii. Recall also the discussion in Chapter 4 of the phenomenological approach adopted in this work.

5. Douglas Berggren, "The Use and Abuse of Metaphor," *Review of Metaphysics* 16, no. 2 (December 1962): 249.

6. Quoted in ibid., p. 240.

7. Quoted in ibid., p. 249 (emphasis added).

8. Ibid., p. 253.

9. Ibid., p. 256.

10. Ibid., p. 254.

11. Ibid., p. 256.

12. The distinction between the poetic and the psychological is not being denied. There is no intention to reduce psychological life to poetry nor the poetic to psychological life. But how this distinction is to be made is beyond the purpose and scope of this work. It remains a question. Suffice it to say that this work acknowledges that this question arises when psychological life is understood on its own terms.

13. Howard Nemerov, *Reflexions on Poetry and Poetics*, p. 40.

14. Ibid., p. 33 (emphasis in original).

15. *Aristotle's "Poetics,"* trans. S. H. Butcher, p. 99.

16. Cyril Dwiggins, "Experiencing Metaphor" (ms.), p. 66.

17. Max Black, *Models and Metaphors*, pp. 35-37.

18. See I. A. Richards, *The Philosophy of Rhetoric*, pp. 115-138.

19. Dwiggins, "Experiencing Metaphor," p. 66.

20. Ibid., p. 60.

21. *Aristotle's "Poetics,"* p. 99.

22. Dwiggins, "Experiencing Metaphor," p. 61.

23. Paul Ricoeur, *The Rule of Metaphor*, p. 248.

24. Richards, *The Philosophy of Rhetoric*, p. 127.

25. Douglas Berggren, "From Myth to Metaphor," *Monist* 50, no 4 (October 1966): 530-552.

26. See, for example, Hillman, *Re-Visioning Psychology*.

27. But if psychological life is a metaphorical reality, then this issue of therapeutics is legitimate. The point is that the recovery of psychological life as a metaphorical reality will have implications for the praxis of therapy.

28. Berggren, "From Myth to Metaphor," p. 547.

29. Ricoeur, *The Rule of Metaphor*, p. 249.

30. Translation by Arthur Waley, *The Way and Its Power*, p. 155.

31. Stevens, *Poems*, pp. 13-14.

32. Kenneth Burke, *A Grammar of Motives*; see especially pp. 503-517.

33. See, for example, Merleau-Ponty, "The Primacy of Perception and Its Philosophical Consequences," trans. James M. Edie, in *The Primacy of Perception*, p. 16.

34. Miller, *George Herbert Mead*, p. 21.

35. Quoted by Marías, *José Ortega y Gasset*, p. 326 (emphasis Marias').

36. Ibid., pp. 285-286 (emphasis in original).

37. Ibid., p. 374.

38. Kanizsa, "Subjective Contours," p. 50.

39. This advice appears beneath the two figures presented on p. 48 of the article. It is an interesting admonition which invites one to strip away the context of the figure, and/or to narrow one's vision. It is a piece of advice totally in agreement with the attitude of science. It recalls the very thing which Newton did in his study of light (see Chapter 2).

40. Kanizsa, "Subjective Contours," p. 52.

41. Ricoeur, *The Rule of Metaphor*, p. 138.

42. Habit and prescription are the two ways in which tensive language becomes steno-language according to Philip Wheelwright, *Metaphor and Reality*, p. 37.

43. Black, *Models and Metaphors*, p. 27 (emphasis added).

44. Cleanth Brooks, *The Well Wrought Urn*, p. 9.

45. Richard Wilbur, "A Voice from under the Table," lines 3-6, from *Things of This World*, p. 19; quoted by Wheelwright, *Metaphor and Reality*, p. 64.

46. Dwiggins, "Experiencing Metaphor," p. 157, n. 28.

47. Quoted by Brooks, *The Well Wrought Urn*, p. 210 (emphasis added).

48. Wheelwright, *Metaphor and Reality*, p. 71 (emphasis added).

49. Dwiggins, "Experiencing Metaphor," pp. 133, 135.

50. I am alluding here to Rafael Lopez-Pedraza, *Hermes and His Children*.

51. See entry for *ludicrous*, in Klein, *Comprehensive Etymological Dictionary*, p. 432.

52. For a full treatment of an issue to which I can only allude, the reader should consult Johan Huizinga, *Homo Ludens: A Study of the Play-Element in Culture.*

53. Quoted by Terence Hawkes, *Metaphor*, pp. 30-31.

54. Ibid., p. 31.

55. Cleanth Brooks, "Metaphor and the Function of Criticism," in *Spiritual Problems in Contemporary Literature*, ed. Stanley R. Hopper, p. 133.

Afterword

1. Keats, J. (1973) The Complete Poems(John Barnard, Ed.) New York: Penguin Books, p. 549

2. Jung, C.G. (1967) Alchemical Studies(R.F.C. Hull, Trans.) The Collected Works of C.G. Jung, Vol.13, Par 414. Princeton: Princeton University Press

3. Merleau-Ponty, M. "Eye and Mind," in The Primacy of Perception, James M. Edie(Editor). Evanston: Northwestern University Press, 1964, p. 162.

4. Neumann, E. Amor and Psyche. Princeton: Princeton University Press, 1956

5. Romanyshyn, R. The Soul in Grief: Love, Death and Transformation. Berkeley: North Atlantic Books, 1999.

6. Corbin,H. Alone with the Alone: Creative Imagination in the Sufism of Ibn' Arabi. Princeton: Princeton University Press, 1969.

7. Descartes, R. Meditations on First Philosophy(L.J. La Fleur, Trans)New York: Library of Liberal Arts, 1960(original work published,1641)

8. Romanyshyn, R.,"Complex Knowing:Toward a Psychological Hermeneutics", in C. Aanstous (ed).) *The Humanistic Psychologist,,* 1991, Vol. 19, No.1. p. 23, n.3

9. Bloom, H. *Preface, Alone with the Alone: Creative Imagination in the Sufism of Ibn' Arabi.* Princeton: Princeton University Press, 1969, p.x.

10. Romanyshyn, R. The Backward Glance: Essays toward an Imaginal Psychology, Pittsburgh: Trivium Publications, in press.

11. Pascal, B. Pensees and other writings (H. Levi, Trans.). New York: Oxford University Press, 1995, p.158.

12. Keats, J. The Complete Poems(John Barnard, Ed.) New York: Penguin Books, 1973, p.539.

13. Shakespeare, W. A Midsummer Night's Dream, Act v, Scene I, ll 14-17, Wolfgang Clemen (Ed.). New York: Signet, 1998.

14. Romanyshyn, R. "For the Moment, That's Enough:Reveries on Therapy and the Poetry of Language," in The San Francisco Jung Institute Library Journal, vol. 18, No.1, 1999, pp. 55-72.

15. Romanyshyn, R. "On Angels and other Anomalies of the Imaginal Life," in Temenos Academy Review, London: The Temenos Academy, Spring 2000, No.3, pp. 171-182.

16. Romanyshyn, R. "The Orphan and the Angel," in Psychological Perspectives, Fall-Winter, 1995, No.32, pp. 90-105.

BIBLIOGRAPHY

Agee, James. *A Death in the Family.* New York: McDowell, Obelensky, 1957.

Arendt, Hannah. *Eichmann in Jerusalem: A Report on the Banality of Evil.* Rev. ed. New York: Penguin Books, 1977.

Arendt, Hannah. *The Life of the Mind.* 3 vols. New York: Harcourt Brace Jovanovich, 1978.

Aristotle's "Poetics". Translated by S. H. Butcher. Introduction by Francis Fergusson. New York: Hill and Wang, 1961.

Bainvel, Jean. *Devotion to the Sacred Heart: The Doctrine and Its History.* Translated by E. Leahy. Edited by George O'Neill. London: Burns Oates and Washbourne, 1924.

Barfield, Owen. *Saving the Appearances: A Study in Idolatry.* New York: Harcourt Brace Jovanovich, n.d.

Becker, Ernest. *The Structure of Evil: An Essay on the Unification of the Science of Man.* New York: Free Press, 1976.

Berggren, Douglas. "From Myth to Metaphor." *Monist* 50, no. 4 (October 1966): 530-552.

Berggren, Douglas. "The Use and Abuse of Metaphor." *Review of Metaphysics* 16, no. 2 (December 1962): 237-258; 16, no. 3 (March 1963): 450-472.

Berlin, Isaiah. *Vico and Herder: Two Studies in the History of Ideas.* New York: Viking Press, 1976.

Black, Max. *Models and Metaphors: Studies in Language and Philosophy.* Ithaca: Cornell University Press, 1962.

Blake, William. *The Poetry and Prose of William Blake.* Edited by David V. Erdman. Garden City: Doubleday and Co., 1970.

Bloch, Marc. *Feudal Society.* 2 vols. Translated by L. A. Manyon. Chicago: University of Chicago Press, 1964.

Bloom, H. *Preface, Alone with the Alone: Creative Imagination in the Sufism of Ibn' Arabi.* Princeton: Princeton University Press, 1969.

Bonah, R. Brent, and Sheila Shively. *The Language Lens.* Englewood Cliffs: Prentice-Hall, 1974.

Brion-Guerry, Liliane. "The Elusive Goal." Translated by John Shepley. In *Cézanne: The Late Works.* Edited by William Rubin. New York: Museum of Modern Art, 1977.

Brooks, Cleanth. "Metaphor and the Function of Criticism." In *Spiritual Problems in Contemporary Literature.* Edited by Stanley R. Hopper. New York: Harper and Row, 1957.

Brooks, Cleanth. *The Well Wrought Urn: Studies in the Structure of Poetry.* New York: Harcourt, Brace and World, 1947.

Burke, Kenneth. *A Grammar of Motives.* New York: Prentice-Hall, 1945.

Burtt, Edwin Arthur. *The Metaphysical Foundations of Modern Physical Science.* Rev. ed. Garden City: Doubleday Anchor Books, 1954.

Cawdrey, Robert. *A table alphabeticall of English wordes.* London: for Edmund Weaver, 1604.

Clouard, Henri, and Robert Leggewie, eds. *Anthologie de la Littérature française.* 2 vols. New York: Oxford University Press, 1960.

Colie, R. L. "Some Paradoxes in the Language of Things." In *Reason and the Imagination: Studies in the History of Ideas (1600-1800).* Edited by J. A. Mazzeo. New York: Columbia University Press, 1956.

Collingwood, R. G. *The Idea of History.* New York: Oxford University Press, 1956.

Copernicus, Nicolaus. *De revolutionibus orbium caelestium libri VI.* Nuremberg, 1543.

Corbin, H. *Alone with the Alone: Creative Imagination in the Sufism of Ibn' Arabi.* Princeton: Princeton University Press, 1969.

Descartes, René. "The Dioptrics." In *Descartes: Philosophical Writings,* edited and translated by Elizabeth Anscombe and Peter Thomas Geach. Indianapolis: Bobbs-Merrill Co., 1970.

Descartes, René. *Treatise of Man.* Translated by Thomas Steele Hall.

Cambridge: Harvard University Press, 1972.

Descartes, René. *Meditations on First Philosophy,* Translated by L. J. La Fleur. New York: Library of Liberal Arts, 1960 (original work pub lished in 1641).

Dunn, Richard S. *The Age of Religious War (1559-1689).* New York: W. W. Norton and Co., 1970.

Dwiggins, Cyril. *Experiencing Metaphor.* Bloomington: Indiana Univer sity Press.

Eccles, Sir John. *All the Strange Hours: The Excavation of a Life.* New York: Charles Scribbner's Sons, 1975.

Eiseley, Loren. *All the Strange Hours: The Excavation of a Life.* New York: Charles Scribner's Sons, 1975.

Elias, Norbert. *The Civilizing Process: The Development of Manners.* Translated by Edmund Jephcott. New York: Urizen Books, 1978.

Eliot, T. S. *Selected Essays: 1917-1932.* New York: Harcourt, Brace and Co., 1932.

Febvre, Lucien. *Le Problème de le'incroyance au XVIᵉ siècle: La religion de Rabelais.* Paris: Michel, 1968.

Foucault, Michel. *The Birth of the Clinic: An Archaeology of Medical Perception.* Translated by A. M. Sheridan Smith. New York: Vin tage Books, 1975.

Freud, Sigmund. *Leonardo da Vinci and a Memory of His Childhood.* In *The Standard Edition of the Complete Psychological Works of Sigmund Freud,* vol. 11. Translated and edited by James Strachey. London: Hogarth Press, 1957.

Freud, Sigmund, and Josef Breuer. *Studies on Hysteria.* Translated by James Strachey. New York: Avon Books, 1966.

Friedman, Meyer, and Ray H. Rosenman. *Type A Behavior and Your Heart.* New York: Fawcett Publications, 1974.

Gardner, Helen. *Art through the Ages.* 6th ed. Revised by Horst de la Croix and Richard G. Tansey. New York: Harcourt Brace Jovanovich, 1975.

Geldard, Frank. *Fundamentals of Psychology.* New York: John Wiley and Sons, 1962.

Haber, Audrey, and Richard P. Runyon. *Fundamentals of Psychology.* Reading: Addison-Wesley Publishing Co., 1974.

Hanak, Miroslav. "The Emergence of Baroque Mentality and Its Cultural Impact on Western Europe after 1550." *Journal of Aesthetics and Art Criticism* 28, no. 3 (Spring 1970): 315-326.

Hanson, Norwood Russell. *Patterns of Discovery: An Inquiry into the Conceptual Foundations of Science.* Cambridge: Cambridge University Press, 1972.

Harvey, William. *Exercitatio anatomica de motu cordis et sanguinis in animalibus.* Frankfurt, 1628.

Harvey, William. *The Works of William Harvey, M. D.* Translated by Robert Willis. London: printed for the Sydenham Society, 1847.

Harwood, A. C. *Shakespeare's Prophetic Mind.* London: Rudolf Steiner Press, 1964.

Hawkes, Terence. *Metaphor.* London: Methuen and Co., 1972.

Hazard, Paul. *The European Mind (1680-1715).* New Haven: Yale University Press, 1953.

Heidegger, Martin. *Poetry, Language, Thought.* Translated by Albert Hoffstadter. New York: Harper and Row, 1975.

Heidegger, Martin. *What Is a Thing?* Translated by W. B. Barton, Jr., and Vera Deutsch. Chicago: Henry Regnery Co., 1970.

Hill, Christopher. "William Harvey and the Idea of Monarchy." *Past and Present: A Journal of Historical Studies* 27 (1964): 54-72.

Hillman, James. "The Fiction of Case History: A Round." In *Religion as Story*, edited by James B. Wiggins. New York: Harper and Row, 1975.

Hillman, James. *Re-Visioning Psychology.* New York: Harper and Row, 1975.

Hillman, James. *Suicide and the Soul.* Zurich: Spring Publications, 1976.

Huizinga, Johan. *Homo Ludens: A Study of the Play-Element in Culture.* Boston: Beacon Press, 1955.

Husserl, Edmund. *The Crisis of European Sciences and Transcendental Phenomenology: An Introduction to Phenomenological Philosophy.* Translated by David Carr. Evanston: Northwestern University Press, 1970.

Jacobs, M. "Depth Psychology: A Passing Cultural Phenomenon." *Humanitas* 7, no 3 (Winter 1971): 371-394.

Jacobs, M. "Geometry, Spirituality, and Architecture in Their Common Historical Development as Related to the Origin of Neurosis: A Summary." *Humanitas* 7, no. 3 (winter 1971): 291-320.

Jager, Bernd. "The Three Dreams of Descartes: A Phenomenological Exploration." *Review of Existential Psychology and Psychiatry* 8, no. 3 (Fall 1968): 195-213.

Janik, Allan, and Stephen Toulmin. *Wittgenstein's Vienna.* New York: Simon and Schuster, 1973.

Jung, C. G. *Alchemical Studies.* Translated by R. F. C. Hull. In *The Collected Works of C. G. Jung,* Princeton: Princeton University Press, 1967.

Kanizsa, Gaetano. "Subjective Contours." *Scientific American* 234, no. 4 (April 1976): 48-52.

Kearney, Hugh. *Science and Change, 1500-1700.* New York: McGraw-Hill Book Co., 1971.

Keats, J. *The Complete Poems* (John Barnard, Ed.) New York: Penguin Books, 1973.

Klein, Ernest. *A Comprehensive Etymological Dictionary of the En glish Language.* Amsterdam: Elsevier Publishing Co., 1971.

Kuhn, Thomas S. *The Structure of Scientific Revolutions.* Chicago: University of Chicago Press, 1962.

Lain Entralgo, Pedro. "Harvey in the History of Scientific Thought." *Journal of the History of Medicine and Allied Sciences* 12 (April 1957): 222-231.

Lao Tse. *See* Waley, Arthur, trans.

Lapointe, Francois, H. "Who Originated the Term 'Psychology'? *Jour nal of the History of the Behavioral Sciences* 8, no. 3 (July 1972): 328-335.

Lopez-Pedraza, Rafael. *Hermes and His Children.* Zurich: Spring Pub lications, 1977.

Lynch, James. *The Broken Heart: The Medical Consequences of Loneli ness.* New York: Basic Books, 1977.

McGratty, Arthur R. *The Sacred Heart: Yesterday and Today.* New

York: Bensinger, 1951.

Macomber, William B. *Anatomy of Disillusion: Heidegger's Notion of Truth.* Evanston: Northwestern University Press, 1967.

Marias, Julian. *The Dream of Descartes.* Translated by Mabelle L. Andison. New York: Philosophical Library, 1944.

Maritain, Jacques. *The Dream of Descartes.* Translated by Mabelle L. Andison. New York: Philosophical Library, 1944.

Mead, George Herbert. *The Philosophy of the Present.* Edited by Arthur E. Murphy. La Salle: Open Court Publishing Co., 1959.

Merleau-Ponty, Maurice. *Phenomenology of Perception.* Translated by Colin Smith. London: Routledge and Kegan Paul, 1962.

Merleau-Ponty, Maurice, *The Primacy of Perception: And Other Essays on Phenomenological Psychology, the Philosophy of Art, History and Politics.* Edited and translated by James M. Edie et al. Evanston: Northwestern University Press, 1964.

Merleau-Ponty, Maurice, *Sense and Non-Sense.* Translated by Hubert L. Dreyfus and Patricia Allen Dreyfus. Evanston: Northwestern University Press, 1964.

Merleau-Ponty, Maurice, *Signs.* Translated by Richard C. McCleary. Evanston: Northwestern University Press, 1964.

Merleau-Ponty, Maurice. *The Visible and the Invisible.* Edited by Claude Lefort. Translated by Alphonso Lingis. Evanston: Northwestern University Press, 1968.

Miller, David L. *George Herbert Mead: Self, Language, and the World.* Austin: University of Texas Press, 1973.

Morgan, Clifford T., Richard A. King, and Nancy M. Robinson. *Introduction to Psychology.* 6th ed. New York: McGraw-Hill, 1979.

Nemerov, Howard. Reflexions on Poetry and Poetics. New Brunswick: Rutgers University Press, 1972.

Neumann, E. *Amor and Psyche.* Princeton: Princeton University Press, 1956.

A New English Dictionary on Historical Principles. Edited by Sir James A. H. Murray et al. 13 vols. Oxford: Clarendon Press, 1888-1933.

Nicolson, Marjorie Hope. *The Breaking of the Circle: Studies in the Effect of the "New Science" in Seventeenth-Century Poetry.* Rev.

ed. New York: Columbia University Press, 1960.

Nicolson, Marjorie Hope. *Newton Demands the Muse: Newton's "Opticks" and the Eighteenth Century Poets.* Princeton: Princeton University Press.

Nietzsche, Friedrich. *Beyond Good and Evil.* Translated by Walter Kaufmann. New York: Vintage Books, 1966.

Norberg-Schulz, Christian. *Existence, Space and Architecture.* New York: Praeger Publishers, 1971.

Norberg-Schulz, Christian. *Meaning in Western Architecture.* New York: Praeger Publishers, 1975.

Okakura, Kakuzo. *The Book of Tea.* Edited by Everett F. Bleiler. New York: Dover Publications, 1964.

Ortega y Gasset, José. *Meditations on Quixote.* Translated by Evelyn Rugg and Diego Marin. New York: W. W. Norton and Co., 1961.

Pagel, Walter. *William Harvey's Biological Ideas: Selected Aspects and Historical Background.* New York: S. Karger, 1967.

Pascal, Blaise. *Pensées.* Translated by W. F. Trotter. New York: E. P. Dutton and Co., 1958.

Pascal, Blaise. *Pensees and Other Writings.* Translated by H. Levi. New York: Oxford University Press, 1995.

Pater, Walter. *The Renaissance: Studies in Art and Poetry.* London: Macmillan and Co., 1925.

Plato. *The Collected Dialogues of Plato.* Edited by Edith Hamilton and Huntington Cairns. Bollingen Series 71. Princeton: Princeton University Press, 1963.

Richards, I. A. *The Philosophy of Rhetoric.* New York: Oxford University Press, 1936.

Ricoeur, Paul. Freud and Philosophy: An Essay on Interpretation. Translated by Denis Savage. New Haven: Yale University Press, 1970.

Ricoeur, Paul. The Rule of Metaphor: Multi-Disciplinary Studies of the Creation of Meaning in Language. Translated by Robert Czerny. Toronto: University of Toronto Press, 1977.

Rilke, Rainer Maria. Selected Prose by Rainer Maria Rilke. Translated by G. Craig Houston. New York: New Directions Publishing Co., 1976.

Robinson, Daniel N. An Intellectual History of Psychology. New York: Macmillan Publishing Co., 1976.

Romanyshyn, Robert. "Copernicus and the Beginnings of Modern Science." Journal of Phenomenological Psychology 3, no. 2 (Spring 1973): 187-199.

Romanyshyn, Robert. "Experience Takes Place." In *Dimensions of Thought: Current Explorations in Time, Space, and Knowledge, vol. 2.* Edited by Ralph H. Moon and Stephen Randall. Berkeley: Dharma Publishing, 1980.

Romanyshyn, Robert. "Psychological Language and the Voice of Things (Part I)." *Dragonflies: Studies in Imaginal Psychology* 1, no. 1 (Fall 1978): 74-90.

Romanyshyn, Robert. "Psychology and the Attitude of Science." In *Existential-Phenomenological Alternatives for Psychology,* edited by Ronald S. Valle and Mark King. New York: Oxford University Press, 1978.

Romanyshyn, Robert. "Unconsciousness, Reflection and the Primacy of Perception." Paper presented at the Merleau-Ponty Circle, Athens, Ohio, 1977.

Romanyshyn, Robert. *The Soul in Grief: Love, Death and Transformation.* Berkeley: North Atlantic Books, 1999.

Romanyshyn, Robert. Complex Knowing: Toward a Psychological Hermeneutics. In C. Aanstoos (Ed.) *The Humanistic Psychologist,* 1991.

Romanyshyn, Robert. *The Backward Glance: Essays Toward an Imaginal Psychology.* Pittsburgh, PA: Trivium Publications, in press.

Romanyshyn, Robert. For the Moment, That's Enough: Reveries on Therapy and the Poetry of Language. In *The San Francisco Jung Institute Library Journal,* 1999.

Romanyshyn, Robert. On Angels and Other Anomalies of the Imaginal Life. In *Temenos Academy Review.* London: The Temenos Academy, 2000.

Romanyshyn, Robert. The Orphan and the Angel. In *Psychological Perspectives,* 1995.

Sallis, John. *Phenomenology and the Return to Beginnings.* Pittsburgh: Duquesne University Press, 1973.

Sartre, Jean-Paul. *No Exit and Three Other Plays.* Translated by Stuart Gilbert et al. New York: Vintage Books, 1955.

Schachter, Stanley, and Jerome E. Singer. "Cognitive, Social, and Physi ological Determinants of Emotional State." *Psychological Review* 69, no. 5 (September 1962): 379-399.

Schwartz, George, and Philip W. Bishop, eds. *Moments of Discovery, vol. I,* The Origins of Science. New York: Basic Books, 1958.

Shakespeare, W. *A Midsummer Night's Dream.* Wolfgang Clemen (Ed.). New York: Signet, 1998.

Skinner, B. F. *About Behaviorism.* New York: Alfred A. Knopf, 1974.

Skinner, B. F. "The Machine That Is Man." *Psychology Today* 2, no. 11 (April 1969): 20-25, 60-63.

Stevens, Wallace. *Poems.* Selected by Samuel French Morse. New York: Vintage Books, 1959.

Strasser, Stephan. *Phenomenology of Feeling: An Essay on the Phenom ena of the Heart.* Translated by Robert E. Wood. Pittsburgh: Duquesne University Press.

Tate, Allen. "The New Provincialism." In *On the Limits of Poetry: Se lected Essays (1928-1948).* New York: Swallow Press and William Morrow and Co., 1948.

Thorn, John, Roger Lockyer, and David Smith. *A History of England.* New York: Thomas Y. Crowell Co., 1961.

Turbayne, Colin Murray. *The Myth of Metaphor.* New Haven: Yale University Press, 1962.

Van den Berg, J. H. *The Changing Nature of Man: Introduction to a Historical Psychology.* New York: Dell Publishing Co., 1975.

Van den Berg, J. H. *A Different Existence: Principles of Phenomenologi cal Psychopathology.* Pittsburgh: Duquesne University Press.

Van den Berg, J. H. *Divided Existence and Complex Society: An Histori cal Approach.* Pittsburgh: Duquesne University Press, 1974.

Van den Berg, J. H. *Dubious Maternal Affection.* Pittsburgh: Duquesne University Press.

Van den Berg, J. H. *Het Menselijk lichaam,* vol. 2, *Het verlaten lichaam.* Nijkerk: Uitgeverij G. F. Callenbach, 1961.

Van den Berg, J. H. "Living in Plurality." *Humanitas* 7, no. 3 (Winter 1971): 395-409.

Van den Berg, J. H. *Medical Power and Medical Ethics.* New York: W. W. Norton and Co., 1978.

Van den Berg, J. H. *The Phenomenological Approach to Psychiatry: An Introduction to Recent Phenomenological Psychopathology.* Springfield: Charles C. Thomas, 1955.

Van den Berg, J. H. *The Psychology of the Sickbed.* Pittsburgh: Duquesne University Press, 1966.

Van den Berg, J. H. *Zien: Verstaan en verklaren van de visuele waarneming.* Sielkundebiblioteek 21. Nijkerk: C. F. Callenbach, 1972.

Vesalius, Andreas. *De humani corporis fabrica libri septem.* Basel, 1543.

Vico, Giambattista. *The New Science.* 3d ed. Abridged and translated by Thomas Goddard Bergin and Max Harold Fisch. Ithaca: Cornell University Press, 1970.

Watkins, Mary M. *Waking Dreams.* New York: Harper and Row, 1977.

Waley, Arthur, trans. *The Way and Its Power.* Boston: Houghton Mifflin, 1934.

Wedgewood, C. V. *Oliver Cromwell.* London: Duckworth, 1939.

Wheeler, John Archibald. "The Universe as Home for Man." *American Scientists* 62, no 6 (November-December 1974): 683-691.

Wheelwright, Philip. *Metaphor and Reality.* Bloomington: Indiana University Press, 1968.

Wilbur, Richard. *Things of This World.* New York: Harcourt Brace, 1956.

Wolfflin, H. *Renaissance und Barock.* Munich: F. Bruckmann, 1908.

Zaner, Richard M. *The Way of Phenomenology: Criticism as a Philo sophical Discipline.* New York: Pegasus, 1970.

INDEX

62. *See also* Mirror reflection
Copernican earth: and human
corpse as imaginal background of
scientific psychology, 23-27. *See
also* Body
Courage: and the heart, 123-126

Death in the Family, A (Agee),
101-102
Descartes, René: "The Dioptrics,"
25; three dreams of, 36-38;
Treatise of Man, 25
Desire: and behaviorism, 229 n.12;
and consideration, 55-56; and
culture, 59; and hope, 60 and
nostalgic sense of home, 60; as
originally a sense of place, 56;
and psychoanalysis, 56; and time,
57; and understanding, 58
De Vanaruum Ostiolis (Fabricus),
127
"Dioptrics, The," (Descartes), 25
Disruption: and the appearance of
psychological life, 21; as
characteristic function of
psychological life, 190-194;
role of, in Heidegger's thought,
224 n.12. *See also* Metaphor:
function of, in psychological life
Donne, John, 146
Dwiggins, Cyril: comparison theory
of metaphor criticized by, 175-
177; and metaphor as deviation,
198; on metaphor and transcen
dence of the real, 200

Eiseley, Loren, 18
Elias, Norbert, 121

Eliot, T.S., 199
Embodiment. *See* Body
Emotions, 90-97; and the body,
95-96; and the mirroring of
experience through behavior, 96-
97; and psychological life, 195
Experience: as illusion, 25-27; as
imaginal understanding of
behavior, 97-103; perspectival
character of, 185-188 (*see
also* Metaphor: as paradox of
identity difference); place and
sense of, in psychological life and
psychology, 54-61; and story, 175;
as subjective, 34; visibility of, as a
world, 44-54. See also Psycho
logical experience.
"Eye and Mind" (Merleau-Ponty),
65-66

Fabricus, 127
Fantasia. *See* Vico, Giambattista
Figure: as distinct from person, 11:
and mirror reflection, 11-13;
transforms person, 12
Frank, Philip, 70
Freud, Sigmund: and the body, 117;
Cartesian influence on, 110; and
the Mona Lisa, 225 n.32; and
scientific psychology, 71. See also
Psychoanalysis

Galen, 131
Galileo, 23
Goethe, Johann Wolfgang von, 80
Guarini, Guarino, 145. *See also*
Heart: and baroque architecture

Printed in the United States
43857LVS00003B